# Processing the News

# LONGMAN PROFESSIONAL STUDIES IN POLITICAL COMMUNICATION AND POLICY

*Editorial Advisor:* Jarol B. Manheim

| | |
|---|---|
| Robert E. Drechsel | *News Making in the Trial Courts* |
| Charles D. Elder and Robert W. Cobb | *The Political Uses of Symbols* |
| Doris A. Graber | *Processing the News: How People Tame the Information Tide* |
| Myles Martel | *Political Campaign Debates: Images, Strategies, and Tactics* |
| Brian Weinstein | *The Civic Tongue: Political Consequences of Language Choices* |

# Processing the News

## How People Tame
## the Information Tide

### Doris A. Graber
UNIVERSITY OF ILLINOIS AT CHICAGO

Longman

New York & London

**PROCESSING THE NEWS**
*How People Tame the Information Tide*

Longman Inc., 1560 Broadway, New York, N.Y. 10036
Associated companies, branches, and representatives
throughout the world.

Developmental Editor: Irving E. Rockwood
Editorial and Design Supervisor: Thomas Bacher
Production/Manufacturing: Ferne Y. Kawahara
Composition: C. L. Hutson Co., Inc.
Printing and Binding: Malloy Lithographing Inc.

**Library of Congress Cataloging in Publication Data**

Graber, Doris Appel, 1923–
    Processing the news.

    (Longman professional studies in political
communication and policy)
    Bibliography: p.
    Includes index.
    1. Public opinion—United States—Case studies.
2. Human information processing—Case studies.
3. Political socialization—United States—Case
studies.   4. Mass media—Political aspects—United
States—Case studies.   5. Democracy.   I. Title.
II. Series.

HM261.G78   1984       306'.2       83-19537
ISBN 0-582-28394-9
ISBN 0-582-28510-0 (pbk.)

Manufactured in the United States of America

Printing: 9 8 7 6 5 4 3 2 1    Year: 92 91 90 89 88 87 86 85 84

*For* TOM

*whose*
*caring and*
*sharing*
*lightens*
*the burdens and*
*doubles*
*the joy.*

# Contents

# □
# Foreword

This book, modeled after Robert Lane's classic, *Political Ideology*, examines the ways in which people seek out, understand, and utilize information presented in the news. *Processing the News* is based on a year-long, multi-wave panel study of 21 residents of Evanston, Illinois, who were selected for their differing interest in and access to the news. Professor Graber employs schema theory, an integrative and particularly context-sensitive extension of social psychological analysis, to chart the patterns of recognition and the retention extant in the news audience.

The highly-detailed picture that emerges is one of people who deal with a potentially overwhelming flow of information more successfully than we might think. They trim, they skim, and they simplify, but for the most part people do obtain enough news to function effectively in their particular sociopolitical locations. More than that, they are very able to take news items that lack background and to position those stories in contexts that are both cumulative and personally meaningful. It is general understanding more than factual detail that is most effectively retained through this process, but over time, Professor Graber argues, general understanding is sufficient to create the relatively well-informed public that is central to the functioning of a genuinely democratic political system. *Processing the News* will be of interest to students of political communication, public opinion, political psychology, and empirical democratic theory. The text will make its mark on our understanding of the political process in much the same way as Lane's work has.

The books in Longman's Professional Studies in Political Communication and Policy Series are intended to illuminate the institutional and theoretical foundations of communication as political phenomena. Through her intensive and insightful examination of the ways that people think about the news, Professor Graber contributes significantly to the attainment of this goal.

*Jarol B. Manheim*

# Preface

In 1957 and 1958, Robert Lane, a political scientist at Yale University, interviewed 15 blue-collar working men in a medium-sized town in the Eastern United States. The records of his lengthy conversations dealing with the men's views about society and politics furnished the raw material for his path-breaking intensive study of *Political Ideology: Why the American Common Man Believes What He Does*. In that book, which is the intellectual godparent of *Processing the News*, Professor Lane accomplished three goals. He analyzed in depth the men's answers to probe for the latent political ideology of urban blue-collar workers in the America of the fifties. He related this ideology to the culture and experiences that blue-collar workers know, and he showed how ideology supports or weakens the institutions of democracy.

For *Processing the News*, I have borrowed much of Robert Lane's methodology for studying thinking patterns through intensive interviews of a small panel of registered voters. But the goals of my research are slightly different. While Lane concentrated on what ordinary Americans think and believe, I focus primarily on the way in which people select and process information that they use to form opinions about current political issues. Hence the emphasis in this book is on selection of information and modes of information processing, rather than on the specific beliefs and opinions that are the end products of information-processing. Modern citizens face a continuous tide of new political information about an ever-changing world. Social scientists, media professionals, and politicians need to know how people tame that tide and use it to build, reinforce, and restructure their views of the political world.

Like Lane, I have tried to place political learning patterns into their particular social and cultural contexts. Communication is an interactive process in which the predispositions of various audiences interact with incoming messages. Contextual information is, therefore, essential to understand what meanings are conveyed. Hence, there are sketches of relevant experiences and life style characteristics of each of the panelists, including the nature of news available to each panelist during the study.

I am also interested, like Lane, in the consequences that patterns of political learning have for the practice of Western-style democracy. Is democracy based on the notion of a well-informed, civic-minded citizenry, possible, or is it a pipe dream or a distant goal that cannot be reached with current communications practices? To construct viable theories about the role of citizens in modern democratic societies, we need better knowledge of information-processing patterns. Such theories are sorely needed because classical theories about the role of citizens in democratic societies are seriously flawed.

In a more practical vein, the knowledge produced by this study is important for various types of social science research. For example, researchers into agenda-setting by the mass media need to know how different types of news are processed and committed to memory to form part of the public's political agenda (i.e., that array of political issues deemed to be most important at any particular period). Scholars interested in news selection and rejection rationales will benefit from news-processing knowledge, as will interview designers who must formulate questions to tap the memories of respondents. These questions must be asked in appropriate ways so that the respondents are able to retrieve the needed information from memory. Knowledge about information processing provides insight into the modes of storage of information and the best approaches for recall.

Finally, this study is aimed at helping political communicators with the difficult task of gaining attention and understanding for their messages. There is great concern among people involved in politics and in the media about reports that most people are ill-informed about the problems of our time and that they harbor a host of misconceptions. To communicate adequately, communicators of political information need to know how to get their audiences' attention, how to bring about initial absorption of their messages, and how to attain long-term storage of their messages in the desired form. Research on processing of political information can supply clues to achieving these goals as effectively as possible.

I have been asked whether I worry that greater knowledge about the political communication process will be used by communicators and their professional advisors to gain politically undesirable ends. I realize the potential for harm. But it does not worry me greatly because the research on which this book is based has strengthened my faith in the ability of average Americans to put most types of information into sound perspectives and to separate the wheat from the chaff. Average people may not be able to spout facts and figures, but they are not gullible and bereft of understanding of public issues.

This book has been many years in the making so that the roster of intellectual contributors is a long one. I owe a deep debt of gratitude for inspiration to many scholars besides Professor Lane. Rather than listing them here, I refer the reader to the list of chapter citations and to the bibliography. I feel especially indebted to the small but growing group of political scientists who are exploring political thinking through schema theory.

Major portions of the research reported here were part of a joint project undertaken by Professors Maxwell McCombs of Syracuse University, David

Weaver of Indiana University, and Chaim Eyal of Hebrew University in Jerusalem. The project involved a large staff of interviewers, news collectors, coders, and research assistants whose contributions formed the backbone of the study. I am deeply indebted to them.

The manuscript for *Processing the News* has benefitted greatly from comments and suggestions made by my colleagues and friends Isaac Balbus and Paul Hiniker, by Jarol Manheim, Editorial Advisor for the Longman Professional Studies in Political Communication and Policy Series, and by my diligent and perceptive research assistant, Robert Cohen. I also want to acknowledge the financial contributions made by the University of Illinois at Chicago, Indiana University, and Syracuse University and various research bodies and computing facilities which are located there. The high cost of content analysis and prolonged interviewing made such assistance indispensable.

Last, but not least, the splendid cooperation of the panelists deserves recognition. Not only did they consent to many long interview sessions in their homes and offices, but they also completed daily diaries recording information that had come to their attention. Experienced hands in diary collection told me that it would be impossible to keep the diaries coming for an entire year. The panelists proved them wrong, and I thank them for doing so.

*Doris A. Graber*

# 1

# Introduction: Current Knowledge about Information Processing

This is a study about how people process political information. For average Americans this means primarily learning political information from the mass media. However extensive their political experiences and contacts may be, the bulk of political information to which they are exposed and which they absorb, is beyond their personal experiences. It comes from the mass media either directly through personal exposure or indirectly through people with whom they talk about current affairs. The evidence that most political information is learned from the mass media is often circumstantial, but it is strong nonetheless. When people know about current happenings that are remote from their daily experiences, there normally is no likely source other than the mass media that could have supplied the information.

Like Paul Ducas's legendary sorcerer's apprentice who drowned in the waters he had brought forth, modern Americans are confronted by a seemingly unmanageable flood tide of information. This is an age of information glut. The average metropolitan paper, served up with breakfast on a daily basis, contains between 50 and 100 pages of fairly fine print, more than enough to cause information indigestion for anyone trying to read it all. Add to this some 25 to 50 stories served up at dinner and bedtime by national and local television newscasts, plus assorted bulletins on radio throughout the day, not to mention news magazines and journals, and you have a tremendous case of information overload. No wonder that consumers of political information, like the panelists whose information processing is reported in this study, feel overwhelmed by the information tide.[1] As Donald Burton, a lawyer well-trained in handling information efficiently, put it: "There's too much information about everything now. That's one reason why I don't remember half the important stuff when I try to think about it. There's more information available than there is time to assimilate and order it."

How do the Burtons and their less well-trained fellow citizens cope with information overloads? What strategies do they use to make choices in selecting information for attention, and what do they extract from the information to which they do pay attention? In sum, what is involved in the process of everyday political learning from mass media news sources?

Prior to the 1980s, few researchers had addressed these questions, despite the fact that the problem of coping with escalating information tides has been steadily growing in Western societies. The difficulties involved in investigating information processing and the relative youth of the modern subfield of political communications partially account for the gap.

The study reported in this book therefore covers much virgin territory of political knowledge. Its explorations have been helped tremendously by prior work on attitude and opinion formation done by psychologists, political scientists, and communications researchers. A very brief review of the nature of this work, particularly as concerns learning of political information from mass media sources, should set the scene for answering our major questions.

## THE STATE OF THE ART

Exploring political learning from the mass media requires answers to *what, why, when,* and *how* questions. In the past, most progress has been made with the *what* questions that deal with the substance of learning. American political scientists first became greatly interested in studying what people learn from the mass media in connection with presidential elections research. They wanted to explore whether voting choices were linked to the information about presidential elections that people had gleaned from the mass media. The first of these studies, published in 1944, was *The People's Choice* by Paul Lazarsfeld, Bernard Berelson, and Hazel Gaudet of Columbia University.[2] The authors reported the impact of various factors, including mass media stories, on voting decisions in the 1940 presidential election. Forty years later, there had been only a handful of major sequels that carried on and expanded earlier traditions.[3] While the early studies dwelled on the impact produced by political learning on voting decisions, later studies looked more carefully at the actual substance of learning during political campaigns. The best example is Thomas Patterson's *The Mass Media Election: How Americans Choose Their President*, which covers the 1976 presidential contest.[4]

The major findings that emerged from these studies was that people pay attention to only a small amount of the available information. They do learn about candidate images and election events and issues from media information, but only to a limited degree.[5] The precise extent and quality of learning are still uncertain, primarily because most studies have involved large-scale survey research. This limits the kinds of questions that can be asked. It also restrains the depth of probing and the examination of the social context in which answers are given. The forthcoming discussion (Chapter 5) pushes the borders of ignorance back a bit, but much remains to be done. At this point, it appears that people learn most about the personalities and qualifications of various candidates, but give spotty attention to information about major campaign issues. As the years go by, most people accumulate a substantial backlog of information about the nature of political campaigns and even about various candidates. This permits them to use new information largely as a filler and refresher for the perceptions that have been previously developed.[6]

The substance of political learning from the mass media has also been tapped through numerous public opinion surveys in which people were asked about facts and attitudes regarding a limited array of current topics. These included questions about support for or opposition to major economic and social policies, queries about the quality of performance of top-level political leaders and institutions, and requests to indicate what the respondents considered to be the most important problems facing the nation at that particular time. The results of such polls have been published in the daily press, as well as the social science literature. Nonetheless, writing in 1981, political scientist Cliff Zukin voiced a widely shared view when he said that

> it is difficult to claim that we know a great deal more about the media-opinion linkage than we did 30 years ago. We know more about how people use the mass media and about the process by which private opinions form and change. However, we know relatively little about formation and change on any specific issue and little about the long-term changes in public opinion that may be attributable to the mass media.[7]

The polls published in the popular press and available from scholarly survey research organizations such as the National Opinion Research Center at the University of Chicago and the Center for Political Studies at the University of Michigan, tell us in a *gross* way what sorts of current information people learn or do not learn—or forget quickly after learning. They indicate that most people become at least temporarily familiar with widely publicized news stories. A spate of studies of media agenda-setting also provides limited insights into the salience that people assign to assorted current political topics.[8] In 1976, for instance, agenda-setting studies showed high concern with inflation, unemployment, and other economic problems and with assorted social problems such as crime. An occasional study sheds light on how people evaluate public policies concerned with these issues.[9]

However, the *array* of topics about which questions have been asked remains quite limited. Most studies have dealt with learning related to elections which points up the fact that scholarly interest in political learning has been very narrowly focused in the past. Knowledge about learning political information is not only lacking in breadth, it also lacks depth because researchers have rarely elicited details by asking people open-endedly what they know about a particular topic and then coding the full range of descriptions and evaluations. While respondents will never fully remember all that they have learned or express all that they recall, open-ended questions can elicit far more expansive and unconstrained answers than is true of the closed-ended questions that have been the norm for this type of research.

The *why* questions have been explored under such headings as "uses and gratifications research," "cognitive balance theories," and "agenda-setting theories." These theories, propounded by psychologists and communications researchers, seek to explain what motivates people to become aware of information and learn or refrain from learning from it. As will be explained more fully (chapter 6), these theories about incentives and disincentives for learning have generally been tested for only a narrow slice of political learning. Again, the emphasis has been on learning from the mass media during elections. Much broadening and deepening of these theories, therefore, remains to be done.[10]

The *when* question has been explored in both its temporal and circumstantial dimensions. Researchers have asked at what time learning occurs, as well as under what circumstances it takes place. The time of learning has been examined in studies of political learning by children at various stages of the developmental process.[11] It has also been examined in adult life cycle studies and in agenda-setting research which assesses how quickly information featured by the mass media becomes a matter of prime concern for mass media audiences.[12] A few studies have tried to establish how much time elapses and how many repetitions must occur before various media presentations produce measurable effects on audiences. But only a handful of scholars have been tillers in that corner of the intellectual vineyard.[13]

Circumstantially, questions have been raised about the conditions which are most conducive to learning. Researchers have focused on dimensions such as the impact of interest in a subject on subsequent learning about it. They have investigated whether a need for information spurs learning and enhances its quality. They have also looked at the format of presentation and the play that media sources give to news stories as possible clues to learning information.[14] In later chapters, our findings will be compared to the results of these studies.

The *how* question, likewise, has several facets. One can ask how people select information for processing and how they go about incorporating it into their thinking. These facets of information processing have been largely ignored by communications researchers and political scientists because they have been considered the preserve of cognitive psychologists. The fact that psychologists have made only small progress in unravelling the mysteries of learning and have disagreed about the validity of various learning paradigms has discouraged outsiders from trespassing on this forbidding territory.

The other facet of the *how* question concerns the shaping of the end product of information processing. Here one asks what categorizations and other cognitive structures people impose on information in order to extract meanings from it and what these meanings are. Sociologists Andre Modigliani and William A. Gamson call this aspect of processing the "grammar" of beliefs.[15] The literature analyzing political belief systems and some voting studies have dealt with such questions. Social scientists have looked at answers to open-ended questions to discover approaches people use in thinking about political parties and candidates during election campaigns. Occasionally, they have examined more broadly how people conceptualize politics.

One representative study is *The American Voter* which identified four major styles of conceptualizing politics.[16] The first of these was called the *ideological style*. Its adherents employ ideological terms and concepts in discussing parties and candidates. They articulate general principles, and their comments are logically consistent. A second approach involves emphasis on *group benefits*. Practitioners of this approach think of politics in terms of its impact on specific groups in society. This is a less global and sophisticated approach than the ideological style, but it is not too different in outcome. Ideologists, too, consider the groups that win and lose in a social system. A third approach has been dubbed *nature of the times*. People using this approach conceptualize politics in terms of specific happenings at a particular time. They see no grand designs or patterns but merely responses to events that happen for reasons beyond their ken. Finally, there are many people who discuss candidates and parties only in terms of personalities or personal likes and dislikes that are unrelated to any substantive political issues or any political ideology. Their views have been labelled as having *no issue content*.

Again, the literature dealing with such thinking patterns has been largely limited to election studies. In addition, a few scholars have investigated a small number of more general conceptualizations, such as the question of whether or not people think of problems in terms of personal or general public concerns, or whether pocketbook considerations are paramount in most of their thinking about politics.[17] Studies dealing with the impact of a liberal or conservative framework of thinking also fall into this category.[18]

## FOCUS ON THE "HOW" QUESTION

The chief focus of this study is on two major facets of the *how* questions. How do people select and process information for incorporation into their thinking and what kinds of patterns do they impose on the information so that it will fit into established belief structures? Answers to these questions will help us understand how people cope with the overabundance of available political information and how they conceptualize politics. Past information on these matters has lacked depth, breadth, and context because it has come predominantly from survey research related to national elections. The answers provided by this study deepen and broaden knowledge about political information processing. The answers also generate a large number of new hypotheses about political learning that should be further tested, broadened, and deepened through in-depth interviews and survey research.

Once we know how individuals select and process political information, we should be able to make better predictions about its likely impact. This will help social scientists as well as the vast army of individuals involved in communicating political messages. As pointed out in the preface, with a better understanding of political information processing, political leaders as well as journalists and social science researchers may be able to match their messages and questions more closely to the processing proclivities of their audiences. Social scientists should also find the information valuable in their continuing quest to discover the limits of the role which citizens do and can play in democratic societies.

## AN OVERVIEW OF THE RESEARCH APPROACH

To study information processing thoroughly, a small-panel design was adopted. It permitted the intense observation of a limited number of average Americans over an extended period of time. As explained more fully in the next chapter, an in-depth approach is necessary because processing of political information is complex and affected by many contingencies. These include the individual's personality, experiences, life-style, and world view, as well as the status of political and economic conditions and events at a particular time, and the substance, format, and manner of presentation of various types of information. All these contingencies must be taken into consideration if one wants to get a reasonably coherent picture of the nature and results of political information processing. The complexity of the enterprise required concentrating the study on a small number of people.

Much of the information for studying cognitive processes necessarily comes from self-assessments by study subjects. Since such assessments are subject to bias and error, it is essential to check them repeatedly for internal consistency and for consistency with actual behaviors. Self-reports must also be supplemented by independent observations and a variety of measurements. If the results obtained from diversified measures are compatible, one can be reasonably confident that the findings are accurate.[19] These approaches have been used to ensure that the results reported here are as reliable as possible.

To answer questions about selection and processing of political information, it became necessary to borrow knowledge of basic research findings on cognitions from cognitive psychologists.[20] These scholars have devoted massive efforts in recent decades to finding answers to questions about information processing and to testing, retesting, and expanding these answers. They have investigated many processing phases, such as attention arousal, information selection, information integration, information storage, and information retrieval and nonretrieval. Most of this work has involved laboratory or field studies of individuals exposed directly to new environmental stimuli from which they extracted information. Only a small portion of these studies has dealt with processing complex, primarily indirect information about abstract concepts, as well as concrete phenomena. Practically none have dealt with processing information about politics.

One needs to ask, therefore, whether general information processing theories require modifications when they are applied to a specific field of knowledge, such as politics. As psychologists Roger C. Schank and Robert P. Abelson argue, it is unlikely that information processing is the same for all knowledge areas.

> [If] you try to imagine the simultaneous storage of knowledge about how to solve partial equations, how to smuggle marijuana from Mexico, how to outmaneuver your opponent in a squash game, how to prepare a legal brief, how to write song lyrics, and how to get fed when you are hungry, you will begin to glimpse the nature of the problems.[21]

Politics in the public sphere, one might argue, is a unique informational realm because it primarily involves a vast number of highly complex vicarious experiences. Unlike many other aspects of learning, these experiences are relayed through an impersonal medium, either print or audiovisual, at frequent intervals throughout the individual's waking hours. Compared to direct perception of persons and events, the stimuli to which individuals react during indirect perception are preselected by others and lacking in detail.[22] Most news stories involve a comparatively narrow array of facts and much of the information contained in the stories has already been preprocessed. Media audiences are apt to accept this information in its preprocessed form because the array of facts that led to journalistic judgments and generalizations is frequently fragmentary or totally missing. Acceptance of the processed product is further encouraged because the new information frequently fits into the stereotypical views already developed by the average media audience thanks to the acquisition of previous mass media information.

Compared to direct perception, the pressure on the individual to interact with the information stimuli and process them correctly often is small. Great emotional involvement with the information is rare. Nonetheless, at times, incentives for learning political information may be quite strong because people believe that many situations which are reported by the media have a powerful impact on their lives. They also need political information periodically for their chief political activity—casting their vote. In addition, most adults have been thoroughly indoctrinated to regard learning of certain types of political information as an important duty.

Given the unique features of political information and its transmission, one may well wonder whether political learning involves fundamentally different mental activities or whether it shares most or all of the features of complex concept learning identified by cognitive psychologists in other contexts. This study sheds light on these intriguing questions. In the words of political scientists Susan Fiske and Donald Kinder: "Politics represents a rich though currently underutilized domain for cognitive research." It therefore is important "to investigate parallels between the burgeoning social cognition literature and research on political cognitions."[23]

## ORGANIZATION OF THE TEXT

This book is divided into ten chapters. The opening chapter has put the study into scientific perspective. It has set forth its significance and outlined the major goals which prompted the research. What immediately follows is a fairly detailed description and explanation of the nature of the research design and its strengths and shortcomings (chapter 2). The reader is then introduced to the panelists whose comments constitute the chief data base and to the social and political context in which they expressed their sentiments (chapter 3). After this discussion, a description of the news supply available to the panelists and a brief report on the substance of their learning about selected news topics is undertaken (chapter 4). The study continues with an analysis of the news selection process which includes a look at the reasons for selecting or rejecting news. Remembering and forgetting are examined in a general manner as well as with reference to particular types of information (chapter 5).

Chapter 6 interprets the panelists' learning scores in light of current learning theories. Incentives and disincentives to learning are explored. Discussion of the context in which information processing typically takes place is followed by a detailed analysis of the process. In Chapter 7, various types of routinely used processing strategies are described, including ways in which special problems are handled. Chapter 8 deals with the kinds of mental constructs people develop to organize their thinking. Chapter 9 deals with variations in conceptual schemas and presents some examples of the types of cognitive maps developed by our panelists. The final chapter (chapter 10) summarizes the significance of the findings and explains how they can be used by scholars and professional communicators.

## Notes

1. The problem of information overload at the individual and at the societal level is discussed in detail in Orrin E. Klapp, *Opening and Closing: Strategies of Information Adaptation in Society*, Cambridge, Cambridge University Press, 1978.

2. Paul Lazarsfeld, Bernard Berelson, and Hazel Gaudet, *The People's Choice*, New York, Columbia University Press, 1944.

3. See, for example, Bernard Berelson, Paul Lazarsfeld, and William McPhee, *Voting: A Study of Opinion Formation in a Presidential Campaign*, Chicago, University of Chicago Press, 1954; Angus Campbell, Gerald Gurin, and Warren Miller, *The Voter Decides*, Evanston, Ill., Row, Peterson, 1954; Angus Campbell, Philip E. Converse, Warren E. Miller, and Donald Stokes, *The American Voter*, New York, Wiley, 1960; Norman H. Nie, Sidney Verba, and John R. Petrocik, *The Changing American Voter*, Cambridge, Mass., Harvard University Press, 1976; Warren E. Miller and Teresa E. Levitan, *Leadership and Change*, Cambridge, Mass., Winthrop, 1976; Thomas E. Patterson and Robert D. McClure, *The Unseeing Eye: The Myth of Television Power in National Elections*, New York, Putnam, 1976; Thomas Patterson, *The Mass Media Election: How Americans Choose Their President*, New York, Praeger, 1980.

4. Patterson, as cited in note 3.

5. For a condensed version of these findings see Garrett J. O'Keefe and L. Erwin Atwood, "Communication and Election Campaigns," in Dan D. Nimmo and Keith R. Sanders (eds.), *Handbook of Political Communication*, Beverly Hills, Sage, 1981, pp. 329–357. Also see the sources cited in note 3.

6. Arthur H. Miller and Michael MacKuen, "Informing the Electorate: A National Study," in Sidney Kraus (ed.), *The Great Debates: Carter vs. Ford, 1976*, Bloomington, Indiana University Press, 1979, pp. 290–291.

7. Cliff Zukin, "Mass Communication and Public Opinion," in Dan D. Nimmo and Keith R. Sanders (eds.), *Handbook of Political Communication*, Beverly Hills, Sage, 1981, p. 360.

8. Recent writings on agenda-setting are summarized in Maxwell E. McCombs, "The Agenda-Setting Approach," in Dan D. Nimmo and Keith R. Sanders (eds.), *Handbook of Political Communication*, Beverly Hills, Sage, 1981, pp. 121–140.

9. David H. Weaver, Doris A. Graber, Maxwell E. McCombs, and Chaim H. Eyal, *Media Agenda-Setting in a Presidential Election: Issues, Images, and Interest*, New York, Praeger, 1981.

10. For reviews of the literature on these concepts, see McCombs, cited in note 8; Jack M. McLeod and Lee B. Becker, "The Uses and Gratifications Approach," in Dan D. Nimmo and Keith R. Sanders (eds.), *Handbook of Political Communication*, Beverly Hills, Sage, 1981, pp. 67–99; Robert B. Zajonc, "Cognitive Theories in Social Psychology," in Gardner Lindzey and Elliot Aronson (eds.), *The Handbook of Social Psychology*, vol. 1, 2nd ed., Reading, Mass., Addison-Wesley, 1968 pp. 320–411.

11. An overview of the literature is presented in Charles K. Atkin, "Communication and Political Socialization," in Dan D. Nimmo and Keith R. Sanders (eds.), *Handbook of Political Communication*, Beverly Hills, Sage, 1981 pp. 299–328.

12. See McCombs, as cited in note 8.

13. See Weaver et al., cited in note 9.

14. Ibid.

15. Andre Modigliani and William A. Gamson, "Thinking About Politics," *Political Behavior*, 1:1, 1979, pp. 6–9.

16. Angus Campbell, Philip E. Converse, Warren E. Miller, and Donald E. Stokes, *The American Voter*, abridged edition, New York, Wiley, 1964, pp. 124–144.

17. See, for example, Stanley Feldman, "Economic Self-Interest and Political Behavior," *American Journal of Political Science*, 26:3, August, 1982, pp. 446–466; Donald R. Kinder, "Presidents, Prosperity and Public Opinion," *Public Opinion Quarterly*, 45, 1981, pp. 1–21.

18. Lloyd A. Free and Hadley Cantril, *The Political Beliefs of Americans: A Study of Public Opinion*, New York, Simon and Schuster, 1968.

19. Robert D. Putnam, *The Beliefs of Politicians: Ideology, Conflict, and Democracy in Britain and Italy*, New Haven, Yale University Press, 1973, pp. 22–25.

20. For a review of this literature, see note 31 in chapter 2.

21. Roger C. Schank and Robert P. Abelson, *Scripts, Plans, Goals and Understanding: An Inquiry into Human Knowledge Structures*, Hillsdale, N.J., Lawrence Erlbaum, 1977, p. 3.

22. Peter B. Warr and Christopher Knapper, *The Perception of People and Events*, New York, Wiley, 1968, pp. 255–288.

23. Susan T. Fiske and Donald R. Kinder, "Involvement, Expertise, and Schema Use: Evidence from Political Cognition," in Nancy Cantor and John F. Kihlstrom (eds.), *Personality, Cognition, and Social Interaction*, Hillsdale, N.J., Lawrence Erlbaum, 1981, p. 171.

# 2

## Through the Microscope: Developing a Research Design

### THE BASIC RESEARCH DESIGN

Three elements are needed for research designed to answer questions about the way people interact with political information. The first element is a group of people whose behavior can be observed to ascertain clues about information processing. The actual brain functions involved in processing information have largely remained beyond the reach of direct examination, aside from a small number of experiments in which brain wave responses to selected information stimuli have been tested.[1] However, it has been possible to record the information stimuli available for processing and to observe the way people reproduce these stimuli verbally after processing. From these verbal expressions, one can make inferences about reasoning processes.[2]

The second vital element in information-processing research is the body of information which provides the respondents with raw materials for information integration. Primary political information sources for our respondents were daily newspapers, a local weekly paper, and national and local television news programs. We examined the content of these sources in detail. News magazines, radio programs, and conversations turned out to be quite minor sources and were therefore checked more cursorily.

A third essential feature of any research design is a suitable theory. The current literature on political learning and information processing points to "schema theory" as the most appropriate approach. It is a theory that has been well-tested and is widely accepted by cognitive psychologists. Its adaptation for this study will be described more fully later in this chapter.

The study was designed as a microanalysis—an intensive study of a small number of people—because this is the preferred research approach whenever human thought processes must be investigated in depth over extended periods of time. Such investigations require exhaustive scrutiny of past and present life styles of individuals and their entire psychological, social, and informational setting. The results must be reported in their full complexity because they do not lend themselves to the shorthand of numerical representation which robs data of richness and realism. These constraints make it impractical to work with more than a limited number of respondents.

As demonstrated by Robert Lane's study of the political ideology of 15 working class men, the intensive study of mental operations performed by a limited number of people can provide insights into patterns of conceptualization which these people share with their counterparts in the larger society. Other researchers have discovered that a number of common human behaviors, such as information processing, exhibit only a limited number of gross patterns.[3] People can; therefore, be classified according to the patterns to which their behaviors correspond. How well one can draw general conclusions from the findings depends, of course, on the investigator's success in choosing a good sample and in properly identifying major behavior patterns. It is also helpful if the investigator is able to ascertain accurately what proportion of the entire population belongs to each of the behavioral types that have been identified.

## Selecting the Panel

The study began with the identification of a small group of respondents. Names were randomly drawn from the 1976 list of registered voters in Evanston, Illinois, until a pool of 200 respondents had been contacted and had completed an introductory interview. Evanston is a university town with a population of 70,000 adjacent to the city fo Chicago. Evanston was selected because it is a community in which political interest tends to be strong and because I was thoroughly familiar with the town's sociopolitical setting, including its print and electronic media. Registered voters were singled out on the assumption that registration signified that these people did have an interest in politics and an incentive to keep themselves informed, particularly prior to the presidential election of 1976. The chances that registered voters would process significant amounts of political information from the mass media were therefore better than might be true of people who had not made themselves eligible to vote.

The success rate in reaching 200 respondents initially and completing the introductory interview was 80%. This means that we had to draw on a pool of 250 names to end up with a pool of 200 completed contacts. Most of the people who could not be reached were students who had moved away from Evanston since compilation of the voter list 20 months earlier. Among the pool of 200 who were reached and who completed the initial filter interview, 84% were willing to participate in the study.

Each of the pool members was interviewed and classified according to interest in politics and ready access to mass media information, as well as the usual demographic characteristics. This classification allowed us to assess how information processing is affected by demographic factors, by eagerness to be informed, and by the effort required to obtain and use information in the face of competing demands on the respondent's time.[4] We assumed that high interest in politics and ease in getting information would encourage attention to news and a high rate of sophisticated processing. Low interest and difficulty in getting news would have the opposite effect.

To test these assumptions, we developed a four cell design that divided people into groups in which high or low interest in politics were each coupled with easy or difficult access to news. Figure 2.1 presents the scheme. People were rated as "high" in interest if they had scored 12 to 15 points on questions testing their interest in politics. They were labeled as "low," if interest was 9 points or less. The borderline group of people scoring 10 to 11 points were excluded from the study.[5] For ease of access, scores of 11 to 12 were called "high," while scores of 8 or less were "low." People scoring in the intermediate range of 9 to 10 points were excluded.[6] Accordingly, the people in cell 1 are high scorers in both interest and ease of access, while cell 4 people are low on both scores. Cell 2 and cell 3 people are mixed, with the former ranking "high" only in interest, and the latter ranking "high" only in ease of access.

The initial plan called for selecting 5 demographically diverse panel members for each of the 4 cells and identifying replacements in anticipation of a 20% dropout rate. When one panel member expected to be transferred out of the Midwest during the first trimester of the study, his substitute was added to the panel. Although the transfer did not materialize, and none of the initial panelists dropped out, the substitute was retained. This accounts for the fact that the final panel contains 6 members in cell 4, rather than 5 members. The 100% retention rate for the panel is exceptionally high. We attribute it to excellent interviewer-panelist rapport, continuous efforts to maintain panelists' interest in the research project, and token compensation for participation in the project.

Table 2.1 depicts the demographic characteristics of the panel members and lists the interest/access classifications to which they were assigned. To check whether a panel of such small size might be reasonably similar to the general

|  |  | ACCESS | |
|---|---|---|---|
|  |  | High | Low |
| INTEREST | High | 1 | 2 |
|  | Low | 3 | 4 |

FIGURE 2.1.   Respondent typology

TABLE 2.1. Panelists' Demographic and Media Use Characteristics

| Name (fictitious) | Age | Sex | Education* | Occupation |
|---|---|---|---|---|
| *1. High-interest, easy-access group* | | | | |
| Karl Adams | 25 | M | College | Research Engineer |
| Donald Burton | 38 | M | College | Administrator |
| Robert Creighton | 45 | M | College | Academic |
| Paul Diedrich | 74 | M | College | Lawyer |
| Leo Evanski | 75 | M | Grade School | Blue-Collar |
| *2. High-interest, difficult-access group* | | | | |
| Carol Fechbach | 28 | F | College | Home/Child Care |
| Martha Gaylord | 28 | F | College | Corporation/Executive |
| Helga Holmquist | 30 | F | College | Consultant/Home/Child Care |
| Cesar Ippolito | 33 | M | College | Government Administrator |
| Max Jackman | 36 | M | College | Editor |
| *3. Low-interest, easy-access group* | | | | |
| Craig Kolarz | 25 | M | College | Grocery Clerk |
| Penny Liebman | 46 | F | High School | Dress Shop Owner |
| Elaine Mullins | 50 | F | College | Homemaker |
| Betty Nystrom | 65 | F | High School | Bookkeeper |
| Sandra Ornstein | 78 | F | High School | Homemaker |
| *4. Low-interest, difficult-access group* | | | | |
| Sven Peterson | 23 | M | High School | Hospital Clerk |
| Tugwell Quentin | 27 | M | College | Retail Sales |
| Darlene Rosswell | 28 | F | High School | Insurance Clerk |
| Deidre Sandelius | 36 | F | High School | Nurse |
| Lettie Tisdale | 56 | F | 3rd Grade | Maid |
| David Utley | 62 | M | College | Plant Manager |

* Each grouping signifies graduates. The high school grouping includes people with partial college educations.

American electorate in responding to political questions, we compared the panelists' responses with results from contemporaneous national surveys. Comparisons were made by replicating a series of questions asked in the 1976 presidential election survey conducted by the Center for Political Studies at the University of Michigan. The answer patterns were sufficiently similar to suggest that this study's findings are common for demographically matching groups in the general population.

Our sample as a whole, it should be noted, included a higher percentage of college-educated people than would have been found in the general population. Previous studies suggest that college training enhances information-processing skills and interest in assimilating political information. It also provides a wide range of previously processed information that might facilitate integration of related new information. Higher education levels are associated with better incomes and, in turn, more leisure, that increases time available for exposure to the mass media.[6]

Our data as a whole, therefore, may reflect above average information-processing activity levels and more intellectually sophisticated performances than one would find in the general population. However, since the panel, as well as a pretest panel for the study, encompassed several people of low educational and socioeconomic status, we could make comparisons between these two types of panelists to assess the impact of socioeconomic and educational differences. These comparisons revealed that "more" and "better" information processing by the well-educated does not mean "basically different" information processing. The general patterns of processing were highly consistent across educational and socioeconomic levels.

In addition to comparing some of the panel's response characteristics with the national sample, we also made comparisons with 3 panels of 48 respondents. These panels were part of a companion study conducted simultaneously under very similar conditions.[7] Many of the questions in the companion study were identical so that direct comparisons on a wide array of answers were possible. We also used the control panels for group interviews to check on variations in response structure produced by small group settings.

The control panels represent populations in communities of diverse socio-economic character and size. While there were some discrepancies in responses traceable to these dissimilar environments, and to the group setting, the similarities were far more striking than the differences.[8] This fact provided additional reassurance that the responses of our panelists were "normal." Differences in geographic location, community size, socioeconomic status, and in the personalities of various interviewers did not produce major variations in results.

## Tapping People's Minds

Field work for the study began in January, 1976 and ended in January, 1977. We chose to study information processing over the course of a year that encompassed a presidential election because the flow of political information of interest to average citizens was likely to peak at such a time. One could, therefore, expect that registered voters would have plenty of material for exercising their processing skills in anticipation of the election.

Each panelist was interviewed ten times during the year and the interviews were (audio) taped. Interviews were spaced at roughly six-week intervals with occasional variations to capture reactions before or following important political events that occurred during the year. Panelists did not know the interview schedule in advance. Rather, interviews were arranged on short notice so that there would be little time for respondents to prepare themselves to answer questions that they might expect to be asked.

Interviews were conducted in the respondent's home or place of business. They averaged 2 hours in length so that the total data set includes approximately 400 hours of recorded interviews, nearly 20 hours for each person. During each interview, 50 to 100 questions were asked about a wide array of political topics. On an average, a 100-question interview yielded 1,500 to 2,000 statements in reply. This massive amount of discourse constitutes a very rich data set for observing the results of information processing. While not all aspects of information processing may have been captured for each individual, there appear to be few gaps in identifying all significant types of processing activities when observations across the total sample are considered.

The questions that we asked in order to assess information processing probed three areas. One was the degree of direct information transfer that had occurred. Here we wanted to know what kinds of information respondents typically extracted from news stories and what types they typically ignored. Secondly, the respondents' interactions with the story were ascertained. How did they conceptualize the information and what meanings did they assign to it? How did they fit the new information into their established belief patterns about the world and how did it modify these patterns? Finally, general thinking patterns were analyzed. This involved such things as looking at the nature and variety of perspectives from which stories were viewed, checking the ability of respondents to draw general conclusions from specific information, and investigating the types of strategies they used in processing information.

The bulk of the questions were open-ended because "closed-ended questions . . . are fatally flawed as instruments for understanding basic beliefs and values."[9] Closed-ended questions force respondents to fit their ideas into thinking patterns suggested by the investigator rather than using their own approaches. To provide an added check on the reliability of our findings, we repeated many questions in successive interviews, either in the same form and question sequence, or in a substantially revised form and during a different part of the interview. In this way, we hoped to guard against judging unique responses, prompted by specific conditions, as typical responses.

This approach is not without pitfalls. Initial questions may influence the answers to later questions when respondents realize that the same subject matter is involved, even though the question is asked several months later. Coders of the interview protocol are subject to a similar halo effect. After forming impressions from coding earlier questions, they may code subsequent ones in light of these early impressions. However, since the main conclusions of the study are based on evidence of the combined records of all the panelists and since each respondent's interview protocols were coded by several persons who were working independently, errors which may occur in the interpretation of individual records were minimized.

Substantively, the questions covered six areas of knowledge. They included (1) a diverse array of general political, social, and economic issues that had been given substantial recent coverage by the news media and (2) impressions about what the panelists and other people in the community considered to be the most important social problems. Such impressions tap the relative salience of many of the issues which have been or are currently receiving media attention. They "tell a great deal about how society perceives and interprets a given historical moment."[10] Knowledge areas also included (3) election-related information about various candidates, key political issues, and the reactions they had produced among potential voters. Questions about these matters were frequently posed as storytelling exercises to allow respondents complete freedom in structuring their answers. A typical question was: "What would you tell a friend about Jimmy Carter if she or he had never heard about him?"

Additionally, (4) there were questions testing the nature and extent of recall of specific current news stories. As with the other questions, answers about the stories involved synthesizing various strands of information. However, in addition, the story recall questions also tested the respondents' ability to report information in the form in which it had been originally presented to them. (5) Several questions related to media use and evaluation. These entailed queries about how often the respondent used various types of media, how well he or she liked them, and more specifically, the sources for particular stories that the respondent recalled. Finally, (6) there were extensive questions about the respondent's family background, past experiences, and current social setting.

Additional data about information processing came from daily diaries. Eighteen of the respondents completed diaries in which they reported what they remembered about news stories that had recently come to their attention. Each respondent was asked to record at least 3 current events stories per day for 5 days of each week, along with personal reactions to the stories. The stories that could come from the mass media, conversation, or personal experiences, were recorded after an average lag of 4 hours or more beyond exposure. The time delay—a minimum of 30 minutes—was requested of the respondents to permit normal forgetting to occur. The diary forms asked for brief reports about the main themes of each story, its source and length, the respondent's reactions to it, as well as the reasons for paying attention to the story and remembering it.

Of the respondents, 13 completed the diaries on their own, while 5 reported the information during telephone interviews. Pretests had shown that the difference in reporting methods did not affect the quantity or quality of the diary stories. These findings were substantiated by analysis of the diaries of two respondents who alternated between writing their own diaries and reporting them via telephone. For reasons of economy, 3 of the respondents were not asked to complete diaries.

The average number of diary stories for each person was 533, with a range from a low of 351 to a high of 969. A majority of the panelists completed diaries on a regular 5-day schedule except for periods of illness in the family and during vacations and business trips. Most respondents claimed that they had not paid attention to the news during those periods and had not kept informed through conversations. Tests of information recall support this contention. Recall was sharply reduced during periods in which daily routines had been interrupted.

## Advantages and Disadvantages of Intensive Interviews

The in-depth interview methods used for this study were particularly well suited for measuring information processing because they permitted listening with "the third ear." As Lane points out in *Political Ideology*, a perceptive interviewer can "read between the lines" because there are sufficient lines available and because the interviewer has had an opportunity to become much better acquainted with the respondent than is possible in less intensive contacts.[11] If properly managed, interview coding is quite reliable with high levels of intra- and intercoder agreement. Nonetheless, the fact that interviewing is costly, and coding is tedious and time-consuming has limited use of in-depth interviews.[12]

Lane identified four special advantages of intensive personal interviews in tapping the thinking processes of respondents.[13] In the first place, such interviews are *discursive*. They allow respondents to pursue their own train of thought. This provides investigators with insights into the meanings that respondents give to words and phrases. For instance, when Robert Creighton was asked whether he ever discussed politics, he answered "no." Then he added, "I only discuss world affairs." Coding his answer as "no" when the investigator's definition of "politics" included world affairs, obviously would have been an error. In a discursive interview, the interviewer also can observe the associations that respondents make in their thinking. This permits systematic study of the structural relationships among assertions and provides insights into the existence and nature of belief systems.[14]

Secondly, intensive interviews are *dialectical*. Reciprocal interchange between the respondent and the interviewer provides opportunities for extensive probing of the respondent's ideas. It also allows examination of the personal meanings that the respondents give to common code words such as identifying people and politicians as "liberal" or "conservative."

In the third place, intensive interviews, when combined with tape recordings, provide an *accurate textual account* of everything said. This permits a precise analysis of the words and word pictures used by the respondents that supply cues to the underlying conceptualizations. The respondents' answers also can be interpreted more readily when they are viewed in their appropriate *contexts*. This is very important because "cognitive operations are structured according to the information patterns in the actual social situations in which mental tasks are performed.[15] In addition, full textual accounts permit checking the degree of consistency in information-processing patterns over time. Long range, repeated observations, furthermore, reveal general patterns of information processing and of reasoning strategies.

Finally, intensive interviews are *biographical*. This allows for life experiences to be related to information processing and reasoning patterns. When typical relationships between life experiences and information processing are identified, the impact that social forces have on thinking patterns can be assessed. The emphasis can be put on detecting common, rather than individual experiences. The personal interview setting also allows direct observation of the particular physical and social environment to which each respondent reacts. Moreover, it reveals nonverbal cues to personality and to depth of emotional involvement with particular issues. Pauses, hesitant answers, and nervous laughs, are examples of typical clues.

Several reservations are often voiced about intensive interviews of small panels of people. As mentioned earlier, using a data set drawn from only 21 individuals creates difficulties when one wants to make statements that are generally applicable to the behavior of larger populations. We reduced these problems somewhat by comparing the respondents in this study to the national sample used by the University of Michigan in 1976, as well as comparing them to three other small panels from different backgrounds whose interview protocols were similar. In each case, there were no major differences. Reservations about the representativeness of the findings are further eased by the fact that recent large-sample studies of selected aspects of cognitive processing corroborate the corresponding findings in this study.[16]

One may also harbor doubts about the willingness and ability of people to report their mental activities, particularly when these activities involve routine situations that may not be vivid in their minds. Memory may be faulty and laced with bias. People may not know their thinking processes. They may base their reports on popular theories about the causal connections between stimuli and responses. These theories may be incorrect. If correct, they may not be applied properly to explain the behavior of the particular respondent.[17] To avoid the danger of relying on self-reports for judging thinking processes, we made inferences directly from the recorded comments. We did not ask the respondents to describe their thinking processes. In this way the data, rather than the respondents' a priori assumptions, supply the clues.

Using this data-based approach also helps to detect insincerity that may be encouraged by the desire to please the interviewer. We found evidence of deliberate skewing of answers in the records of only one of our panelists. Betty Nystrom repeatedly tried to make her responses conform to what she perceived to be socially desirable stances. For instance, she habitually expressed her lack of racial prejudice and retracted prejudicial remarks after uttering them. Nonetheless, her interview protocols are laced with evidence of racial bigotry. She also overstated her knowledge of news events and tried to bluff when it became obvious that she did not know what she professed to know. Her case demonstrates that it is difficult to mask ordinary patterns of thinking and knowledge in the face of multiple intensive questions spread out over a long span of time.

Omission of known information is a bigger problem than deliberate distortion. Respondents may tell only parts of what they know about news stories. They may edit their remarks randomly or systematically to weed out information that makes them feel uncomfortable or that seems self-evident to them. The use of multiple probing questions eases the problem only partially. Moreover, as Putnam has warned,

> some important political attitudes rarely if ever reach the stage of explicit formulation. Such unstated assumptions, or "cognitive predispositions," silently structure more explicit and more ephemeral political action. The predispositions serve as implicit premises for conscious reasoning that leads men to act as they do.[18]

However, these assumptions may become apparent from the patterns of conceptualizations that emerge from examining a large number of responses by the same individual.

The validity of findings from interview studies is based on the assumption that respondents are reacting normally in an essentially normal setting. When interviews are conducted in the respondents' homes and are repeated sufficiently so that respondents become accustomed to the interviewer and the questioning process, normality would seem assured. Granting that skilled interviewing conducted in familiar settings can achieve a relaxed attitude among respondents, interviewing nonetheless remains a reactive research technique. The interview situation as such becomes part of the context in which comments are formulated. The personality of the interviewer, the nature and sequence of the questions, the environmental factors of the particular day, and the setting all produce reactions in the respondent which may not be totally "typical."

There is no escape from this problem. Yet, the types of responses gathered for this study could not become available in sufficient scope and quantity through unobtrusive eavesdropping. A person's written messages do not constitute an acceptable alternative because they, too, are usually produced in reaction to a specific, potentially biasing, stimulus. The reactivity problem is diminished somewhat when massive bodies of data are accumulated over an extended-period of time. This assures a large number of variations in the contexts in which questions are asked, minimizing the impact of particular conditions that might be present in a single interview.

Taping the interviews apparently created no problems, especially since few questions were potentially sensitive for the respondents.[19] Most people seemed to forget about the recorder. I was asked only once to turn the recorder off when a respondent discussed improper behavior by his boss that, he claimed, was unknown to his colleagues. During pretests for the study, comparisons of taped and hand-recorded interviews showed no difference in the openness of respondents, their willingness to answer questions, and in the completeness of their responses.

Panel studies also raise questions about the effects of earlier interviews on later ones. Being an interview subject may raise a person's interest level in the topics of discussion and may stimulate increased attention to relevant information. To check whether significant sensitization had occurred, we conducted periodic interviews with people from the original pool of respondents who had not been interviewwed except at the original screening. We found no significant differences in the answers given by panel members and outsiders. For instance, a comparison of the ability to recall news stories, rated on a 4-point scale, showed a ranking of 2.3 for panel members and 2.4 for the control group.

Apparently, sensitization was not a problem because of the scope and length of the study. During each interview, so many different questions were asked that the respondents found it difficult to remember their answers or to be alerted to the type of question that might be asked in subsequent interviews. Furthermore, the year-long time span of the study made it too inconvenient to maintain enhanced attentiveness to information. Although information seeking increased moderately for a few respondents during the first six weeks of the study, it returned to normal levels thereafter. Data from group interviews conducted with members of the control panels confirm this observation.

## ANALYZING INTERVIEW AND MEDIA DATA

Attention arousal and information processing were examined by a two-stage analysis of the interview tapes and diaries. The first coding ascertained the substance of the interview responses and the diary contents. Topics of recall, frequencies, direction and strength of opinions, and the like were noted. Most of this work was done by a single coder, with intercoder reliability checks performed on 10% of the work. For questions involving discretion, intercoder reliability averaged 91%. It did not drop below 83% for any single category.

The second, and more difficult, coding task involved conceptual coding. Here coders were asked to infer thinking processes from the respondents' comments. We checked the interview protocols for such matters as conceptualizations of political situations, ability to generalize and produce analogies, cause-and-effect linkages, rationales and rationalizations, and consistencies and inconsistencies in thought.[20]

A total of seven coders were involved in conceptual coding. Interview protocols for each respondent were parcelled out to three or more coders to guard against idiosyncratic coding. Each individual interview was coded independently by at least two trained coders. At the start of the project, three coders were used. Ultimately, two codings were deemed sufficient since intercoder reliability rates were good—averaging 85% agreement on choice of statements to be coded and selection of a specific code.[21] Intercoder reliability was equally good when coders interpreted what the respondent meant, in light of all responses, as when they stuck strictly to what the respondents said.[22] Coders also reached high levels of agreement when coding latent features, such as the ability to generalize, and when making overall judgments of certain traits of the respondents, based on the whole interview.

The second portion of data presented in this book—the mass media messages available to our panelists—came from daily content analyses of the print and broadcast media used by our respondents. The panelists included in this study relied most heavily on the *Chicago Tribune*, as their daily newspaper, and on the *Evanston Review* for weekly news.[23] They used the *Chicago Daily News* and the *Chicago Sun Times* only occasionally. For this reason, we limited content analysis of the latter two papers to two constructed weeks for comparison with daily *Tribune* coverage. A constructed week is composed of seven successive weekdays, each drawn from a different week.

Our panelists watched the early evening news broadcasts of the three national television networks. For local newscasts, most used the 5 P.M. NBC and 10 P.M. CBS news. Local news was viewed, taped, and coded from the actual telecast. National news was coded from printed abstracts provided by the Vanderbilt Television News Archives. Comparisons between codings from these abstracts and codings done directly from newscasts showed only very minor differences for the information required for this study. Use of the abstracts of national newscasts simplified and reduced costs substantially. At the local level, no abstracts were available.

While we did not code radio broadcasts and news magazines, information provided during interviews and in the daily news diaries furnished by respondents gives some insights about the news obtained from these sources. These audience comments suggest that radio newscasts yielded information that was quite similar to information gained from local television newscasts. News magazines, on the other hand, while they dealt with the same information as daily newspapers, provided more news interpretations and context for the panelists. However, compared to newspapers and television, they were seldom mentioned as sources of information in the diaries or during interviews. On balance, it appears that the addition of detailed coding of radio and news magazine offerings would not have altered the substance of findings presented in this book.

The content of the panelists' major news sources was analyzed on a daily basis for the entire year of 1976. This permitted us to capture the daily flow of news available to the panel members and to assess its cumulative impact. It also prevented sampling problems that arise because major news events are not randomly distributed. We coded up to three topics for each news story to capture its main themes. News was categorized into 67 subject areas, dealing with major social institutions, interest groups, individual actors, as well as with policies, and individual and group activities at various political levels.

Two subject areas were selected for especially intensive analysis. They were the 1976 presidential election and crime news. We had anticipated that these would be areas of particular interest to all of the panelists, so that there would be many instances of news processing available in all of the interview protocols. Therefore it was helpful to have more detailed information about the media treatment of these stories.

Election stories were analyzed for details about candidate images and about linkages made between policy issues and specific politicians. Stories were also checked for the kinds of information they provided about the major problems facing the nation. Besides checking story substance, we noted how often particular types of stories and story elements were mentioned and how prominently they were featured. In the crime story content analysis, coding emphasis was on features such as the nature of the crimes that were covered, causes and motivations of crimes, details revealed about particular crimes, and information about apprehension of offenders, prosecution, conviction rates, and penalties. Stories dealing primarily with the police, the courts, and the correctional system were also included in the intensive analysis.

The coding unit used in all these content analyses was the individual story. All news stories were coded for each newspaper and news broadcast, except for features in the entertainment sections of the paper. "Stories" for newspapers were defined as including editorials, letters to the editor, features, and cartoons, as well as ordinary news reports. Excluded were advertisements, obituaries, puzzles, radio and television listings, and similar types of announcements. For television, "stories" encompassed all information conveyed during regularly scheduled newscasts, except for commercials.

The reliability of coding for the content analysis was carefully controlled.

It is difficult to report a single reliability figure since many different coders were involved in this project. The same coding supervisor checked and recoded a portion of each coder's work following the initial training period and at various times thereafter. Excluding simple identification categories, such as newspaper or station name and date, which might inflate reliability figures, intercoder reliability averaged 85% and intracoder reliability averaged 90%. These figures are based on using the ratio of coding agreements to the total number of coding decisions. Considering the complexity of coding, these results are good.

## THE THEORETICAL BASE: SCHEMA THEORY

Finally, the most important element in any research design is the theoretical perspective from which the data are collected and processed. Social scientists interested in human learning have developed many different theories about the ways in which people process information. We formulated hypotheses on the basis of these theories and tested them out with the data. Theories which were tested in this manner included classical learning theories, gestalt theories, various cognitive consistency theories, as well as a spate of cognitive processing and schema theories.[24]

To some degree, the data are consistent with at least a portion of all of these theories. However, the best fit of theory and data, by far, occurred when we used schema theories.[25] As is true of many terms used by social scientists, there is considerable disagreement about the precise definition to be given to "schema theory." This makes it necessary to define carefully how the term is used. To make the semantic confusion worse, various terms other than "schema" have been used by scholars for schematic information-processing models. Roger Schank and Robert Abelson, for instance, talk about "social scripts."[26] Other scholars, using slightly different perspectives on the same phenomenon, have talked about "preliminary cognitive representations (PCR)," about prototypes, or about "constructs" and the "constructivist approach."[27] Scholars investigating decision-making by political elites have dealt with schemas when they have examined "cognitive maps." Such maps delineate how various elements of a leader's belief structures are interrelated.[28]

A number of social scientists have talked about schemas without labelling them as such. These include, among others, Philip Converse in his search for ideologically constrained belief systems and Robert Lane in his discussions of the way in which his respondents "contextualized" their beliefs.[29] Some of the literature dealing with attitude clusters also borders on schema theory.[30] Thus schema theory does not constitute a sharp break with other theories that deal with cognitive functions. Rather, it builds on them but goes farther.

As will become clear when we describe the nature of schemas more fully, where other theories are vague about mental configurations that affect the manner in which people assign meaning to incoming information, schema theories present more concrete and detailed hypotheses. Confirmation of these hypotheses leads to a much better understanding of what goes on inside peoples' heads when they process information than is possible when research takes its cues from other theories about cognitive functioning.

Schema theories have been tested repeatedly and substantiated experimentally by various teams of scholars using non-political data.[31] At the present time, cognitive processing models, such as schema theory are, in the view of respected social psychologists, "the most comprehensive and comprehensible way" to understand and explain higher mental processes such as thinking, perception, concept formation, and memory.[32] Among political scientists, these theories have come into vogue more recently, starting with studies of thinking processes of political elites, and then moving to studies of selected aspects of the political thinking of average people. The focus has been on schemas about specific politicians, policies, rules, events, and institutions that tap the lay person's theories about the political world.[33]

The chief criticism of cognitive processing models has been that they have relied heavily, in the past, on testing through laboratory experiments. Since this is an unnatural setting, the models may, therefore, lack ecological validity. Moreover, there is little assurance that all aspects of information processing have been fully detected. People's capacity for information processing may be far more diverse and complex than revealed by evidence from verbalized descriptions and evaluations. A few critics have also complained that there is no absolute proof that the schemas that have been inferred actually exist in human minds. The schema paradigm has stood up well in the face of such criticisms and has attracted a larger following than any competing theory. By applying the model to political data, the findings presented here expand the study of information processing in general, as well as providing information about processing strategies in a particular area of knowledge.

What then is a schema, and why is it useful for processing information? In a nutshell, a schema is a cognitive structure consisting of organized knowledge about situations and individuals that has been abstracted from prior experiences. It is used for processing new information and retrieving stored information.[34] In the words of Fiske and Kinder, "Schemata constitute serviceable although imperfect devices for coping with complexity. They direct attention to relevant information, guide its interpretation and evaluation, provide inferences when information is missing or ambiguous, and facilitate its retention."[35]

Cognitive psychologists have described schemas as pyramidal structures "hierarchically organized with more abstract or general information at the top and categories of more specific information nested within the general categories."[36] More simply, this means that most schemas contain conceptions of general patterns, along with a limited repertoire of prototypical examples to illustrate these patterns. The general patterns usually are commonsense models of life situations that individuals have experienced personally or encountered vicariously. They may be embedded in an overarching ideological conception that helps to structure the subordinate levels of the schema, or they may exist, side by side, with only casual connections.

Most schemas appear to have a limited number of basic components. For instance, when people think about election campaigns, their thoughts may dwell exclusively on the personal qualities and backgrounds of particular candidates, on their political background and ideology, and on their campaign style and a limited number of specific issue stands. These categories are the six slots in their mental filing system into which people generally place campaign information. These slots may be part of a general conception of politicians and campaigns, or they may form part of the schema for a particular politician.[37]

Schemas include information about the main features of situations or individuals and about the relationships among these features.[38] They also include information about the expected sequences of occurrences or behaviors under various contingencies. Thus people may have definite ideas about what can be expected to happen in election campaigns or when teachers go on strike in the public schools. They can envision the characters in such scenarios, the props, the actions, and the sequence of actions. They also may have an array of ready-made evaluations and feelings about all aspects of these scenarios, and they may make inferences based on the scenarios. The actual situation encountered at a particular time may be mentally restructured by adding, subtracting, or altering features so that the situation fits more readily into the established mental image.

Several schemas may be linked to each other so that thinking progresses readily from one schema to the next. Thus, thoughts about a variety of social programs may be closely linked to thoughts about the costs of government and the effects of these costs on the economy. When one schema is tapped, the others are also likely to be tapped either for storing information or for retrieving it. Many schemas may overlap so that the same bits of information may be stored in different contexts and often from different perspectives.

According to schema theory, people are "cognitive misers" whose limited capacity for dealing with information forces them to practice "cognitive economies" by forming simplified mental models (what Fiske and Kinder call "generic knowledge structures") about the world.[39] Simplified representation seems particularly important for a knowledge sphere, such as politics, which presents flood tides of information through the mass media, yet is far removed from the personal experience and interests of average citizens.

Schemas perform four major functions. (1) They determine what information will be noticed, processed, and stored so that it becomes available for retrieval from memory. (2) They help individuals organize and evaluate new information so that it fits into their established perceptions. This makes it unnecessary to construct new concepts whenever familiar information is presented. (3) Schemas make it possible for people to go beyond the immediate information presented to them and fill in missing information. This permits making sense from abbreviated communications. (4) Schemas also help people in solving problems because they contain information about likely scenarios and ways to cope with them. This makes them an important element in deciding whether and how to act.[40]

How do we know that schemas actually exist and are not merely figments of the imagination of social scientists? Sir Frederick Bartlett, one of the earliest proponents of schema theory, provided an answer. Bartlett noted that English audiences, who were asked to retell Kwakiutl Indian folktales, would frequently change story details as if the action had taken place in familiar British cultural settings. From this pattern of story revisions, Bartlett concluded that his British audiences had mental frameworks about story scenarios and were fitting facts from an alien culture into these frameworks to make them meaningful.[41] Bartlett's work, which was published in 1932, was ignored for nearly 30 years. Then, it was picked up again by cognitive psychologists who demonstrated in laboratory settings that people will fill in missing parts of stories in line with standard story scenarios in their memories.

The same phenomenon is apparent in the interview protocols of our respondents. Remarks like "it's one of those periodic crackdowns the police go through" or "the media always pick on this kind of thing," are evidence that people have mental pictures of corresponding events.[42] In fact, several respondents would actually supply imaginary dialogues while they were speculating about what had probably happened in a particular situation. Darlene Rosswell, for instance, considered President Ford a puppet for Richard Nixon, his predecessor. She invented a dialogue to match this schema.

> And when Nixon says, "Say, I'm going to China." President Ford might have felt "well, being the President, I should go." But that's the only thing he thought. If Nixon said, "I'm going and I'm going to tell them what has to be said." Then, Ford said "well o.k., I'd rather go, but if you feel you should go, then go ahead, you know."

There currently is no consensus on how one can best test what kinds of schemas people use.[43] Most social psychologists test people with specific information in laboratory settings to gauge from their recall what schemas, if any, they have used for processing.[44] Several recent studies by political scientists have tested schemas by using survey research or small panel interviews to study the manner of recall of generally available information. The research reported in this book presents examples. Alternatively, one can explore schemas by suggesting certain traits to respondents or creating prototypical situations or individuals for them and then asking them to supply additional details or to provide story scenarios.[45] For instance, we asked our respondents to describe their conceptions of the typical criminal and the typical crime victim. We also asked them to describe the main features involved in major political issues, such as welfare policy, or to describe in their own words specific political figures, such as President Ford or Governor Carter. In this way, we were able to establish that the panelists did, indeed, have mental pictures. We were also able to glimpse at the dimensions of these pictures and some of the specific details that had been stored.

## THE FINISHED RESEARCH DESIGN

When carried out, the research design produced a panel of 21 registered voters, with diverse demographic characteristics, but all living in the same community.

They were a reasonably "average" group, compared to their demographic counterparts in the nation. Repeated lengthy interviews did not turn them into news freaks or change their behaviors markedly in any other way.

If one wants to know how people process information, one must check the raw materials. To do this, we carefully examined the content of the major information sources that the panelists used. This required content analyzing 1 major newspaper and 5 versions of evening news broadcast by the 3 major networks.[46] In this way we knew the content, format, and context of the major stories to which our panelists were exposed as long as they followed their usual patterns of media attention. When we asked them questions about news stories, we could judge the relationship between their answers and the stories because we knew how the stories had been presented.

Finally, we formulated hypotheses, on the basis of various theories about political learning and about the kinds of findings one could expect if the theories were valid. When we tested data from the initial interviews in light of these hypotheses, schema theory emerged as the best fit. To confirm the accuracy of this conclusion, we developed schema and information-processing profiles for each of the panelists on the basis of the initial interviews. We used these profiles to project the kinds of patterns we expected to find in subsequent interviews. These projections turned out to be accurate in all major respects.

Accordingly, it seemed reasonable to conclude that information processing and the development and use of schema are stable cognitive operations that are worth investigating. Once the patterns that groups of individuals exhibit for these behaviors are known, one can predict how they are likely to handle new information and questions about stored information, as long as the context for storing and retrieval of information remains constant. More importantly, one can understand how individuals use mass media information in the process of keeping abreast of their political world.

And now we are ready to enter the world of the panelists. We shall examine their social-psychological cocoons and the political currents that buffet them. And we shall meet them individually.

## Notes

1. See, for example, Herbert E. Krugman, "Brain Wave Measures of Media Involvement," *Journal of Advertising Research*, 11, 1971, pp. 3–9. A full discussion of the physiological bases for learning is presented in Thomas S. Brown and Patricia M. Wallace, *Physiological Psychology*, New York, Academic Press, 1980. A brief summary can be found in Jarol B. Manheim, *The Politics Within: A Primer in Political Attitudes and Behavior*, 2nd ed., New York, Longman, 1982, pp. 168–191.

2. For a psycholinguistic perspective, see Roy Lachman, Janet L. Lachman, and Earl C. Butterfield, *Cognitive Psychology and Information Processing: An Introduction*, Hillsdale, N.J., Lawrence Erlbaum, 1979, chapter 11.

3. Steven R. Brown, *Political Subjectivity: Application of Q Methodology in Political*

*Science*, New Haven, Yale University Press, 1980; Steven R., Brown, "Intensive Analysis in Political Research," *Political Methodology*, 1, 1974, pp. 1–25; Karl A. Lamb, *As Orange Goes: Twelve California Families and the Future of American Politics*, New York, Norton, 1974; Robert E. Lane, *Political Ideology: Why the American Common Man Believes What He Does*, New York, Free Press, 1962; Jennifer L. Hochschild, *What's Fair? American Beliefs about Distributive Justice*, Cambridge, Harvard University Press, 1981; Kay Lehman Schlozman and Sidney Verba, *Injury to Insult: Unemployment, Class, and Political Response*, Cambridge, Harvard University Press, 1979.

4. The degree of each respondent's interest in politics was assessed on the basis of variations in answers to five questions. Three levels of interest were scored for each of the following questions: (1) How much do you use newspapers for news about political issues and events? (2) How much do you use television for news about political issues and events? (3) In general, how often do you discuss politics with others? (4) Overall, how interested are you in politics? (5) How far did you go in school?

5. Three levels of answers to four questions were used as cues to the ease of access to the media: (1) How often do you read a daily newspaper? (2) How often do you watch the news on television? (3) Do you subscribe to a newspaper, buy it at a newsstand, or secure it in specified other ways? (4) How often do you watch television? Follow-up questions were used to elicit reasons for the behaviors reported in the answers so that the answers could be interpreted more accurately.

6. Numerous studies of political knowledge have produced evidence that people with more formal education, as a group, acquire more political information than their less well-educated counterparts. See, for example, Norman H. Nie, Sidney Verba, and John R. Petrocik, *The Changing American Voter*, Cambridge, Mass., Harvard University Press, 1976, pp. 119–121; Robert S. Erikson, Norman R. Luttbeg, and Kent L. Tedin, *American Public Opinion: Its Origins, Content, And Impact*, 2nd ed., New York, Wiley, 1980, pp. 127–133; Stephen Earl Bennett, Robert Oldendick, Alfred J. Tuchfarber, and George F. Bishop, "Education and Mass Belief Systems: An Extension and Some New Questions," *Political Behavior*, 1, 1979, pp. 53–72. Hans D. Klingemann, "The Background of Ideological Conceptualizations," in Samuel H. Barnes et al. (eds.), *Political Action: Mass Participation in Five Western Democracies*, Beverly Hills, Sage, 1979, pp. 255–277.

7. The companion panels were located in Evanston, Illinois, Indianapolis, Indiana, and Lebanon, New Hampshire. These sites were chosen to represent people in a large metropolitan area, a medium-size town, and a small community in a rural setting. The socioeconomic and educational levels of the Indianapolis and Lebanon panels were considerably lower than those of the Evanston panel.

8. For a description of some of these differences, see Doris A. Graber, *Crime News and the Public*, New York, Praeger, 1980, pp. 104–115.

9. Robert D. Putnam, *The Beliefs of Politicians: Ideology, Conflict, and Democracy in Britain and Italy*, New Haven, Yale University Press, 1973, p. 18.

10. Tom W. Smith, "America's Most Important Problem—A Trend Analysis, 1946–1976," *Public Opinion Quarterly*, 44, Summer 1980, p. 164. Smith reports and analyzes trends on the "most important problem" question. He recorded 1.1 to 1.35 responses per respondent. He also undertook a time series analysis of demographic variables.

11. Robert E. Lane, *Political Ideology: Why the American Common Man Believes What He Does*, New York, Free Press, 1962, pp. 9–10.

12. The method has been used in a number of studies. See for example the works by Lamb and Hochschild, cited in note 3. When conceptualizations have been examined

in connection with larger surveys, answers to open-ended questions have been used as the data base. See, for example, Angus Campbell, Philip E. Converse, Warren E. Miller, and Donald E. Stokes, *The American Voter*, New York, Wiley, 1960; Hans D. Klingemann, "Measuring Ideological Conceptualization," in Samuel H. Barnes and Max Kaase (eds.), *Political Action: Mass Participation in Five Western Democracies*, Beverly Hills, Sage, 1979, pp. 215–254.

13. Lane, as cited in note 11, pp. 8–11.

14. Samuel Freeman, "The Elitist-Populist Debate on Mass Belief Systems," *Midwest Political Science Association Paper*, 1981.

15. W. Lance Bennett, "Perception and Cognition: An Information-Processing Framework for Politics," in Samuel L. Long (ed.), *The Handbook of Political Behavior*, vol. 1, New York, Plenum Press, 1981, p. 82.

16. See, for example, David O. Sears and Jack Citrin, *Tax Revolt: Something for Nothing in California*, Cambridge, Mass., Harvard University Press, 1982; Arthur H. Miller, Martin P. Wattenberg, and Oksana Malanchuk, "Cognitive Representations of Candidate Assessments," *American Political Science Association Paper*, 1982.

17. Richard E. Nisbett and Timothy DeCamp Wilson, "Telling More Than We Can Know: Verbal Reports on Mental Processes," *Psychological Review*, 84:3, 1977, pp. 248–252. The authors argue that the source of these theories lies in cultural and subcultural rules theories, in empirical observation of cause and effect, and in rational linking of phenomena—if I have insomnia, I must be worried. Moreover, people are more likely to give stereotypical causal explanations for stimuli that are remote in time than for more recent stimuli. Nisbett and Wilson's findings are based on experimental research.

18. Putnam, as cited in note 9, p. 126.

19. For similar experiences see Lane, as cited in note 3, p. 7; and Putnam, as cited in note 9, pp. 20–22.

20. Category construction was left open throughout the coding process so that new categories could be added when needed. the second coder could then fill in any information skipped prior to the expansion of catagories. Each coded item was accompanied by a verbatim or summarized account of the statements which were coded and the context in which the statement was made. Coding categories fell into seven major groups. (1) Under "Evidence of Schemas" we coded statements that indicated that the respondents had a persistent, detailed mental picture of the situation they mentioned. We also coded the nature of this picture. For example, did it involve a judgment of persons, and who was judged in what way? Did it involve statements about cause-effect relationships? (2) Under "Schema Variations" we coded such features as the level of abstraction of the statement, its complexity, its consistency with previous schemas, and elements of inferential thinking which might be involved. (3) "Processing Strategies" required coding evidence of the respondents' efforts to relate new information to previous knowledge or established thinking categories. (4) Evidence of detail retention, patterns of remembering and forgetting, and the like, fell into the "Memory" category. (5) We also recorded all evidence of reasons for paying attention or ignoring stories about current affairs under the rubric of "Story Choice Criteria." (6) The category of "Perspectives" was used to code general response patterns, such as the tendency to put problems into a public or private-regarding perspective or view them in the light of past history. (7) The final group of coding categories, called "Idiosyncracies" was reserved for recording the respondents' definitions of various political concepts, their appraisals of media performance, and references to unique personal experiences. No attempt was made to count the number of times each coding category occurred because this was a function of the kind of news available to the respondents in

1976 and the kinds of questions we asked them. Although news topics, over all, are fairly consistent from year to year, the frequencies would have been different if we had worked with another set of news stories. However, for purposes of analysis we used only those data which appeared repeatedly.

21. Other researchers have achieved equally high reliability levels when they used trained, sensitive coders, See, for example, Putnam, as cited in note 9, p. 23.

22. Putnam, as cited in note 9, p. 262, found the same. Also see John C. Pierce and Paul R. Hagner, "Conceptualization and Party Identification: 1956–1976," *American Journal of Political Science*, 26:2, May 1982, p. 378.

23. Comparisons of *Tribune* readers with *Sun Times* and *Daily News* readers did not show any significant differences in demographic or psychosocial characteristics.

24. For a brief review of learning theories see Philip E. Freedman and Anne Freedman, "Political Learning," in Samuel L. Long (ed.), *The Handbook of Political Behavior*, vol. 1, New York, Plenum Press, 1981, pp. 255–303.

25. The discussion that follows merely samples the extensive literature on this topic. For an exhaustive analysis and rich bibliography see Lachman et al., as cited in note 2.

26. Roger C. Schank and Robert P. Abelson, *Scripts, Plans, Goals, and Understanding: An Inquiry into Human Knowledge Structures*, Hillsdale, N.J., Lawrence Erlbaum, 1977.

27. Nancy Cantor, "A Cognitive-Social Approach to Personality," in Nancy Cantor and John F. Kihlstrom (eds.), *Personality, Cognition, and Social Interaction*, Hillsdale, N.J., Lawrence Erlbaum, 1981, pp. 23–44; David L. Swanson, "A Constructivist Approach," in Dan D. Nimmo and Keith R. Sanders (eds.), *Handbook of Political Communication*, Beverly Hills, Sage, 1981, pp. 169–191.

28. Bennett, as cited in note 15, p. 165; Robert Axelrod, *Structure of Decision: The Cognitive Maps of Political Elites*, Princeton, Princeton University Press, 1976, p. 20.

29. For a discussion of schema-related analyses, see Susan T. Fiske and Donald R. Kinder, "Involvement, Expertise, and Schema Use: Evidence from Political Cognition," in Cantor and Kihlstrom, cited in note 27, pp. 176–181.

30. See, e.g., Martin Fishbein and Icek Ajzen, *Belief, Attitude, Intention and Behavior: An Introduction to Theory and Research*, Reading, Mass., Addison Wesley, 1975.

31. Examples are contained in the following works: Cantor and Kihlstrom, as cited in notes 27 and 29; Mardi Jon Horowitz, *Image Formation and Cognition*, 2nd ed., New York, Appleton-Century-Crofts, 1978; Lachman et al., as cited in note 2; Peter H. Lindsay and Donald A. Norman, *Human Information Processing*, New York, Academic Press, 1977; Schank and Abelson, as cited in note 26; Constance Scheerer (ed.), *Cognition: Theory, Research, Promise*. New York: Harper and Row, 1964. The psychobiological roots of schemas are discussed by Ulric Neisser, *Cognition and Reality*, San Francisco, W. H. Freeman, 1976.

32. Lachman et al., as cited in note 2, p. 33.

33. Axelrod, as cited in note 28; Putnam, as cited in note 9; Fiske and Kinder, as cited in note 29; Sears and Citrin, as cited in note 16; Miller et al., as cited in note 16; Pamela Johnston Conover and Stanley Feldman, "Belief System Organization in the American Electorate: An Alternate Approach," in John C. Pierce and John L. Sullivan (eds.), *The Electorate Reconsidered*, Beverly Hills, Sage, 1980; and Milton Lodge and John C. Wahlke, "Politicos, Apoliticals, and the Processing of Political Information," *International Political Science Review*, 3:1, 1982, pp. 131–150.

34. This definition rests on the work of Pamela Johnston Conover and Stanley Feldman, "Schema Theory and the Use of Q-Methodology in the Study of Mass Belief

Systems," *American Political Science Association Paper*, 1982, p. 2; and Susan T. Fiske and Patricia Linville, "What Does the Schema Concept Buy Us?," *Personality and Social Psychology Bulletin*, 6, December 1980, p. 543.

35. Fiske and Kinder, cited in note 29, p. 173.

36. Shelley E. Taylor and Jennifer Crocker, "Schematic Bases of Social Information Processing," in E. Tory Higgins, C. Peter Herman, and Mark P. Zanna (eds.), *Social Cognition: The Ontario Symposium*, vol. 1, Hillsdale, N.J., Lawrence Erlbaum, 1981, p. 92.

37. Bennett, as cited in note 15, p. 168.

38. See Fiske and Kinder, and Nancy Cantor, both cited in note 29; and Bennett, cited in note 15.

39. The terms, in order, are from Conover and Feldman, as cited in note 33; Walter Mischel, "Personality and Cognition: Something Borrowed, Something New?," In Cantor and Kihlstrom, cited in note 27, p. 14; and Fiske and Kinder, as cited in note 29, p. 176.

40. The link between schemas and actions is examined in Kenneth P. Langton and Octavian Petrescu, "Cognitive and Situational Antecedents to Worker Participation," *American Political Science Association Paper*, 1982.

41. Lachman et al., as cited in note 2, p. 453.

42. For a discussion of the use of schema concepts in American social psychology, starting with the work of Kurt Lewin in the late 1930s, see Schank and Ableson, as cited in note 26, p. 10. The term "schema" came into wide use in the 70s through the work of scholars such as David E. Rumelhart, David Bobrow, Donald R. Norman, and Andrew Ortony.

43. Fiske and Linville, as cited in note 34.

44. For methods of measurement, see Thomas M. Ostrom, John B. Pryor, and David D. Simpson, "The Organization of Social Information," in E. Tory Higgins et al., cited in note 36.

45. For research along these lines, see Nancy Cantor and Walter Mischel, "Prototypes in Person Perception," in Leonard Berkowitz (ed.), *Advances in Experimental Social Psychology*, vol. 12, New York, Academic Press, 1979; Hazel Markus and Jeanne Smith, "The Influence of Self-Schema on the Perception of Others," in Cantor and Kihlstrom, cited in note 27, pp. 233–262; and Pamela Johnston Conover and Stanley Feldman, "The Origins and Meaning of Liberal/Conservative Self-Identification," *American Journal of Political Science*, 25, November 1981, pp. 617–645.

46. For the matching panels, two papers were analyzed in Indianapolis and one in New Hampshire.

# 3

# Everyman in Middletown: Portraits of the Panelists

As John Donne observed many centuries ago, "no man is an island." People act and react in a number of microenvironments that are "informationally biased and interpersonally reactive. It is in these politically nonneutral and interactive contexts that political information is received, nurtured, matured, and ultimately brought to bear on individual" thinking about politics.[1] To understand why people process news the way hey do requires, therefore, scrutiny of their environment and some knowledge, or at least informed guessing, about the likely impacts of this environment on the individual's thinking processes and actions. In this chapter, we will briefly describe psychosocial, economic, and political settings that contributed to the patterns of information processing observed in our panelists. We will discuss the apparent impact of these settings on information choices, on modes of processing, and on the nature of schemas developed by the panelists.

## PSYCHOSOCIAL SETTINGS

### Gender, Age, Race, Ethnicity and Geography

In survey research, it is an accepted procedure to define psychosocial context in terms of various demographic variables. The more common ones are sex, age, race or ethnicity, and geographic location. These criteria will be used here with the understanding that they are merely a shorthand expression for differences in life-style. I do not subscribe to demographic determinism. Age, sex, race, ethnicity, and geographic location may give us clues to likely behaviors, but they indicate probabilities only, rather than certainties. They are also ". . . inadequate indicators of self-interest, because they inextricably confound it with socialization and therefore the origins of symbolic predispositions."[2] For example, women, as a group, have life experiences and are socialized to be more sensitive to human welfare issues than men. They are, therefore, more likely to absorb information about the misfortunes of other people. However, when men are privy to the same experiences and socialized to sensitivity, their reactions differ little from those of women. Linking reactions to various types of environmental stimuli to sex identity is therefore questionable. This is all the more true because most individuals are psychologically and socially cross-pressured. The impact of sex influence on life-style may be counteracted by the pressures of occupation or social setting and may be confounded by economic and religious concerns.[3]

Of our respondents, 11 were men and 10 were women. At the time of the interviews, 10 were married, 4 were widows, and 7 were single. The latter group was a mixture of divorced individuals, unmarried couples, and true singles. There are measurable differences between men and women in the kinds of information selected for processing and in the nature of detail retention. These differences, which will be discussed in greater detail in subsequent chapters, diminish sharply when women adopt life-styles that resemble current male patterns. Differences also diminish for women who have lost their mates. Each of the four widows on the panel told us at some point during the interview year that she had relied on her mate for scanning the news to make sure that no essential information was missed. When this culturally sanctioned division of labor was no longer possible and could not be shifted to another male family member, the woman assumed the burden of news surveillance.

The panel represented a broad, evenly spaced span of ages, ranging from 23 to 78. Again, as will be discussed in more detail later, age is related to the attention paid to news and the manner in which details are retained because age affects life-style. By and large, the younger panelists, particularly single males and couples with small children, lead the most crowded lives. Consequently, they paid least attention to current information. This inclination was enhanced by the fact that most younger people's fund of life experiences is smaller than that of older people. Accordingly, most younger panelists had a narrower range of schemas for incorporating the kind of information presented by the mass media. Therefore they rejected more current news because they could not relate to it. However, a few younger panelists with unusually rich experiences provided the exceptions that demonstrate the weakness of demographic rules.

The panel was not well balanced in terms of race. Only 2 of the 21 respondents were black, both of them women. However, black males were included in the pool of respondents who were pretested for this study and in the companion panels. The pretest and test results provide no indication that blacks present patterns which differ from their white counterparts drawn from similar social settings. The blacks in our sample did not even show unusually great interest in stories involving the black community, locally, nationally, or abroad. The fact that all interviewers were white may have dampened their inclination to report such stories in their diaries or in open-ended questions. But it should not have affected their ability to recall stories that presumably were of special concern to blacks when such stories were mentioned by the interviewer.

Ethnic origins and religious preferences do appear to influence the type of information that is selected for processing and the types of schemas that people hold. For example, the two Jewish panelists had an exceptionally high interest in stories about Israel and the Middle East, while the seven Catholic respondents showed an above average interest in stories about the Catholic clergy. People of Polish extraction were more likely to absorb stories about Poland than was true of people whose ethnic ties were linked to Germany. Altogether, our sample represents seven major ethnic groups with people with Northern European roots predominating.

The panel was totally homogeneous in terms of its geographic location in 1976 and the influences that this implies. All of the panelists had lived for many years in Evanston, a university town adjacent to Chicago. This means that they were exposed to Midwestern cultural forces. Presumably this implies a fairly conservative approach to life, an emphasis on work, rather than leisure, and a strong sense of civic obligation. The Evanston location also means that the panelists were thoroughly familiar with urban problems. However, they could view these problems with some detachment because of the more sheltered existence possible in a town just beyond the reach of the city.

Our panelists differed in the amount of domestic and foreign travel they had experienced and in the number of places other than Evanston in which they had lived. Nearly half the panel had been raised elsewhere, but mostly at other Midwestern locations. Of the panelists, 12 had travelled to 10 or more cities outside of Illinois and 11 had been abroad, primarily to Western Europe. Extensive travel seemed to have little independent effect on interest in news and the nature of news processing. In particular, there appeared to be no correlation between foreign travel exposure and interest in foreign countries, which was generally quite low.

## Income, Education, Social Interactions and Partisanship

Similar to demographic settings, social settings are merely indications of likely trends, rather than accurate predictors. As Gerald Pomper has pointed out in a slightly different context: "It is simply untrue that 'social characteristics determine political preferences.' Attempts to predict votes on the combined basis of class, religion, and residence succeed in only 60 percent of the cases (even excluding nonvoters)."[4] However, social characteristics may determine the life situations in which individuals become enmeshed. People living in similar social situations are likely to have similar experiences and encounter similar pressures. These may then lead to similar outlooks.

Compared to the national electorate, our panel was somewhat skewed in terms of education and social settings. Of the panelists, 13 had completed college and only 2 stopped with a grade school education. Nearly half did professional work. All of them were registered voters. This means that many, though by no means all of our panelists, had above average interest in politics, above average understanding, and above average information processing capabilities.[5] As will be discussed later, education and interest affect the quantity and sophistication of processing, but *not* its basic nature.

The panelists' economic status was more diverse: 5 were in comfortable economic circumstances with few worries about making ends meet; 10 fell into a middle range where income and outflow were reasonably well balanced but where extraordinary expenses would cause real hardships; and 6 were economically marginal, with 1 depending largely on social security income and the other relying on public assistance. However, personal economic circumstances, aside from their effects on life-style, appeared to have no impact on news-processing behavior. When they had time available, poor and rich alike were apt to indulge in mass media exposure, which remains one of the least expensive and most readily available forms of diversion in modern America.

Judging by the kinds of policies that the panelists supported, 14 had strong Democratic leanings while 7 favored Republican approaches. This, however, did not prevent the Democrats from voting for Republican candidates. Such behavior is in line with the political behavior of Americans in general. As Gerald Pomper has pointed out, based on national survey data, "five out of eight Americans still feel a meaningful attachment to either the Democrats or Republicans, and only about 15 percent are confirmed Independents." Nonetheless, "over half the voters have supported the opposition party at least once in a presidential election."[6] Similarly, our panelists were not dyed-in-the-wool partisans who stuck with their party no matter what its positions or who its candidates were. They were, nonetheless, predisposed, other things being equal, to align with the policy position of the party with which they had generally identified since childhood. Given the tentativeness of party support, the panelists were quite willing to expose themselves to information that bore the stamp of either party and to accept agreeable views, regardless of party labels. We found no evidence of outright rejection of any information simply because it came from the opposition party.

Pomper also says that "party identification affects not only the vote but the individual's perception of the entire political world."[7] That seems to put the cart before the horse. The social conditions in which our respondents operated, including their information environment, seemed to predispose them to political outlooks that corresponded, to those advocated by one or the other of America's major parties. None of our panelists ever acknowledged that her or his political beliefs were the consequence of party affiliation. By contrast, our respondents frequently stated that their religious beliefs were the direct consequence of formal or informal affiliation with a particular religion. On the other hand, party affiliation, once established, becomes "an enormously efficient schematic device in the organization of beliefs, evaluations, and feelings toward the political world."[8] When new evaluations need to be made and the individual looks for guidance, the party label becomes a beacon that attracts the uncertain.

John Sprague has argued that an individual's daily interactions with others is a powerful molder of political views. He likens the situation to operant conditioning, through which a person is reinforced with praise to adopt and repeat certain behaviors and discouraged from pursuing behaviors which earn disapproval.[9] Mindful of the importance of such conditioning effects, we asked our panelists repeatedly about their conversational contacts, about the intellectual level of discussion, and about their role in the discussion. We also routinely asked about the sources of information and opinions for every news story that came into focus through the interviews or diaries.

The findings are mixed: 15 panelists discussed current news with others, though only 3 (Rosswell, Adams, Ippolito) claimed to discuss it at length. Men generally engaged in discussions in a more serious and specific vein than women. But both men and women tended to limit discussions to consensual remarks and to avoid political discussions that were likely to be controversial. In fact, several panelists expressed strong reluctance to discuss politics at all. Some said that politics and religion were topics that they avoided because they considered them potentially divisive. Only one panelist (Liebman) reported that she was frequently involved in political conversations with people whose views deviated sharply from her own.

The linkage between politics and religion is revealing. For many panelists, politics is a private affair, based on beliefs about which one should not and cannot argue. Arguing about politics is viewed as a more or less hostile encounter and *not* as a way to clarify thinking. Even those panelists who discussed politics freely rarely did so in the spirit of intellectual exchanges from which acceptable truths emerged. Rather, the purpose was to find and reinforce shared views and learn which areas of discourse to avoid because they might produce controversy, hurt, and anger.

During group interviews, when people were thrust into a situation that required discussing political matters with strangers, conversation appeared to be influential. The participants obviously strove to adjust their expressed views, and possibly their actual views, to what they perceived to be the shared norms. When silent members of the group were later asked the reason for their silence, they indicated that they had abstained from participation because they perceived their own views to be substantially out of line with those already articulated by the group.[10] The picture that emerged is that most of our panelists discussed political matters rarely unless they involved a sharing of mutually acceptable information. Furthermore, attention to news was often guided by the desire to find news items that might reinforce shared beliefs. The fact that conversations mostly involved mutually familiar facts and opinions explains why the panelists routinely claimed that conversations about the news had little impact on their thinking—although they improved memory—and why they rarely mentioned learning anything new from their everyday contacts.

The exceptions to this pattern were three people who had little mass media exposure and a fourth person whose job involved monitoring news events and discussing them with his staff. Rosswell and Peterson, who had little interest in the news and little time for it, had very limited mass media exposure and therefore received most of their information through conversations with friends. Fechbach was dependent on her husband for relaying mass media information because her two small children kept her occupied for most of her waking hours. Ippolito had a professional concern with discussing the news. Among these four, only Rosswell thought that her views were strongly affected by her conversation partners. Fechbach conceded some influence, and Peterson and Ippolito felt that they were dominating the conversations.

The influence of learning news attention patterns from experiences in their childhood homes seemed to be greater than the impact of discussions. Of the 10 panelists who reported that they were highly interested in politics and discussed it frequently, 7 also reported similar patterns from their childhood homes. Of the panelists, 10 of 11 who reported little interest in politics and few conversations, likewise indicated that this was a pattern similar to their childhood experiences. Since the information about childhood experiences rests entirely on recall, its accuracy may be limited.

## THE IMPACT OF PSYCHOSOCIAL SETTINGS: AN OVERVIEW

What conclusions can we draw about the importance of various psychosocial factors on the manner in which our panelists selected news and processed it? The key factor is life-style. It generates interest in certain events and creates needs for particular information and it determines how much time is available to get the desired information. Demographic factors have a strong impact on life-style. What one does during one's waking hours is strongly affected by whether one is a woman or a man, old or young or middle-aged, married or single, with young or grown children or no children at all. But gender, or race, or age, or any other demographic determinant, is *not* destiny. Variations in life-style which run contrary to stereotypes are quite common. When they occur, media behavior corresponds to life-style, rather than to demographic or social characteristics.

Interpreted in terms of life-style, gender means more or less serious interest in politics and more or less available time. It has only a slight impact on the kinds of subjects in which our panelists were interested. Age parallels gender, with the additional factor that greater age means more experience which tends to broaden interests and receptivity. Ethnicity, in a limited way, focuses interest on specific types of news. Living in the Midwest affects the cultural values which our panelists brought to information processing. The same holds true for childhood experiences and for identification with the political thrust of the major parties. The panelists interpreted news in line with the predispositions formed as children. They continued these patterns in adulthood, using parties as frequent reference groups for political values when processing political news.

The impact of various demographic factors was enhanced or diminished by the amount of formal education that our panelists had and by the type of job they held. The combination of higher education and a professional job meant greater interest in current affairs because of a wider knowledge background and greater need for keeping abreast of current information. It, therefore, meant paying more attention to news and processing it with greater sophistication. However, when higher education is not paired with a professional job, it loses much of its impact as a stimulus to more and better information processing.

For our panelists, the sprightly art of conversation appeared to be at a low ebb when it came to politics. Most of them avoided controversy, sought out information that conformed to the views that they believed to be current among their associates, and learned from conversations only when independent learning was at a low ebb. For them, there was little reality to the notion of the two-step flow of information, through which opinion leaders relay most media news to willing listeners who absorb the leaders' perspectives. Similarly, there was little reality to the view that economic status is a powerful mediator of interactions with the world outside one's door. Neither information selection nor processing appeared to be shaped by the panelist's economic fortunes or misfortunes.

## GENERAL POLITICAL SETTINGS

Thus far, we have described the general psychosocial factors that provide the context for information selection and processing by our panelists. There is a larger environment of current social conditions in which these factors operate. The impact of these environmental factors, therefore, must be examined.

### The National Political Climate in 1976

In 1976, the United States celebrated the 200th anniversary of the Declaration of Independence. There were parades, exhibits, concerts, and fireworks displays. The most spectacular event was Operation Sail in which 53 warships from 22 countries, along with 16 tall-masted, large, square-rigged sailing vessels, gathered in New York harbor for a Fourth-of-July celebration. Six million people watched and cheered the boat parade in a remarkable display of old-fashioned patriotism. Yet there was a wide gulf between the mood of the bicentennial celebrations and the everyday mood of Americans, including our panelists, in 1976.

As the year opened, Gerald Ford, the first unelected president of the United States, was in the White House. Bad memories about the disastrous Vietnam war and the disillusionment it brought about the morality of America's goals still lingered. Public confidence in government had been shaken by a major scandal in the White House that had led to the resignation of President Nixon. When President Ford quickly pardoned his predecessor to end what he called "our long national nightmare," his popularity and the belief in White House integrity, dropped sharply.

In addition to the White House scandals, there were reports of major scandals in the C.I.A. and F.B.I. A number of scandals involving improper financial and sexual conduct proved embarrassing to Congress. They included serious misconduct by the powerful chairman of the House Administration Committee, illegal corporate contributions to Congressmen, bribery of Congressmen by agents of the South Korean government, and bribery of foreign government officials by American exporters. These various scandals heightened the mistrust in government and made the question of morality in politics painfully salient to Americans. As Carol Fechbach put it: "After Watergate, there isn't anything bad about the government that I won't believe."

Our panelists, like other Americans were also deeply concerned about the nation's economy. In the fall of 1974, the country had reached the deepest recession since the Great Depression of the 1930s. The unemployment rate had risen sharply. The period from 1972 to 1976 had produced the worst four-year record for inflation since World War II, with costs of food, fuel, housing and medical care particularly high. While rampant inflation eroded incomes, escalating unemployment swelled relief costs. Widespread economic suffering led to demands for economy in government and for an end to deficit spending, as well as requests for measures to stimulate employment.

In foreign policy, maintaining the peace in the Middle East remained a major concern. American policy focused on ending the civil war in Lebanon, safe-guarding Israeli interests in the Middle East, and keeping foreign intervention out of the area. United States diplomats also were active in trying to forestall adverse changes in the volatile political situation in southern Africa. These efforts led to a worsening of United States-Soviet relations because of Soviet intervention in African conflicts.

None of these foreign policy problems seemed to distract the panelists and the general public from its major concern—the frightening combination of high inflation and high unemployment. An analysis of the ten issues that people throughout the country ranked as most important in connection with the elections of 1976 showed "honesty in government" in first place. It was followed by inflation, unemployment and high taxes. At some distance came crime and drugs, energy, foreign relations, and pollution. The last place in this ten-issue list went to racial issues and consumer protection.[11] As Pomper put it,

> The principal concerns of Americans in 1976, and typically in other elections as well, are those matters that have an immediate impact on their own well-being: their prospects for a job, the prices they pay, the gas lines at the corner pump. Voters are aroused by what affects them personally. [12]

The news about the presidential election was viewed by our panelists and other Americans against the backdrop of these public concerns.

> Against this background of Watergate and economic problems, questions of which candidate could be trusted and who could manage the economy loomed large in 1976. [In] the aftermath of the social upheavals, corruption, and alienation of previous

years, the voters were seeking a means to revive their underlying trust and affection for American government.[13]

Among lesser current issues, most Americans cheered for an Israeli commando unit which flew a daring mission to Uganda to rescue nearly 100 Israeli hostages held after the hijacking of a French jetliner. A hot public debate also developed over the "right to die." It was sparked by court action over the rights of a New Jersey couple to terminate artificial life-sustaining measures that kept their irreversibly comatose daughter alive. Likewise, our panelists and people throughout the country became caught up in the trial of Patricia Hearst, the socially-prominent, young kidnap victim who had joined her captors in bank robberies and other illegal activities.

In general, 1976 was a year of major public worries that touched the lives of all of our panelists. Coupled with the fact that it was also a presidential election year, the impetus for following national news was undoubtedly above average. The same, as we shall see, was not true for local news.

## Life in Evanston, Illinois

Evanston, Illinois, the home of our panelists, is a university town of 77,000 people. In 1976, it ranked as the sixth largest city in the state of Illinois. However, its location adjacent to the northern boundary of Chicago gives it the aura of a Chicago suburb. Evanstonians think of themselves as suburbanites whose jobs and cultural interests frequently draw them into the city. One in three Evanstonians actually works in the city of Chicago, traveling there through an integrated metropolitan transportation system. Evanstonians also rely on Chicago print and electronic news media for most of their news, although there is a local weekly newspaper and several local radio stations. Because of the close ties to Chicago, Chicago politics have always been matters of major interest and concern to Evanstonians. This is reflected in the fact that all of our panelists used Chicago media and that they knew more about political happenings in Chicago than in Evanston.

Evanston's social and cultural life revolves around Northwestern University and a number of smaller colleges and seminaries. Hence, "town and gown" issues are a prominent part of local politics. Northwestern is Evanston's largest employer and land owner. Questions concerning tax exemption for some of this property and disputes over new land purchases by the university have been a perennial source of friction between the university and the city. The year 1976 was no exception. Other major problems in Evanston concerned competition for scarce vacant lands by housing, business, and recreational interests; the comparatively low socioeconomic status of Evanston's sizable black community; the difficulty of maintaining excellent schools in the face of rising costs; and the general problem of raising sufficient taxes. Lesser concerns included revitalization of business areas through building shopping malls and coping with issues related to traffic, parking, and public transportation. Most of our panelists were aware of at least some of these issues, but the level of concern was well below concern for national issues.

The citizens of Evanston are a heterogeneous, relatively prosperous and well-educated lot. The average Evanstonian has completed two years of school beyond the national average, owns or rents a home of above average value, and earns more money than the national norm. While the range in levels of income and education is wide, the town has no unusually severe poverty or school problems. Most Evanstonians are native born Americans, with the largest number claiming a northern European ethnic heritage. Nationality groups are fairly evenly distributed throughout all neighborhoods. The most notable exception is the concentration of black families in the southwestern part of the city. Although that part of the city remains integrated and is by no means a slum area, it does contain the poorest housing and has a reputation for a relatively high incidence of crime. Throughout 1976, the problem of youth gangs and their illegal activities began to emerge as a public concern.

There appeared to be a consensus among our panelists that the town, which has a council–manager form of government, was reasonably well administered. Major controversies and scandals had been rare. Consequently, panel members showed little cynicism about local government performance in general or even with regard to specific policies. By the same token, interest in local Evanston problems was ordinarily far lower than interest in Chicago affairs. Although turnout for national elections always exceeded national averages in Evanston, turnout for local elections was high only when spirited contests occurred or controversial issues were involved. Most of our panelists had frequently skipped voting in local elections.

On balance, then, our Evanstonians in 1976 were primarily concerned with national economic issues. They kept a fairly close watch on Chicago politics, but from the stance of an interested outsider. And they regarded local affairs as a matter of brushfire politics—to be minded only when and if blazes seemed to get out of hand.

## PANELIST SKETCHES

We have sketched out the general psychosocial setting for our panelists. Now we are ready to briefly describe them as individuals, noting their salient demographic and psychological characteristics, as well as major factors of background and current life-style that are likely to affect the way they select and process news. Childhood examples and conditioning, basic attitudes of optimism and pessimism, basic tenets of conservatism and liberalism, pressures that support or suppress media use, and concerns created by vulnerability to social ills such as crime and unemployment, are among the factors to be outlined.

The sketches are arranged according to interest in political news and ease of access to mass media information sources. Groups range from those with high interest in politics and ready access to media, who, as expected, processed the largest amount of information in the most sophisticated manner, to those with low interest and difficulties in attending to the media, who learned the least and treated information in the simplest manner. In between are those with high interest but difficulties in exposing themselves to information and those with ready access to information but little interest in acquiring it. Their news selection and news-processing performance fell in between the ratings of the other two groups.

## High-Interest, Easy-Access Group

Looking at this group as a whole, several features stand out. Each of the five panelists was raised in a home where politics and political discussions were considered important and where media were readily available. The panelists were willing to adopt these patterns because they had positive feelings about their parents and their childhood settings in general and because they believed in patterning themselves after cherished models. Perpetuation of childhood patterns was further fostered by ample formal educational opportunities and, in one case, wide individual reading outside a college environment.

All but one member of the group were professionals who needed to be well-informed. The exception was a retired blue-collar worker who had been involved in professional participation in local politics. As with the other professions, this made knowledge about current affairs essential to him. Though several members of the group were cynical about many aspects of politics, they retained an overall belief that the political system was sound and influential and that citizens could have an impact on it. These panelists felt the same about the media: though there is much to criticize, there is also much to praise. On balance, attention to the media was deemed worthwhile. Cameo profiles of the group members, as they appeared in 1976, follow.

*Karl Adams.* Adams is a 25-year-old, college-trained research engineer. He is single and shares an apartment with several professional peers in a middle-income neighborhood. Among young male panelists, he is by far the most avid consumer of mass media information, despite substantial dissatisfaction with the accuracy of news reporting. He also engages in frequent conversations about the news at work and in his home setting and has an excellent memory for details. His appetite for news and discussion was whetted in childhood by his parents and teachers.

His outlook on politics appears to have changed over the years. Trust in government and people has turned into distrust because of numerous personal experiences with bureaucratic bungling and obstructive institutional politics. He has also turned away from the liberal political stance of his college days to fairly conservative views, having switched his party loyalties from Democratic leanings to Republican leanings. He is intolerant of personal failings, such as laziness and criminal behavior, believing that they should be dealt with more harshly than is done at present. Despite his disillusionments, he retains an optimistic outlook on life, believing that change for the better is possible, though not likely.

***Donald Burton.*** Burton is 38 years old and works as an administrator in an organization dealing with legal problems. He has travelled widely, both domestically and internationally. Despite the conservative influence of his legal training and service in the military, Burton has remained true to the liberal political atmosphere in which he was raised. His views on society are optimistic, and he is an enthusiastic participant in a variety of community social and political causes, in line with a family tradition of political discussion and activism. He often talks about politics in social settings and on the job.

Burton is married and has three young daughters. Family and community obligations leave him little spare time. However, he commutes on public transportation from his home in an upper-class residential neighborhood to his job on Chicago's South Side and uses the long commuting time to read several newspapers. Given the distractions during such a trip and the fact that he is constantly faced with an overload of information at his job and in his other pursuits, he remembers comparatively few details from his ample reading. Nonetheless, he perceives himself as having an excellent memory and retaining details for long periods of time. He holds generally favorable views of print media, particularly news magazines, but not of television.

***Robert Creighton.*** Creighton is a 45-year-old bachelor who lives alone in a large apartment building in a high crime neighborhood. He is a college graduate whose work in adult professional education requires a lot of travel away from home. This does not keep him from his life-long habit of reading several newspapers each day and consuming a vast amount of professional literature. When out-of-town trips keep him from reading all of the papers to which he subscribes, he saves them and reads them later, often several months after publication. While he appraises the news critically, he does not generally question the credibility of the media. His memory for detail is excellent.

Due to the nature of his work and life and career experiences, he is very interested in public policy issues in general and law and order issues in particular. He discusses these issues frequently on the job and in social settings. His political leanings are Republican, mixed with a liberal tinge on social issues. Societal concerns, rather than personal concerns, dominate his evaluations. His outlook on life, including politics, is optimistic, and his life-long respect for government, trust in most political leaders, and a strong sense of civic obligation remain firm.

***Paul Diedrich.*** Diedrich is a respected lawyer who, at age 74, continues to practice at a downtown Chicago location. He commutes to his job by public transportation from his home in an upper-class residential neighborhood. He and his wife also travel a great deal, including trips abroad, to spend time with their grown children and to enjoy various leisure pursuits. His outlook on life is a mixture of optimism and pessimism that he regards as realism. Diedrich has a low regard for politicians but considers their amoral behavior a normal characteristic of the breed. It neither worries him nor diminishes his generally supportive attitude towards government. In general, his political leanings are middle-of-the-road, though he tends to swing towards conservatism and the Republican party.

Diedrich reads extensively but very selectively, focusing on matters of law and economics. He expresses lack of interest in most events that are beyond his professional concerns. This narrowness appears to be a life-long trait despite ample exposure to a vast variety of information during his youth and in his current social contacts and his travels. Diedrich rarely discusses politics. His memory is good for stories which interest him; otherwise, he tends to be sketchy on details or completely forgetful. Diedrich is somewhat critical of the tone and quality of print media stories and has little respect for television which he watches only rarely.

*Leo Evanski.* Evanski is 75 years old and has retired from a blue-collar job. Yet, he remains physically active in gardening and home maintenance activities in Evanston and in a summer house in northern Michigan. His modest home is located in a changing, crime-prone neighborhood. Although he worries about personal security, he is determined to keep his home because it harbors his memories. Evanski has a strong life-long interest in current affairs, enhanced by his leadership roles in precinct politics in his younger years and by his penchant for political discussions with his large family and friends. He is an avid news consumer who spends many hours each day reading the newspaper and watching television. He conveys much of what he reads and sees to his wife who does little reading and watching on her own. He occasionally has trouble recalling specific facts quickly and blames these lapses on his advanced age.

Evanski has only a grade school education, but his children are college graduates. He has developed a wide fund of knowledge through reading and through his life experiences. He is more likely to accept information from interpersonal sources than from the media because he distrusts media accuracy. While he is concerned about crime and many other problems, Evanski retains an essentially optimistic and liberal outlook on life. This explains his high ratings on scales measuring support for civil rights and trust in government.

## High-Interest, Difficult-Access Group

In many ways, the high-interest, difficult-access group is indistinguishable from the high-interest, easy-access group. All five panel members had childhood experiences that encouraged interest in news and attention to mass media. All of them are college-trained and have worked or are working now as professionals in fields where news awareness is important and useful. What is different is that all members of the group have exceedingly tight time budgets. Three of them (Fechbach, Holmquist, and Jackman) spend much of their time in the exhausting task of caring for small children. The remaining two (Gaylord and Ippolito) have job obligations which devour leisure hours.

The consequences are that these panelists pay much less attention to news. When they do read, listen, or watch, they are much more selective in the kinds of stories to which they pay attention. Their memory for stories is often weakened because they do not pay undivided attention to them. Most of these panelists feel frustrated by their inability to get all the information they would like. When the opportunity presents itself to catch up quickly, as happened for instance during the presidential debates of 1976, they seize it eagerly. Let us now meet these panelists.

*Carol Fechbach.* Fechbach is a 28-year-old homemaker who is married to a professional man and lives in a middle-class neighborhood. She has two preschool children whose care she finds very taxing. If she has free time when the children are sleeping, she is generally too tired to pay much attention to either the newspaper or television. She is a college graduate, interested primarily in education, fine arts, and sports. Interest in politics is a secondary concern but she does make an effort to keep up with the news because she discusses it with her husband who is very interested and because talk about politics is socially useful to her. When she pays attention to stories, she shies away from economic and foreign affairs, news which she considers boring. She considers the news to be generally accurate. Because her total news intake is limited, she remembers those stories to which she can give undivided attention exceptionally well.

Although Carol Fechbach is by nature optimistic and trustful, a constant barrage of stories in the past two years about public and private misbehavior has left its mark. This explains her turn toward a middle-of-the-road position, away from the liberalism of her college days, as well as her low trust in government. She also harbors suspicions about various population groups such as businessmen or blacks. However, she remains liberal on civil rights and views politics from the perspective of the community in general, rather than from a self-interested perspective.

*Martha Gaylord.* Gaylord is a 28-year-old corporate executive with a job that keeps her travelling nearly half of the time. Since she has not acquired the habit of reading during travel, she has little opportunity for consistent media exposure. The demands of her job also curb her social contacts so that she rarely engages in sustained political discussions. She is unmarried and lives alone in a middle-class neighborhood in an apartment selected because of its excellent security system.

Martha Gaylord is a college graduate who was originally bound for a career in teaching. She would like to be as well-informed about current affairs as she was in the past and frequently expresses regret that her job provides insufficient leisure time. She considers the media generally credible and tries to keep in touch with the world through sporadic attention to television news. Her memory of news stories is erratic; most are quickly forgotten, but a few leave a lasting imprint. She is optimistic about people and politics with a basic trust in government. Her political stance remains liberal, but her job in a large corporation has made her far more sympathetic to the role of "big business" than was true in earlier years.

*Helga Holmquist.* Holmquist is a 30-year-old college graduate who splits her time between household chores, care of an infant, and a part-time professional job. Her husband, too, is a professional and both are much concerned about government issues. Both come from homes where political interest and attention flourished. Despite high interest in the political world, Holmquist's busy schedule prevents her from paying much attention to mass media news in general. She does make time for news about crime and the justice system because this is an area of professional concern for the family. As part of her personal, social, and professional life, she also gets involved in a lot of political discussions, particularly about local politics. Her memory for stories is short and often inaccurate. The reason may be that attention to news is frequently combined with supervision of her child.

Helga Holmquist started life as a liberal, but marriage to a well-informed conservative has brought her to a center position. Life experiences have pushed her towards the middle as well. She has been a crime victim and now lives on the edge of a high crime neighborhood. Her trust in government has been eroded by an unending barrage of news about misconduct by public officials and by corroborating experiences when she worked for the state of Illinois. She also has some qualms about the accuracy of print and electronic media, accusing them of distortions to make stories sensational. However, her basic optimism about the "American system" remains intact.

*Cesar Ippolito.* Ippolito works in downtown Chicago as a professional for a federal agency. He is 33 years old and lives with his wife and two young children, adjacent to a high crime neighborhood. Personal safety for himself and his family is a major concern, especially since his job involves a fair amount of out-of-town travel, and he also works part-time in the late evening. This tight schedule keeps his media exposure moderate, despite the availability of a variety of newspapers and magazines that he reads selectively on the commuter train to work. He also watches television news occasionally, even though he thinks that it is dull and formula-ridden and, like print news, occasionally distorted by newspeople's bent of mind. As with many of the men in this study, conversations at work fill in the information gaps whenever he neglects his own reading and listening. Since he discusses politics frequently with co-workers, his memory is constantly refreshed and sharpened so that matters of professional relevance are current. Otherwise, his knowledge is hazy. He does not discuss politics with his wife, characterizing her as "not too smart. Calling Hubert Humphrey a 'neat guy' is about the level of her political thinking."

His interest in politics is high and long standing. His family was involved in local politics at the precinct level and political discussion abounded in the home. While in college, Ippolito worked as a political reporter for the electronic media and later prepared for a career in journalism. His current jobs involve politics and politicking on a non-partisan basis. He regards himself as a liberal and he defines the term as "somebody willing to try new ideas." He is also an occasional ideologue, blaming assorted social problems on the capitalist system and viewing them from the perspective of various political and economic groups.

*Max Jackman.* Jackman is a 36-year-old, college-educated copy editor who lives with his wife and two children in a decaying old house in a neighborhood rapidly slipping into disrepair. He is an unstable character, given to bouts of drinking and alternating between high optimism and stark pessimism. He can be garrulous and quarrelsome or withdrawn and passive, and, depending on his mood, he is a leader in discussions or a silent observer. He has travelled widely and served with the armed forces in Europe and the Far East.

Living in small towns during his childhood, he became personally aware of and interested in politics and politicians. His grandparents, with whom he lived much of the time, were very conservative, and Jackman adopted a liberal outlook partly as a form of rebellion against their strictness. There were ample news sources available in his childhood home and politics was discussed frequently. He would like to continue this pattern, but his work schedule interferes. When he is not on his night-time job, he has substantial childcare chores because his wife goes to work during the day.

Jackman is skeptical about the objectivity of mass media sources and criticizes them for shallow coverage and failure to take stands. In fact, he is skeptical about all aspects of society. Based on personal experiences, he distrusts all power holders and frequently complains that the average citizen is powerless to control politics in government and in the business community. He also complains about the unequal opportunities of people in various economic sectors.

## Low-Interest, Easy-Access Group

A variety of reasons account for the low interest which members of this group have in politics. The women grew up at a time when social patterns ordained that an interest in politics and political discussions was not part of the feminine mystique. Two of them remember being warned against becoming involved in political controversies. The single male member of the group grew up in a fatherless home and lacked male role models. In terms of education, only two of these panelists are college graduates. Although all panel members recalled having media available in their childhood homes, none thought that they had been amply used.

No panelist in this group has ever held a professional job where knowledge of current affairs was essential or even useful. Therefore none feels any strong pressures to keep informed. Moreover, probably most important, all of these panelists have other interests in their lives that seem far more important to them than paying attention to media. When sports events beckon or travel lures, when one can while away time with friends, or go to movies, or watch television entertainment shows, attention to news lóses out. Overall, it is a low priority. Like their time-short fellow panelists in the previous group, these panelists become very selective in news attention when their chief priorities fill up their leisure time.

*Craig Kolarz.* Kolarz is 25 years old and single. He lives with his mother and siblings in a deteriorating neighborhood. His family has little interest in politics and rarely discusses it. His father died while Kolarz was young, forcing his mother to work outside the home to support the family. Although Kolarz has an engineering degree, he works as a grocery clerk because he has been unable to find work in his field. In the winter, he attends night school classes to advance his engineering skills. Summer leisure hours are taken up by outdoor sports.

Kolarz has ready access to newspapers and electronic media but uses them irregularly because his interests in night school and in sports take precedence. When he does make time for media, he concentrates on stories that touch him personally and remembers these exceedingly well. He has a generally high regard for the media but is cynical about most other institutions. Given his reserved, colorless personality, which occasionally borders on sullenness, neither his job nor his home and social life provide much conversational information about political events. Hence, knowledge gaps remain unfilled whenever his mass media exposure is low.

*Penny Liebman.* Liebman is a high school graduate with two years of college training. She is 46 years old, married, and the mother of two young adults. She runs her own business and combines the very liberal orientations learned in her childhood with the more conservative outlooks of business people on matters that affect her business. She is not troubled by contradictions and doubts produced by this mixture of liberalism and conservatism. Her comments about a story raising the issue of the United States withdrawal from the Panama canal zone are typical. "I think that every country is entitled to control their own problems, but I don't know if they're educated enough and have enough leadership to do this. Perhaps they need a little guidance from us yet."

Liebman frequently complains about government corruption, poor public services, crime, and racial problems, speaking on the basis of personal experience. But she is optimistic that such problems can be solved. She believes that "if you set your mind to it, you can do anything; just like we cleaned up the lakes and cleared our cities of pollution and decaying buildings." She discusses selected political issues frequently, often heatedly, with her family and her business partner, but only if the conversation is initiated by others.

Liebman does not take much time to read or watch the news in general because she is preoccupied with her personal and business affairs. The exceptions are topics of special interest to her, such as news about Israel, business news, and news about crime in the area where her store is located. She keeps the radio on most of the day and, when cue words about these topics are mentioned, her attention suddenly perks up. But her memory of stories she has heard is short and often inaccurate.

*Elaine Mullins.* Mullins is a 50-year-old college-educated homemaker who lives alone in a fine residential neighborhood. She has been widowed for many years but retains close social ties with her husband's professional colleagues. Since she has no regular out-of-the-home job, she is able to spend a good deal of time travelling, visiting friends, and running errands for her disabled mother. She was victimized by serious crime—armed robbery and home invasion—during the course of this study. This traumatic experience did not change her news attention patterns, or even her life-style, since she believed that the crime was a freak occurrence that was unlikely to recur and that could not be prevented.

Although not currently interested in ongoing politics, and somewhat spotty in her attention to the mass media, she has a good grasp of political matters, especially on the local level at which her husband was active in the Democratic party. By her own description, she is a conservative Democrat, with fairly positive feelings about politics and politicians. She thinks that, aside from occasional bias, the media do a good job in presenting the news, but she sharply limits her attention to highly personalized stories or stories of direct concern to her. Mullins apologizes for being so selective and for forgetting important facts that are not of personal interest to her. However, though she has the time, she makes little effort to improve her news scanning and learning techniques.

*Betty Nystrom.* Nystrom is a 65-year-old widowed bookkeeper who lives alone in a small high-rise apartment. She finished high school and a few college courses. The one word that best summarizes her life is "frustration." She recalls her family stifling her childhood ambitions and losing all their worldly possessions during the Depression. Illness and death also plagued the family. She received her introduction to politics when her father became involved in precinct politics. She also worked for many years as a bookkeeper for various local governments to support herself and her ailing husband and always felt that her jobs were beneath her capabilities. This has left her with a permanent distaste for the political world, a world that she views in a highly stereotypical way.

Nystrom seems to think that it is chic to be cynical and suspicious about life and not to be shocked by anything. She mistrusts the media, saying "They are told what to say" by unnamed powerbrokers. Therefore, she exposes herself to news only on an irregular basis. She limits political discussions to members of her family because "I was taught you never get into an argument about religion or politics." When she disagrees with family members, she acquiesces nonetheless. Her memory for details is poor, except for stories with a strong human disaster focus. Of all the panelists, Nystrom was the only one who frequently conveyed the impression of insincerity. Outright contradictions between her open-ended conversations and answers to more directed questions support this impression. She obviously tried to cater to what she believed to be the interviewer's tastes.

*Sandra Ornstein.* At age 78, Sandra Ornstein is the oldest member of the panel. She is a high school graduate who married early and never joined the paid labor force. Despite her advanced age, she lives alone, spending much of her time in the well-kept high-rise apartment that she shared with her husband who died 13 years previously. Fear of crime keeps her indoors after dark unless members of her family escort her. She has a generally cheerful outlook on life, although comparisons between the world of her youth and the present invariably show the present to be inferior. Of politicians she says that "they are all alike. They are all a bunch of bums." However, she blames their jobs, rather than their personalities, for their failings. She considers herself a staunch Democrat.

Sandra Ornstein maintains contact with life in the local community through regular social service volunteer work and through her children and grandchildren. Because she lives alone, television and radio are steady, much appreciated companions. As is true of other older respondents, she feels personally close to a number of media figures, including commentators as well as fictional characters and stars who portray them. When she reads the newspaper, she does so very selectively, avoiding foreign affairs and other matters that she claims she cannot understand, that are likely to upset her, or that are unsuitable for sharing with her friends. Her opportunities for talking about current affairs with others are limited. Like Betty Nystrom, she feels political discussion is apt to lead to conflict and should be avoided. Nonetheless, she feels a strong obligation to be fully informed "so that I can talk intelligently about politics," and disparages herself whenever she fails to recall an important political story.

## Low-Interest, Difficult-Access Group

The chief shared characteristic of members of this group is that they do not feel that news is useful to them. Two of these panelists, both college educated and working in business management positions, characterize news as a "waste." They feel that information is important, but that the manner in which the media supply it is totally unsatisfactory. Therefore, they prefer to learn by other means or devote their time to other pursuits. The two black women in this group were raised in environments that made it difficult to cope with the complexity of much current information. One is a grade school dropout, the other completed high school. These women prefer to receive their news in simplified form from conversations with friends and family members, preferably males. As was true of members of the low-interest, easy-access group, their other pursuits take priority over being well-informed.

The two remaining panelists have abandoned their childhood news-consumption traditions. Both are high school graduates working in the health field and neither feels the need for news in their daily occupation. Sven Peterson thinks of news largely as entertainment. He will pay attention only if it seems intrinsically amusing. Deidre Sandelius has become so overburdened with work that she has given up all efforts to keep informed.

Lacking interest in current news and finding it difficult to make time for news consumption does not mean that these panelists are totally uninformed. All of them pick up scraps of news, off and on, in a completely unsystematic fashion. All of them have sufficient understanding of the world around them to make reasonably intelligent use of the bits of information they pick up. In fact, the two professionals in the group are quite astute in guessing accurately about the course of events without being privy to actual information. Here are profiles of this final group of panelists.

*Sven Peterson.* Peterson is a 23-year-old hospital clerk who grew up in a well-to-do family in which media abounded but political discourse was scarce. He contrasts his parents' conservatism with his own liberalism that was spurred by high school friends and the anti-Vietnam war movement. In fact, he characterizes himself as having "a romance with socialism." He dropped out of college during his freshman year and worked for a while in a steel plant before switching to a low-level clerical job. He shares a cluttered apartment in a run-down neighborhood with a co-worker and spends much of his leisure time in social activities and with his hobby, which is reconstructing current and past military battles in all parts of the world.

Although Peterson thinks that the media do a good job covering the news, he pays relatively little attention to them except for off-beat stories reported by a rock music radio station to which he listens regularly. He views news attention as an amusement activity, rather than a civic or human obligation. However, because he talks with many people throughout the day, he picks up much current information through casual conversations. He selectively remembers what he hears. As a history buff, he pays particular attention to new information that puts past events, like the turmoil of the sixties, into new perspectives.

*Tugwell Quentin.* Quentin, a 27-year-old bachelor, lives in Peterson's neighborhood, but in a better-kept building. He finished college, has travelled extensively, and now works in Chicago as a buyer for a large retailer. Although he comes from an upper-class, media-rich, socioeconomic setting that is quite similar to Peterson's, the two men are poles apart in their oulook on life. Unlike Peterson, Quentin is highly motivated to succeed, keeps his activities in line with mainstream ideals, and has a strong sense of civic obligation to be informed about current affairs. His religious and family background predispose him to take a public rather than personal benefit stance towards political problems. His liberalism in the social policy area is combined with a preference for conservative policies in other areas. He is optimistic about ultimate improvement of public moral and ethical standards.

Nonetheless, Quentin has little interest in extensive mass media use because his time pressures are severe. His job, involving frequent overtime work, his active social life, and numerous hobbies crowd his schedule. He feels that, at best, papers and television would provide him with only a very superficial view of the world. Much newspaper reading and television watching is therefore a waste. However, like other societally involved low-media-use males with outgoing personalities and good listening and memory skills, he picks up a good deal of information from his co-workers and social contacts, without getting involved in extensive discussions. This makes him and other such males far better informed than most low-media-use women, who ordinarily lack the information-rich contacts available to employed males.

*Darlene Rosswell.* Rosswell is a 28-year-old unmarried black woman who works in Evanston as an insurance clerk. She completed high school and tried her hand at college, but admits that she does not care much for academic subjects nor, for that matter, about current events. She lives with her parents, both of whom work in Chicago, in a neatly-kept townhouse in an area plagued by teenage gang activities. Rosswell is generally liberal in outlook, though a bit cynical about the motives of politicians and other power figures whom she accuses at times of conspiracies against the public interest. However, her liberalism wanes whenever it conflicts with her personal concerns. For instance, she favors strict punishment for lawbreakers, deeming them a threat to the possessions she and her family have acquired through hard work.

Darlene Rosswell does not generally pay much attention to the media. The reasons are twofold. Her active social life leaves her with little spare time for media consumption and she has serious doubts about the credibility of many news stories. She thinks they are incomplete, often deceptive, and usually overly sensationalized. She also finds most of them boring. Therefore, she gets much of her information about current affairs through interpersonal conversations. She prefers to rely on her father and her friends for most political judgments, feeling that they know more about politics so that "it is wise to go along with them." Asked what position she plays in discussions, she says: "To be truthful, people can sway me more than I can sway them. I listen to what they say." She apparently listens well, though selectively. For matters of interest to her, her memory is excellent. Otherwise, she remembers little more than her overall reaction to stories, such as "I was surprised" or "I thought it was terrible."

*Deidre Sandelius.* Sandelius is a registered nurse who has two middle-grade school children and a husband in a white-collar job. She is a pleasant, cheerful woman, 36 years old, who takes the view that all of life's problems can be solved satisfactorily, if people of good will work hard. However, she doubts that politicians are doing their best. During the course of our interviews, Sandelius was working a number of night shifts as well as attending classes to upgrade her nursing skills. Homemaking, job, and school tasks left her with little time to pay attention to the news and sapped whatever interest in the news she had in the past when her life provided her with more leisure time. "I just don't care any more. I have too many other things to worry about." She exemplifies how changes in life-style can bring about changes in attitudes towards news and in media use patterns.

Sandelius currently relies heavily on her husband for political judgments, including voting choices, and, therefore, feels little pressure to make time for news exposure, even in an election year. Moreover, she has stored up a good fund of knowledge and opinions from earlier years, that she applies readily to current political issues. She was raised on a midwestern farm, in a family with a keen interest in politics and an ample supply of media in the home. She has some doubts about the accuracy of media stories, complaining about omissions and slants that distort the truth. She is involved in numerous political conversations but prefers to be a listener rather than an active participant. Like many women, she routinely pleads incompetence to understand complex issues that "completely throw me."

***Lettie Tisdale.*** Tisdale is a poorly-educated black woman, of somewhat precarious health, who lives in a tiny apartment on the edge of a high-crime area. She is 56 years old and spent the first 40 years of her life in a small southern community where she raised three children and worked part-time as a farm hand. The family has always been too poor to subscribe to newspapers and magazines. Aside from the move to Evanston, she has not travelled. Lettie Tisdale has been a widow for four years and shares her cramped living quarters with an extended family, including several young grandchildren. She works as a maid in the daytime and spends many evening hours participating in church affairs. She is very much concerned about the crime danger in her neighborhood, especially when her grandchildren are outside the home.

Her interest in, and attention to, mass media information are low. She has little spare time and therefore has always relied on the men in her family for political information. Her comprehension of complex information is limited except when it is put into simple terms. She disapproves of the political scene because her husband did so, and she believes that society makes life more difficult for blacks than for whites. But she is optimistic about the future and remains a staunch Democrat who loyally votes a straight Democratic ticket. She acquires information about a limited number of local news items through listening to friends and family members and through news bulletins on the radio. But she does not discuss political issues and shows little concern for their significance or impact on her life.

***David Utley.*** Utley is a 62-year-old, college-educated plant manager. He is married and has four children, two of them still living at home. He has travelled widely and is active in professional engineering associations. He describes himself as a science buff who has never been interested in politics and did not participate in political discussions in his childhood home. This pattern has continued. He rarely discusses politics at home or on the job. When he becomes involved in political conversations, he listens rather than talks because he does not like to foist his views on anyone. This goes along with his ideal that thinking should be independent and free from outside pressures.

David Utley is cynical about the motives of governments and politicians. He considers himself a conservative, turned liberal through his own reasoning about political matters and through watching social legislation in operation. He has excellent insight into human relations so that his guesses of what was likely to happen as the year 1976 unfolded turned out to be exceedingly accurate. He believes that history over the last 2,000 years shows that little has changed in human behavior and motivations and their consequences.

When he devotes a little time to newspapers and television, he does so "with a jaundiced eye," to glimpse facts from which he can then draw his own conclusions. His opinions about mass media were formed early in life when he was exposed to an abundant array of newspapers and magazines in his childhood home. He thinks most news stories in the daily press are shallow, overly neutral, and lacking in appropriate societal perspectives. He prefers instead to rely on the occasional political stories in his professional journals. He claims to have an excellent memory, but when asked what he remembers about last night's news, he answers, "Nothing, because there was nothing worth remembering." Nonetheless, he absorbs sufficient information about current events from his haphazard contacts with news sources so that he can comment on most well-covered news topics.

## THE BELIEF INFRASTRUCTURE OF THE PANELISTS

Despite their obvious uniqueness, our panelists share a political culture that has produced many striking similarities among them. As Rokeach has argued in *The Open and Closed Mind*, people have central beliefs that guide their thinking.[14] These central beliefs or "cognitive predispositions," to use a term coined by Putnam, structure man's understanding of "the nature of the physical world he lives in, the nature of the 'self,' and of the 'generalized other.' " They form the backdrop for assimilating new information.[15]

Here we will sketch out a few of the cognitive predispositions that surfaced repeatedly, during the course of the interviews, in the thinking of all of our panelists. We will speculate about their likely impact on our panelists' processing of current information.

### Life Satisfaction

Except for Craig Kolarz and Betty Nystrom, most of our panelists appear to be reasonably well-satisfied with life. Their generally favorable outlook on politics may therefore spring from what is called "stimulus generalization," with general satisfaction casting a glow of good feeling over all aspects of life. Basic American institutions seem sound to them, although a few panelists have intermittent doubts about the economic viability of the capitalist system. None of the panelists, not even Kolarz and Nystrom, appeared to feel alienated and powerless and deliberately aloof from the political environment. All had a surprisingly high tolerance for unsatisfactory performance by government, blaming problems, rather than individuals, for ongoing difficulties. Apparently they wanted to understand rather than condemn. The fact that they were drawn from a pool of registered voters may account for the low level of alienation and the substantial concern, albeit at varying levels of intensity, with the political process.

Despite occasional twinges of doubt, the panelists, as a group, believe very much in the American, Horatio Alger dream. With hard work and a good education, any American, with the possible exception of blacks, can achieve his or her life's ambitions. Personal experiences may paint a different picture, but the dream persists. It engenders optimism and a sense of personal rather than societal responsibility for solving social problems. At the same time, government is viewed as facilitator of equal opportunities and as the provider of last resort. If personal efforts fail, then government is expected to be an effective provider and a solver of intractable problems.[16]

Similar sentiments have been measured in national samples. Kay Schlozman and Sidney Verba, for instance, concluded from a national survey:

> On the whole, Americans' beliefs about the social order seem to be characterized by a relatively high level of commitment to the American Dream of success and a very low level of class consciousness. Furthermore, the attitudes seem to be fairly uniform across classes. . . . An unhappy experience with the economic system—and the unemployed can clearly be said to have had such an experience—does not appear to reduce belief in the extent or fairness of opportunities in America. . . . There is virtually no relationship between beliefs about opportunities in general and evaluation of personal opportunities.[17]

## Tolerance and Fairness

Our respondents generally are open-minded. They see two or more sides to each question and feel compelled by canons of fairness to listen to them.[18] "You have to hear both sides of the story" is a common remark. Hence the panelists are willing to expose themselves to opposing views, even though this complicates their opinion formation or contradicts what they already believe. The panelists routinely assume that there are counterarguments to any position that is publicized by the media even when these counterarguments are not stated. They often try to fathom what these counterarguments might be. They also are "not easily persuaded that differences with another group are irreconcilable . . . there is a positive search for neutral and central ground undertaken whenever differences appear."[19] Our panelists tried to accommodate the positions stated by others without necessarily yielding their own.

Because of the incredible complexity of political and social conditions, many of our panelists are uncertain about some of their views or take ambivalent positions. Frequently, they have built up repertoires of schemas embodying diverse perspectives. This explains why they often express multiple and even divergent views about issues in the news, depending on how these issues are presented and how questions are framed. Such inconsistencies usually are a sign of the ability to view the world from a variety of perspectives, rather than a sign of confused thinking.

Although many political views fluctuate because they are not firmly held or because they are context-dependent, a number of basic beliefs are steadfast and shared by nearly all panelists. Belief in the "American way" is one example. Sven Peterson, for example, expressed shock about F.B.I. spying on President Nixon. "We're not supposed to have secret police here. This is shocking . . . spying on the President, throwing the President out of office . . . that's fantastic! That's not what America is supposed to be like." Such beliefs have the quality of political religion, learned early in childhood and never questioned. New information is processed so that it accords with these beliefs and contrary evidence is not generally permitted to undermine their strengths. Because these beliefs are so widely shared and constantly reinforced, they "may account for the mysterious processes in which large numbers of individuals seem to think and act in similar ways."[20]

## Feelings about Politics

Politics is a spectator, not a participant, sport for our panelists. They watch it because they deem it important or useful or because they feel a social obligation to keep aware of major political developments. But they rarely are passionate about politics or perceive it as a force that directly and immediately affects their personal lives in major ways. This detached attitude has several consequences. It prevents people from taking great pains to keep up with the news and encourages them to process it in ways which reduce time and effort spent on cognitive operations. It explains why people are sloppy in scanning news and why they totally ignore much of it. It also means that our panelists, most of the time, neglect to pass judgments about the events that come to their attention and rarely try to think about solutions to problems.

Detachment also meant that panelists felt that they could normally afford to act the role of the "good citizen" when making political choices since the role appeared to involve few obvious costs. Accordingly, when pressed to do so, they judged on the basis of symbolic considerations, such as political altruism or party allegiance or human sympathy, rather than personal self-interest. However, when the impact of political issues appeared more direct, as happened when busing or tax policies were at stake, our panelists took a more self-regarding stance.[21]

Lack of deep concern about politics does not mean that the panelists were unaware of social and political inequities and problems that required urgent action. Many of them were supportive of such changes, even though they were unwilling to participate in a major way in social activism through personal service or donations. Neither was lukewarm interest in politics and scattered attention a bar to acquiring a substantial fund of political knowledge. Political news is so pervasive and comes to people's attention so often in the course of their daily lives, that even the most passive learners cannot avoid acquiring a sense of how the system operates and a stock of incidents to illustrate the general principles. It is this combination of comparatively low motivation to learn along with plentiful opportunities for learning that explains why our panelists learned less than one might hope, yet knew more than one might expect. By and large, they had a good grasp of how the political system works, even when they were short on specific facts and details.

One would think that the combination of giving a low priority to the acquisition of political knowledge (compared to other pursuits) and the awareness of knowing a good deal about politics, would give our panelists a sense of adequacy and satisfaction. This was not the case. There was a pervading sense among all of them that they did not really know enough to adequately understand the complex social environment in which they lived. They felt that expertise is required to grasp most problems and that they lack this expertise. Many panelists had a sense that they could acquire expertise, if only they worked harder to get and assimilate information. This reflects the typical American view that all problems have solutions that hard work makes available. Most panelists expressed guilt for insufficient attention to news. However, this is coupled with unwillingness to make the efforts that their civic consciences seemed to demand.

## The National Focus

In their reading habits, as well as in their general concerns, our panelists focused primarily on national politics and secondarily on local politics. As Lane has pointed out: "The county, the state senatorial district, the congressional district have no trace lines in psychic space . . . There are only two areas of importance — local and national."[22] For most panelists, most of the time, this distinction narrows down to a single area, national politics. They are not interested in local politics unless major upheavals or scandals are involved or, their lives are touched in mundane matters like the need for snow removal or parking facilities, or in matters of greater but sporadic concern, like the desire for more street safety. Since most political news does not usually deal with ordinary local concerns, interest in local affairs is piqued only intermittently. On the other hand, interest in international affairs was also sporadic. Most of the panelists paid attention to international events only if they affected United States' politics, particularly the conduct of foreign affairs. Also, if the matters related to the panelists' ethnic ties, the panelists were more aware of the events. But, at best, interest was quite limited even for those respondents who had travelled extensively abroad.

The media, especially television, contribute to this priority structure by putting heaviest emphasis on national news or the national aspects of local and international news. The media even have nationalized political gossip so that people know more about the pecadillos of Washington personalities than of local political leaders.

Another major factor in this national orientation is the increasing mobility of Americans. Lane argues that "community identity is a product of an immobile society, a static society; the cost of labor mobility, equality of opportunity, and technical change is a lost community identity. . . ."[23] This means that political space is no longer "congruent with psychic space (the area of interest, friendship, knowledge)." Therefore, it has become difficult "to enlist men's private motives for local political affairs." Our panelists, like Lane's Eastport sample, lacked" a sense of localism, a feeling of being rooted, a genuine community identity. . . ."[24]

How is the impact of this belief infrastructure reflected in the panelists' news-processing behavior? The next chapter tells part of the story. After describing the news environment in 1976, it shows what happens when people who lack a passion for politics, try to keep up with the news in the face of many other demands on their time. The outcome is a compromise. The shape of that compromise will be outlined in chapter 4.

## Notes

1. John Sprague, "Is There a Micro Theory Consistent with Contextual Analysis?", in Elinor Ostrom (ed.), *Strategies of Political Inquiry*, Beverly Hills, Sage, 1982, p. 108.
2. David O. Sears, Richard R. Lau, Tom R. Tyler, and Harris M. Allen, Jr., "Self-Interest vs. Symbolic Politics in Policy Attitudes and Presidential Voting," *American Political Science Review*, 74, 1980, p. 672.
3. Gerald M. Pomper (with Susan Lederman), *Elections in America*, 2nd ed., New York, Longman, 1980, p. 65.
4. Ibid.
5. In the Indiana and New Hampshire control panels, college graduates made up less than one-third of each panel. Only 13% of the panelists held professional jobs.
6. Pomper, as cited in note 3, pp. 56, 66.
7. Ibid., p. 56.
8. Susan T. Fiske and Donald R. Kinder, "Involvement, Expertise, and Schema Use: Evidence from Political Cognition," in Nancy Cantor and John F. Kihlstrom, (eds.), *Personality, Cognition, and Social Interaction*, Hillsdale, N.J., Lawrence Erlbaum, 1981, p. 180.
9. Sprague, as cited in note 1, pp. 112–118.
10. For similar observations, see Elizabeth Noelle-Neuman, *Die Schweigespirale*, Munich, R. Piper, 1980.
11. Pomper, as cited in note 3, p. 63. For monthly variations in such lists, based on responses from panelists from all four study panels, see David H. Weaver, Doris A. Graber, Maxwell E. McCombs, and Chaim Eyal, *Media Agenda-Setting in a Presidential Election: Issues, Images, and Interest*, New York, Praeger, 1981, pp. 86–88, 120–121, 146–148.
12. Pomper, as cited in note 3. For a different interpretation of the nature of these concerns, see the spate of recent "sociotropic" literature, such as Donald R. Kinder, "Sociotropic Politics: The American Case," *British Journal of Political Science*, 11:1981, 129–162; or Kay Lehman Schlozman and Sidney Verba, *Injury to Insult: Unemployment, Class, and Political Response*, Cambridge, Harvard University Press, 1979.

13. John Kessel, *Presidential Campaign Politics: Coalition Strategies and Citizen Response*, Homewood, Ill., Dorsey Press, 1980, p. 159.

14. Milton Rokeach, *The Open and Closed Mind: Investigations into the Nature of Belief Systems and Personality Systems*, New York, Basic Books, 1960, pp. 39–51.

15. Robert Putnam, *The Beliefs of Politicians: Ideology, Conflict, and Democracy in Britain and Italy*, New Haven, Yale University Press, 1973, p. 5.

16. See also, Karl A. Lamb, *As Orange Goes: Twelve California Families and the Future of American Politics*, New York, Norton, 1974, pp. 153–154.

17. The quotes, respectively come from Schlozman and Verba, as cited in note 12, pp. 129, 140, 150–151. See also, Robert E. Lane, *Political Ideology: Why the American Common Man Believes What He Does*, New York, Free Press, 1962, pp. 150–151; and Richard Sennett and Jonathan Cobb, *The Hidden Injuries of Class*, New York, Random House, 1972, p. 92.

18. See also, Lane as cited in note 17, p. 31. For a detailed examination of this belief see, Jennifer L. Hochschild, *What's Fair? American Beliefs about Distributive Justice*, Cambridge, Harvard University Press, 1981.

19. Lane, as cited in note 17, p. 448.

20. W. Lance Bennett, "Perception and Cognition: An Information-Processing Framework for Politics," in Samuel L. Long, (ed.), *The Handbook of Political Behavior*, vol. 1, New York, Plenum Press, 1981, p. 131.

21. For similar observations see David O. Sears, Richard R. Lau, Tom R. Tyler, and Harris M. Allen, Jr. "Self-Interest vs. Symbolic Politics in Policy Attitudes and Presidential Voting," *American Political Science Review*, 74, 1980, pp. 670–684; Donald R. Kinder and D. Roderick Kiewiet, "Economic Grievances and Political Behavior: The Role of Personal Discontents and Collective Judgments in Congressional Voting," *American Journal of Political Science*, 23, 1979, pp. 495–527; and Stanley Feldman, "Economic Self-Interest and Political Behavior," *American Journal of Political Science*, 26:3, August 1982, pp. 446–466.

22. Lane, as cited in note 17, p. 299.

23. Ibid., p. 305.

24. Ibid., pp. 457–458.

# 4

## What's New? Information Supply and Learning Scores

Putnam opens his book on *The Beliefs of Politicians* with the statement that "most men are not political animals. The world of public affairs is not their world. It is alien to them—possibly benevolent, more probably threatening, but nearly always alien. Most men are not interested in politics. Most do not participate in politics. And few have much power or influence."[1] To a degree this statement seems to be true for our panelists. Politics seemed alien to them in the sense that they perceived it as something that others were doing. But it was not so alien that they felt totally unable to understand it. They did have a large number of perceptions about the ways in which politics operated and a large number of judgments about the quality of general and specific operations. Moreover, though politics was not a top priority for them, our panelists were interested in it and spent a substantial amount of time and effort in surveying the political scene.

What sorts of information did this surveillance yield for our respondents in 1976? To answer this question, we shall look first at the information which was available to them from the media. Then, we shall look at some of the uses that they made of their media information.

### THE PANELISTS' INFORMATION SUPPLY

#### Television and Newspaper Content Analysis Data

To assess the panelists' news supply, we coded their chief newspaper source, the *Chicago Tribune*, on a daily basis during the entire year of the study. This yielded 19,068 news stories. Since most news stories cover more than one topic, triple coding was used to capture the substance of coverage more fully, Accordingly, a total of 33,200 news topics were coded for the *Tribune*. Since several panelists also read the *Chicago Sun Times* and the *Chicago Daily News*, or were exposed to stories from these papers during conversations with others, we decided to code samples from these papers to compare story distribution with the *Tribune* scores. The differences turned out to be minor. Altogether, we coded seven days of news, each day from a different week, for each of these extra papers. This yielded 335 stories, involving 581 topics from the *Sun Times* and 282 stories, encompassing 506 topics from the *Daily News*. Had we coded every theme mentioned in each story, this would have multiplied the coded items by a factor of 20, as compared to triple coding.[2] These figures give some indication of the scale of the information flood that confronts readers of major newspapers.

Since our panelists regularly watched several television newscasts, we also coded these on a daily basis. The national network news yielded 4,763 stories (7,962 topics) for ABC; 4,879 stories (8,193 topics) for CBS; and 4,561 stories (7,667 topics) for NBC for the last 9 months of the study.[3] The local newscasts yielded 4,592 CBS and 7,371 NBC stories, encompassing 7,597 and 12,274 topics respectively.[4]

We coded these data by subject matter into 67 separate topics. Table 4.1 presents a condensed version of 21 topics. The table reveals that all news sources were strikingly similar in the proportion of news devoted to various topic and subtopic areas. The similarity was particularly pronounced within the television groups. However, there were differences between the relative frequency of various stories when one compares the print media as a group with national television newscasts on the one hand and local television newscasts on the other. This meant that regardless of which national or local news broadcasts the panelists watched, or which paper they read, the proportions of various types of news presented to them were almost identical. Therefore, we did not have to worry that panelists who used different news broadcasts would be exposed to different patterns of news and would be unaware of major topic areas.

Major newspaper topics in 1976 encompassed stories about the national government, including the President, Congress, the courts, and the bureaucracy (13%); domestic policy of the national government (13%); street crime, corruption, and terrorism (12%); foreign affairs (10%); elections (8%); and the state of the economy, business, and labor (8%). Corresponding figures for CBS broadcasts, the national and local program used most widely by our panelists, included the President, Congress, the courts, and the bureaucracy (17% for national, 11% for local); domestic national policy (8% for national, 7% for local); street crime, corruption, and terrorism (7% for national, 12% for local); foreign affairs (17% for national, 5% for local); elections (15% for national, 7% for local); and the state of the economy, business, and labor (9% for national, 11% for local).

## Fluctuations in News Coverage Trends

These patterns of topics and even of particular stories were exceedingly stable, assuring a constant stream of novel and not-so-novel information to deepen and broaden, or merely refresh, knowledge about familiar topics. An analysis of semi-monthly fluctuations in news topic coverage shows a very narrow dispersion around the mean, especially in the major "hard" news areas.[5] Soft news topics, for example, human interest stories and news about hobbies, tended to vary most. But even here, the fluctuations were quite minor.

As far as the news audience is concerned, on most days there is very little that is geniunely new. The news mix is the same and most stories are simply minor updates of previous news or new examples of old themes. The fact that news is a standardized product—the "standardized exceptional," to use a phrase coined by Leon Sigal—eases the news consumer's task tremendously.[6] The bulk of news can be scanned and discarded as "nothing new," or it can be readily processed and stored as just one more example of familiar happenings.

## An Overview of Story Topics

The following is a roster of news stories that were displayed prominently in the print and electronic media in 1976. Many of them appeared off and on throughout the entire year, featuring the same locale and the same actors. Others surfaced frequently, but with different actors and in different locales. Most of them involved perennial prototypical news events —the kinds of stories that have been and are continuing to be the mainstay of American news. Undoubtedly, the reader in the 1980s and beyond will feel déjà vu when comparing current news with 1976 happenings.

In the 1976 American-style version of news, domestic policy stories reported various changes in allotments for social services such as social security, food stamps, and veterans' benefits, as well as outlays for defense and the procurement of specific weapons. Abortion, the right to discontinue artificial life support, and the scope of affirmative action were also common topics. So were major court decisions, particularly by the Supreme Court, that further developed well-established trends.

A large number of stories dealt with the presidential primary elections, the nominating conventions, the presidential debates, the final election, and various candidates and major issues in the campaign. A few faces were new, but most were familiar, and the rhetoric followed established patterns. Overall, the tone of news stories was respectful towards government and the American system of politics, notwithstanding frequent specific criticisms. If anything, the news reinforced the audience's respect for the American version of democratic government. Most stories were presented from a public-good, rather than private-advantage perspective, encouraging the audience to view their world altruistically.

In foreign affairs, Soviet and Cuban efforts to assist in the establishment of pro-Soviet regimes in Africa received repeated coverage. So did stories about unrest in the Middle East, instability in Latin America, terrorism in Ireland, and the possibility of Communist gains in various European elections. The scope of American military and economic aid to various countries was another staple of

TABLE 4.1. Frequency of Mention of News Topics (*scores are in percentages*)

| | Chicago Tribune* | Sun Times | Daily News | CBS local | NBC local | ABC national | CBS national | NBC national |
|---|---|---|---|---|---|---|---|---|
| *Government/politics* | | | | | | | | |
| National government | 35.2 | 34.8 | 34.5 | 20.7 | 19.5 | 39.8 | 41.2 | 38.8 |
| Elections | 7.6 | 10.0 | 11.5 | 6.8 | 6.2 | 15.7 | 15.2 | 15.2 |
| State government | 1.8 | 1.4 | 0.8 | 2.7 | 2.2 | 0.6 | 0.9 | 0.8 |
| City government | 1.9 | 0.3 | 1.2 | 4.3 | 3.2 | 0.7 | 0.5 | 0.5 |
| Miscellaneous | 0.6 | 0.7 | 0.0 | 0.9 | 1.0 | 0.7 | 0.6 | 0.4 |
| | 47.1 | 47.2 | 48.0 | 35.4 | 32.1 | 57.5 | 58.4 | 55.7 |
| *Economic issues* | | | | | | | | |
| Economy status | 2.4 | 2.1 | 2.4 | 1.1 | 1.0 | 1.7 | 1.7 | 1.9 |
| Business/labor | 5.9 | 6.4 | 4.9 | 6.6 | 10.2 | 7.8 | 6.8 | 6.8 |
| Environment/transportation | 3.2 | 4.1 | 1.8 | 9.1 | 9.1 | 3.5 | 4.0 | 4.0 |
| Medicine/health | 2.5 | 2.4 | 1.6 | 3.3 | 4.6 | 2.1 | 2.8 | 3.2 |
| | 14.0 | 15.0 | 10.7 | 20.1 | 24.9 | 15.1 | 15.3 | 15.9 |

| | | | | | | | | |
|---|---|---|---|---|---|---|---|---|
| *Social issues* | | | | | | | | |
| Deprived groups | 2.7 | 2.9 | 3.8 | 2.1 | 2.0 | 2.7 | 2.9 | 2.4 |
| Education/media/religion | 4.4 | 2.2 | 2.8 | 4.0 | 4.0 | 2.8 | 3.0 | 2.5 |
| Leadership style | 1.2 | 1.5 | 1.4 | 0.2 | 0.2 | 0.8 | 0.7 | 0.6 |
| Disaster/accident | 2.2 | 1.9 | 2.4 | 3.8 | 5.0 | 3.2 | 2.8 | 3.3 |
| Police/security | 4.7 | 7.2 | 7.7 | 3.3 | 3.1 | 1.5 | 1.6 | 1.5 |
| Corruption/terrorism | 4.0 | 5.7 | 5.5 | 4.0 | 3.3 | 3.1 | 3.3 | 3.1 |
| Individual crime | 7.5 | 10.2 | 9.5 | 7.8 | 8.5 | 4.1 | 4.0 | 4.6 |
| Miscellaneous | 1.7 | 0.7 | 0.6 | 1.3 | 1.2 | 1.8 | 1.4 | 1.5 |
| | 28.4 | 32.3 | 33.7 | 26.5 | 27.3 | 20.0 | 19.7 | 19.5 |
| *Human interest/hobbies*** | | | | | | | | |
| General stories | 2.9 | 1.9 | 3.4 | 6.0 | 6.8 | 1.8 | 1.8 | 2.3 |
| Celebrities | 3.6 | 1.4 | 2.0 | 2.2 | 2.1 | 1.4 | 1.5 | 1.7 |
| Political gossip | 1.6 | 0.5 | 1.2 | 1.4 | 1.4 | 1.4 | 1.1 | 1.4 |
| Sports/arts | 2.6 | 1.7 | 1.4 | 8.3 | 5.3 | 2.9 | 2.1 | 3.4 |
| | 10.7 | 5.5 | 8.0 | 17.9 | 15.6 | 7.5 | 6.5 | 8.8 |

* $N$ = 33,200 for the *Tribune*; 581 for the *Sun Times*; 506 for the *Daily News*; 7507 for CBS local; 12,274 for NBC local; 7,962 for ABC national; 8,193 for CBS national; and 7,667 for NBC national news.

** When stories of this type appeared in special sections, the entire section was coded as one story (e.g., People, Leisure, Food). This depresses the Human Interest/Hobbies count.

foreign news. So were stories about disarmament talks with the Soviet Union. The only mildly unusual story in 1976 concerned rioting in China and the arrest of Mao Tse-tung's widow Chiang Ch'ing, along with three other out-of-power politicians. The general impression created by the flow of stories was one of the United States' inability to stop advances by pro-Communist forces. However, the advances were depicted as quite limited, reassuring the audience that it need not worry very much about foreign policy.

Stories about the economy mainly concerned inflation, taxes, and the plight of various public institutions. Occasional stories reported unemployment and inflation figures, along with general economic indicators. But most stories were only illustrations of these economic trends, such as reports about rising telephone and transportation rates, increased college tuition and cutbacks at the elementary and secondary education level, financial crunches in public hospitals and strikes by unionized labor for higher wages. The activities of the Organization of Petroleum Exporting Countries (OPEC) in producing oil and pricing it received substantial attention. Again, the overall impression was one of impotence of the American government to cope with economic ills, a tip-off for many panelists to ignore such stories because "nothing can be done anyhow."

In the aftermath of Watergate, the issue of corruption in government remained a topic of major interest. Stories about payoffs in return for election support were plentiful, along with stories about the bribery of legislators and sexual misconduct by people in high places. As in the past, these incidents were pictured as exceptions, rather than the rule, and, therefore, produced more titillation than genuine concern. Corruption in the private sector was also a popular topic, with stories about corrupt unions, corporate graft, Medicaid fraud, and welfare fraud heading the list. Rich and poor alike were shown as capable of fraud. Two scandals involving the Military Academy at West Point were a bit out of the ordinary, one concerning examination cheating by cadets and the other dealing with fraud in meat purchases.

The 1976 news also featured its normal share of major disasters and crimes. There were severe earthquakes, volcanic eruptions, tornados, along with ruptured dams, oil spills in the ocean, commuter train crashes, plunging cable cars, and nursing home fires. The safety of atomic energy plants and the chemical pollution of housing areas and food stuffs spawned speculations about future disasters and steps needed to prevent them. On the crime front, the trial of Patricia Hearst received ample attention over many months. There were numerous reports about airline hijackings, terrorist murders, kidnappings and threatened assassinations, and more routine stories about revenge murders and child abuse. Organized crime activity also received a good deal of coverage. Most panelists, but especially those with little interest in politics, paid substantial attention to these stories because they were easy to grasp and emotionally stimulating.

Finally, stories about well-known personalities and organized groups made the news. These included football coaches, players, and their teams, boxers and tennis professionals, along with famous entertainers, political interest groups, and prominent figures. Henry Kissinger, the peripatetic Secretary of State, rated several stories each month. A few well-known senators fared nearly as well, particularly those who were also involved in the election contest. The never-ending parade of visiting heads of states was well covered, as were the activities of black leaders during racial disturbances. Sprinkled throughout the year were the notices about the deaths of famous people, along with reviews of their major achievements. Again, the human drama played out by these stories made them an attractive form of entertainment for many panelists.

From the perspective of news coverage, 1976 was a routine election year. The bulk of the stories dealt with familiar subjects and familiar activities and caused little surprise. Even the more unusual stories were fairly predictable, with the possible exception of photographs from outer space. There were few major surprises in the activities surrounding the celebration of the American bicentennial in the summer of 1976 and few geniune breakthroughs in medical, environmental, or technological news.

The frequency with which these various types of stories were covered in 1976 matched neither the rising or ebbing significance of real world problems, nor the expressed major interests of media audiences. For example, environmental protection and dependence on Mideastern oil continued to be matters that received ample media attention in 1976, although there were no unusual developments meriting such plentiful coverage. For our panelists, inflation, unemployment, and taxes were prime concerns during the interview year, while foreign affairs were of far lesser interest. Yet the media emphasized foreign affairs far more than the economic issues, obviously because the foreign stories contained more dramatic developments. Similarly, many panelists complained about an overabundance of election stories which covered topics of little interest to them and omitted needed information about the candidates' past experiences. Such disjunctions between desired news and available news put a damper on learning from the media.

## Coverage of the 1976 Presidential Election

From a variety of perspectives, the presidential election was the major news story for which the public had strong learning incentives. Most panelists were interested in the election because they felt obliged to be at least moderately informed, so that they would be able to vote intelligently. They also knew that election events were likely topics of social and business conversation. We will, therefore, look closely at the information supplied by the *Tribune* for making electoral choices, so that we can test the degree of learning when motivation was high and the most ample medium was used. We will supplement election learning data with information about learning from crime stories because crime was also an area of major news attention for the panelists.[7] In fact, crime was the most frequent news topic in the diaries. Even panelists with poor memories could recall crime stories comparatively well and remembered them longer than other stories. While election stories often presented novel situations with which media audiences might have been unfamiliar, most crime stories followed familiar patterns for which people were likely to have well-established schemas. The impact of the differences between these two learning situations will be examined.

There was ample media coverage of the election in the *Tribune*. The paper carried 426 stories about President Ford and 599 about Governor Carter during the year. It also had 516 stories about other candidates and 457 dealing with candidates in general. While these stories were not exceptionally prominent, they fared reasonably well in terms of placement in forward sections of the paper, space allotments, and inclusion of pictures. The issues featured in these stories, therefore, had a good chance of coming to the attention of media audiences. In fact, our study shows that even stories which were infrequently covered and which did not benefit from prominent display might soar to the top of the audience's attention once a threshold of coverage had been reached.[8] While the quantity of coverage was ample, the quality of the mix of information provided was open to question on several counts. These related to the adequacy of information, especially during the primaries, the appropriateness of patterns of topics, and the depth and slant of the coverage.

*Tribune* coverage was open to some criticism on all these counts, especially during the primaries. Most importantly, during the primaries, information supply concentrated on just three of the candidates. Of the information, 70% about the qualifications of the contenders, and 77% of the news about campaign events and public policy issues, referred to Ford, Carter, and Reagan, leaving seven other candidates sparsely covered. Our panelists learned little about Wallace, Bayh, Brown, Harris, Udall, Jackson, or Church. Third party candidates and vice-presidential candidates were almost completely ignored by the *Tribune*, even though the chances of a vice-president becoming president are substantial. A look at the description of personal qualities of the ten most-covered presidential contenders shows that there were gaps in information about professional skills for half the candidates.

The impact of sparse coverage can be demonstrated by examining name recognition patterns among our panelists, as well as other Americans, following the New Hampshire primary. Benefitting from ample media coverage, Carter's name recognition skyrocketed from 16%—the average figure for most of the New Hampshire entries—to 80%. By contrast, name recognition levels for sparsely publicized candidates remained low. They rose only 14% for Udall, Brown, and Jackson and 9% for Church. Recognition levels remained constant for Harris and declined for Bayh. Recognition levels, of course, are a highly important aspect of political learning because voters tend to pay careful attention to, and vote for, those candidates whom they have learned to recognize.

Although the need to acquaint the voters with a host of unfamiliar personalities is greatest during primaries, the proportion of information devoted to personal qualities of candidates was less during the primaries than during later phases of the campaign. During the primaries, 40% of all stories dealt with such qualities, compared to 60% in the general election.

Throughout the entire election, personal qualities were covered more heavily than professional capabilities. The general human qualities encompassed in personality traits, style, and professional image made up 75% or more of the qualities mentioned for the candidates (85% for Carter and 71% for Ford during the primaries). Trustworthiness, strength of character, and compassion were mentioned most often. These characteristics, while important for job performance, were not specifically related to qualification for the presidency. Much less exposure was given to such professionally relevant characteristics as the ability to conduct domestic and foreign affairs well and to keep the peace at home and abroad. Similarly, there were few mentions of the ability to lead public opinion or of the general political philosophy by which the candidates would guide governmental organization and operations.

In line with usual news practice, there was heavy emphasis on negative aspects of the qualities of the candidates and the quality of their policy proposals. The consequences must be interpreted in light of the fact that negative information tends to have a stronger impact than positive information. Only 45% of the comments publicized in *Tribune* stories were positive. The news made it seem that none of the contenders would be able to handle the presidency effectively. The mood conveyed by such stories did, indeed, cast a pall over the enthusiasm with which the panelists faced the election and dampened their eagerness to continue reading what one panelist termed "that sorry story." Its effect on voting intentions apparently was less marked. In response to a direct question about willingness to vote when no good choices are available, our panelists split evenly between those who said they would be discouraged and those who felt it would make no difference in their decision to vote.

For the leading contenders, Ford and Carter, negative remarks were unevenly distributed during various phases of the campaign. During the primaries, Ford had received a preponderance of negative comments—57%, compared to 46% for Carter. The balance shifted in the summer when Carter references became 51% negative, compared to 44% for Ford. The overall figures for the entire campaign showed 60% of the remarks about Carter as negative, compared to 49% for Ford. The *Tribune's* differential treatment of the two candidates, which is statistically significant, was paralleled by trends in the panelists' appraisals of the two leading contenders. When asked to describe the candidates to a friend, they had fewer negative comments about Ford than about Carter, especially during the later phases of the campaign.

Coverage of issues and events during the primaries concentrated very heavily on fleeting campaign activities and vote tallies in state contests, slighting a discussion of the policy stands taken by the candidates. Of the 663 stories about the primaries published in the *Tribune*, the bulk (65%) dealt largely with ongoing campaign events. Only 7% of the stories were devoted to the domestic and foreign policy preferences of the main contenders. Another 3% of the stories covered major economic issues, including unemployment and inflation, with which the new president would have to cope. Stories about race relations and busing for school integration constituted 3% of the election coverage. Two percent of the coverage was devoted to stories about government spending and taxes. Other topics were covered even more sparsely. Overall, some 25 issues surfaced fairly regularly in the press and some 20 on television, but only half of these received substantial attention. It is obvious from these figures that no single policy issue received in-depth coverage during the primary season, notwithstanding that this is the most crucial period for predetermining who will have the chance to win the final election.

Moreover, information provided for various candidates covered different dimensions, for issues as well as personality characteristics, so that comparisons were difficult. With regard to Ford, for example, general domestic and foreign policies received chief attention, with lesser emphasis on economic and social policy positions. For Reagan, the media put the spotlight on his foreign policy plans and economic policy positions, with only slight emphasis on domestic and social policies. For Carter, discussion of social problems ranked first, followed by domestic politics. Attention to his views on foreign policies and economic problems was slight. Overall, 56% of the stories about Ford dealt with public policies, compared to 42% for Reagan and 32% for Carter.

Throughout the entire campaign, the media focused heavily on clear-cut, readily definable issues, such as busing or détente. Such issues could be cast in the form of battleground scenarios where candidates gain firm victories or suffer solid defeats. They make better stories than the diffuse discussions that candidates prefer when they consider complex questions of public policy. Despite their clarity, the winner–loser stories contribute to the confusion often felt by media audiences because the media report conflicting claims about who the losers or winners are in a particular issue battle.[9] Analytical pieces, exploring particular issues and policy options in depth and clarifying the scope and impact of particular victories and defeats, were comparatively rare.

For the post-primary period, the patterns set during the primaries persisted, although there was a decrease in the proportion of stories dealing with campaign events—from 65% to 51%—and a corresponding increase in stories covering policy issues. As mentioned, the proportion of stories dealing with candidate qualifications increased in the post-primary period.

On balance, despite all the deficiencies in media coverage, panelists who wanted to be well-informed about the qualities of the candidates and the relevant policy issues could usually find that information if they were willing to devote time and effort. Close attention to all *Tribune* election stories, along with watching television news regularly and reading analytical essays in news magazines, could supply a well-rounded picture, albeit a picture clouded by many unresolved inconsistencies. Few of the panelists, like their countrymen in general, were willing to make such a concerted effort. The motivation to become a political expert was simply not strong enough.

Most of the panelists resolved open questions, including their voting choices, by assessing the general trustworthiness of the candidates and weighing their capacity to make intelligent decisions and by looking for evidence that the candidates' past experiences could be brought to bear on the job. They used all kinds of stories as raw material to yield information about these characteristics.

Making evaluations and choices on the basis of such personal qualities is quite rational. Most people have experience with judging others by their personal attributes. Most find it too time-consuming and too difficult to form opinions about complex issues on the basis of mass media stories, particularly when the experts differ about the merits of conflicting policy recommendations. Those panelists who did consider the candidates' issue positions usually focused on only a few major concerns such as the Vietnam war, law and order problems, the Watergate scandal, inflation, or energy shortages. Other issues rolled off their minds like water off the proverbial duck.

## THE PANELISTS' INFORMATION GAIN

### The Substance of Learning

We used several measures to examine the amount of factual information ascertained from the media. To test how many election stories had left a mark, we asked the panelists during each interview about 5 specific election stories. For the 4 interviews during the primaries, we found that an average of 2 of the 5 stories were recalled. The rate rose to an average of 3 stories later in the campaign. This recall rate was average for important political stories.

To check learning about candidates and issues, we asked open-ended questions during each interview about what the panelists had learned on each score. Additionally, the panelists were asked to briefly describe each candidate to a friend and to indicate the most important issues on which the candidates had taken or should take a stand. The questions were: "Suppose you had some friends who had been away for a long time and were unfamiliar with the presidential candidates. What would you tell them about Candidate X?" Also, "About what issues has Candidate X been talking? What else should he talk about?"

We found that our panelists, like their counterparts in the general electorate, talked most about personality traits and background factors of the candidates.[10] For Jimmy Carter, image qualities constituted 67, 82, 80, and 79% respectively of the open-ended descriptions derived from interviews in March, July, August, and October. The corresponding figures for Ford were 90, 88, 89, and 87%. The specific image attributes stressed by the panelists and the patterns of attributes closely resembled those found in *Tribune* coverage. Changes in emphases in successive interviews also ran along lines that paralleled *Tribune* coverage. However, the imbalance of media coverage with respect to individual candidates was less clearly reflected among the panelists. Knowledge was uniformly low on all. But the panelists did supply proportionally more information about two familiar old-timers, Humphrey and Wallace, than was the case for the *Tribune*.[11]

Contrary to much of political science folklore, stress on image qualities was higher among the best-educated panelists. These panelists frequently mentioned that personality is crucial to a president's performance in office. It is important to know whether a candidate is honest, experienced, capable, strong, and trustworthy. One cannot appraise issue stands or estimate future performance until one has some sense of these character traits. Moreover, the stands of various candidates on issues were usually perceived as quite close, so that there was really no choice on the basis of issues.

These findings are substantiated by actual data. A group of investigators from the University of Michigan point out: "In every presidential election survey since 1952 better educated respondents volunteered more personal comments about the candidates than did the less well educated, a finding that remains true even after controlling for articulation."[12] To find people who respond in terms of issues, one must look to political interest, rather than education, as a distinguishing mark.

As is true for news stories, the elements making up the candidate portraits were distributed in different proportions. For instance, the panelists assessed Ford far more frequently on his past activities and abilities than Carter. For Carter, the emphasis on physical attributes and current social connections was much stronger. These differences are readily understandable. Ford was the incumbent whose performance record was well-known; for Carter, the newcomer, it was more important to establish what kind of an individual he was and how he had interacted with others in the past. Image dimensions pertaining to personality traits and styles of the candidates were better remembered than those pertaining to job qualifications and ideology.[13]

Comments about policy issues were infrequent throughout the campaign. They averaged 14%, but increased sharply just prior to the election, especially for Carter. We cannot tell whether this change reflected the panelists' own judgments of what was important in voting, the feeling that the absent friends for whom the candidates were described were interested in these matters, or the sense that issues ought be more important. In line with cultural norms, our panelists frequently indicated that they believed their election choices should be based on issues and that choices made on the basis of personal qualifications were ill-informed.

Issue knowledge was also tested by asking the panelists which of a list of 40 prominent news issues had been mentioned "a lot, a little, or not at all," by the media. With one exception, the panel's rankings coincided broadly with measurements of *Tribune* coverage, with only slight scrambling of the precise order. The exception was foreign policy, which was a frequent *Tribune* topic (though occurring less frequently on television), but which the panelists apparently missed. There were moderate differences in individual ratings which indicated that panelists differ in their alertness to various story topics. But all were obviously aware that the *Tribune* had covered numerous public policy issues amply. However, most panelists failed to link these issues to the election, even when the news story had made the connection explicit.

The panelist evidently were keenly aware of their sparse knowledge about the relation of policy issues to the election. When they were asked in midsummer, after the primaries, how much they had learned about the important issues of the election, only one panelist claimed to have learned a lot. Twelve of the panelists said that they had learned a moderate amount, 6 admitted to learning only a little and 2 said that they had learned nothing. Since the panelists knew that we had exact data on their learning, their self-evaluations were apt to be realistic. They certainly were correct.[14]

## The Quality of Learning

"Learning" involves various levels of complexity. To determine at which levels political news is learned from mass media stories, we rated responses to open-ended questions according to their complexity and accuracy. We distinguished four levels of learning about issues and candidates. For example, during the week after the 1976 presidential debates, we measured how much the panelists had learned about selected issue positions that the candidates had discussed at length. Half of these issue positions had been mentioned more than ten times during the debates. Panelists displayed *bare recall* if, following a question that provided them with minimal cues, they could recognize that an issue had been discussed, but they could not give additional facts. *Recall with facts* meant that the panelists remembered one or more comments made about the issue more or less accurately. A third level was reached whenever respondents were able *to relate specific issue positions to at least one of the candidates*. Ability to link *both candidates to specific positions on the same issue* received the highest score because it requires the most complex level of discrimination.

The six issues for which we tested these levels of knowledge concerned policy regarding jobs, taxes, draft evaders, United States policy in Africa, United States relations with the Soviet Union and the adequacy of national defense. The 1976 presidential debates constituted a rehearsal of this information because the panelists had been repeatedly exposed to it many times during the course of the year. Except for the treatment of draft evaders, all of the issues had been mentioned frequently by most of the panelists as personally important to them. This, then, was the ideal learning situation—ample, repeated information, dramatically re-hearsed at a time when the information was likely to be highly salient to the panelists because the election was imminent. Judging from our data, the fact that 11 of the panelists had definitely decided for whom they would vote by the time of the debates, and 5 had made tentative voting decisions, did not reduce their interest in watching the debates.[15]

Indeed, as Table 4.2 shows, the scores were good, indicating that all types of people can master fairly complex information when they are motivated to learn, the lessons are frequently repeated, and their knowledge is tested fairly promptly after learning. Of the 21 panelists, 17 knew the positions of both candidates regarding the treatment of draft evaders; 16 also reached the top level of learning regarding the candidates' defense policies; 10 panelists made top scores on tax policy, 7 on jobs policies and 7 on plans regarding relations with the Soviet Union. Only 3 knew the positions of both candidates regarding U.S.

TABLE 4.2. Panelists' Learning Levels (*n* = 21 respondents)

| Issue | No awareness | Aware-ness | Know issue only | Know issue + stand of 1 candidate | Know issue + stand of 2 candidates |
|-------|-----------|---------|------------|-----------|-----------|
| Employment policies | 4 | 3 | 4 | 3 | 7 |
| Tax policies | 3 | 3 | 0 | 5 | 10 |
| Draft evaders | 1 | 0 | 1 | 2 | 17 |
| U.S. policies in Africa | 6 | 2 | 4 | 6 | 3 |
| U.S./Soviet relations | 5 | 0 | 5 | 4 | 7 |
| Defense policies | 3 | 0 | 2 | 0 | 16 |

policies in Africa. At the other end of the spectrum, 6 panelists were totally unaware that African policy had been discussed, 5 did not recall that relations with the Soviet Union had been mentioned, 4 claimed to be totally unaware of proposals regarding employment, 3 had heard nothing about tax policy or about defense policy, and 1 was totally ignorant of the fact that the fate of draft evaders had been debated.

The panelists were aware of the fact that much of the information that surfaced during the debates had been previously learned. Asked about learning new things about the candidates from watching the three 90-minute presidential debates, and the 60-minute vice-presidential debate, only two panelists reported learning "a lot." One learned a lot about Ford in the second debate, another gained a lot of knowledge about Carter during the third. By contrast, there were 5 reports about learning a lot from the one-hour vice-presidential debate. 3 respondents thought they had learned a lot about Senator Dole and 2 thought the same about Senator Mondale. Both of these candidates were, of course, far less familiar to the panelists than President Ford and Governor Carter, his main challenger. Approximately half of the panel members claimed to have learned nothing new at all about the candidates in the course of the four debates.

Claims about learning something new about the issues were even more modest, despite the fact that the debates presumably were structured to enhance the public's knowledge about the salient issues and the positions of the candidates on these issues. Judging from self-appraisals, the panelists learned nothing about issues from the first debate. About 4 of the panelists reported moderate learning from the third presidential debate and 6 from the vice-presidential debate, and 12 learned about issues from the second debate. Only two respondents claimed to learn a lot about the issues from any one of the debates, in this case the third one. Only one respondent learned a lot about the issues from the vice-presidential debate. In each case, those who claimed to learn a lot were respondents from the high-interest, difficult-access group. They had found it impossible to stay on top of the news. For these respondents, the debates presented a chance to "catch up" on desired information to which they had been unable to expose themselves earlier.

The record of learning about candidates and issues looked far more meager when the panelists were asked to recall spontaneously and specifically what they had learned about each candidate and about the issues. As will be discussed in chapter 7, most respondents found it difficult to answer totally open-ended questions about specific facts because such questions lacked cues pointing to specific schemas in their memories. Following an open-ended question, some panelists were unable to recall anything; others recalled just one item of information, usually about candidates rather than issues. Few could give a coherent spontaneous account of complex policy considerations as presented by the candidates.[16] When the panelists were asked about their knowledge of specific news items to which they had been infrequently exposed, their knowledge, for the most part, was at the bare awareness level. They recognized that they had heard or seen something about the item in question, but they could not supply additional facts. Learning, it seems, generally requires repeated exposure over prolonged time periods.

When stories were remembered, certain types of details were widely recalled while others appeared to be particularly elusive. Politicians' names fell into the elusive category, except for those that were very frequently in the news. This does not mean that names were rarely learned; the names of sports figures and entertainers were remembered quite readily. As will be discussed more fully in the next chapter, people learn those parts of descriptive information that fit neatly into the verbal pictures that they customarily paint of certain situations. Politicians' names are not a staple of this type of learning. Similarly, 51% of *Tribune* crime stories mentioned the occupation of criminals. Yet few panelists could recall this type of information because they did not usually think of criminals in occupational categories. They were able to describe criminals in terms of their emotional status, childhood traumas, and drug use. These latter features were rarely covered in media crime stories, so that the panelists had to dredge their memories for appropriate comments.

Of course, the fact that so little specific information can be recalled from a story does not mean that learning has not taken place. The information base from which conclusions are drawn may be forgotten, while the conclusions are still retained. This seems to happen routinely. Voting choices, for instance, often match approval of a candidate's policy positions, even when voters cannot recall the candidate's positions or the specifics of the policy. In such cases, media facts apparently have been converted into politically significant feelings and attitudes and the facts themselves forgotten. Such general impressions, formed from media stories and other information, are likely to have a more profound impact on political thinking than the specific facts that are remembered only vaguely.

Our respondents freely admitted on numerous occasions that they had not learned recent candidate or issue information but were willing to guess. We kept track of such guesses with regard to election information. We found that politically astute individuals frequently were able to deduce information from a general knowledge of party stands or from the candidates' past performances. These clues allowed them to tap their relevant schemas. Most of these deductions were correct, especially when there had been some rehearsal of a related knowledge area. For example, conjectures about what the presidential candidates might have said improved following the first debate because these conjectures had provided likely patterns. We observed similar peaks in political insight when the primaries and conventions served as a refresher course for political information. The fact that there is no certain way to know whether information represents genuinely new learning, whether it is merely refreshed knowledge drawn from existing schemas, or whether it is an astute guess, makes it difficult to get totally accurate learning scores.

Learning patterns are not constant over time, across topic areas, or across groups of individuals. This happens because the combination of factors that affect attention to media content, as well as its perception, interpretation and acceptance, varies from time to time and from individual to individual. We mentioned earlier, for instance, that most panelists could recall crime stories well. Most panel members had learned a lot—not always accurately—about policemen, courts, and prisons. They could talk about suspended sentences, bail, parole, and the difficulties of creating multiracial police forces. But they had picked up little information about several recent, amply publicized, developments in criminal justice.

Public programs to aid crime victims were one example. The panelists' knowledge about such programs paralleled the novelty of particular programs. More had been learned about older programs than about more recent ones. This suggests that considerable time might be required to acquaint the public with new social services. Information about programs that particular panelists might be likely to use was learned more readily than information about less personally relevant programs.

As discussed in chapter 3, there also are variations in patterns of learning that frequently coincide with differences in sex, age, and education, because these connote differences in life-style. People with limited education, younger age groups, and particularly women with small children, usually were least interested in news and frequently had greatest difficulty in finding time for attention to news. Hence, they learned less than other panel members. However, panelists whose life-styles differed from the norms of their age, sex, and education group showed few of the presumably age or sex or social status-linked characteristics.

Restricted learning meant not only that fewer stories were processed, but also that the topic areas from which stories were selected became narrower. Panelists whose news interests and exposure were low, tended to focus more on soft news such as human interest and crime stories. When they learned about political candidates, the panelists thought primarily in terms of personal traits and characteristics of the candidates' families. Evaluations were nonspecific, referring to general likes and dislikes. By contrast, well-educated panelists spoke more often about the intellectual abilities of political candidates and cited specific reasons for liking or disliking them. Diaries of panelists with limited education, particularly when they were women and when they were black, contained above average percentages of crime and justice system stories. Evidently, this increased attentiveness to crime and justice system stories reflects perceived vulnerability to crime. These panelists often reported that home and work locations and social pressures forced them and their families to expose themselves to crime-prone situations.

## ALTERNATIVES TO CURRENT MEDIA SOURCES

### Past Experiences and Reasoning

The media are not the sole sources of information for many news topics. For instance, when we tested our panelists' learning about crime and justice system topics, we found that 38% of the information for their answers had come partly from the media and partly from other sources. The latter included information based on more or less vicarious personal experiences (14%). In general, our panelists used the media as the prime source for factual data; for inferences about the implications of reported events and for evaluations, they frequently turned to other sources.[17] As Cesar Ippolito put it: "You can't get everything from mass media. You have to balance it with your own perceptions out in the street." Generally, these alternative sources were represented by personal experiences or judgments that had been distilled over long periods of time from information provided by a combination of media and interpersonal sources.

Most panelists, for instance, judged the severity of inflation on the basis of its impact on their own budgets. Donald Burton said: "My ideas come from the news, but even more than that, that just tends to reinforce what I see on the supermarket shelves." When panelists cited specific incidents, they drew these incidents from their own experiences rather than from cases reported by the media, demonstrating that there is an intermixture of information. Betty Nystrom's comments on a television news report that candidate Reagan had $1.4 million in assets is a good example of using her own thoughts to evaluate a story. Going beyond the reported facts, she said "I think he earned it mostly. He is a good, honest man. He got it through acting and when he was on television." Another example is Darlene Rosswell's heavy reliance on her father and her friends for evaluations. "I never disagree with what they tell me, unless it's something really important, 'cause they usually know more than I do." Most panelists were able to speculate on their own about the causes of the events which were reported by the media. Occasionally, and far more rarely, they were able to speculate about the remedies.

One reason for making independent evaluations and speculations about cause-and-effect sequences is the fact that most people are interested in such matters but that evaluations and projections rarely receive explicit media coverage, except in occasional editorials or feature articles. For instance, in the area of crime and justice in 1976, slightly more than 1% of the stories appraising the police, the courts, and the prison system contained evaluations and only 4% mentioned causes. In addition, there were implicit evaluations conveyed through mentions of the ability of the system to apprehend criminals, to convict and punish them when apprehended, and to return them to society as reformed individuals unlikely to repeat their crimes. But many panelists were unable to recognize that this information constituted criteria by which the system might be appraised.

It is not at all surprising that people have well-founded ideas about current news topics. The topics of many of these stories have been covered for long periods of time, often ranging over the entire lifespan of adults. The specific incidents vary, of course, but the themes are the same. Stories about these topics, therefore, are not genuinely "news" in the sense of something that has not happened before. They are episodes in a continuing story that simply reinforce whatever has been previously perceived as the main story theme. For such topics, people are likely to have developed firm conceptions about likely scenarios, causes, consequences, and occasionally, remedies. These are not readily altered or replaced, irrespective of current media coverage, because rethinking and restructuring one's conceptions is a difficult, often painful task.

When concept and image formation are based on personal experiences, or on information provided through respected personal sources, changes in the light of fresh media information are even less likely. Current media data, if noted at all, are interpreted to fit into existing beliefs or are taken as examples of media inaccuracies and distortions. Judging by our panelists' experiences, gradual, incremental reshaping does occur for some topics bringing media and audience images into line. But for many other topics, such adjustments appear to be exceedingly slow or totally lacking.

For instance, many aspects of crime news were firmly fixed in the minds of our panelists, based on personal experiences or community wisdom, media stories, to the contrary, notwithstanding. Examples are the panelists' descriptions of crime as largely the work of young, non-white males, although *Tribune* stories identified 70% of the criminals as white, over 25 years old, with substantially more females involved than the panelists had indicated. Likewise, the panelists pictured victims more often as black, female, old, and poor than did *Tribune* stories. The *Tribune* blamed crime largely on the criminal justice system and on personal failings. The panelists saw social causes, such as poverty and economic stress, as equally major motivations, even though media stories did not make that point.

## Coping with Media Distortions

All of our panelists were fully aware of the kinds of distortions that occurred routinely in media coverage and all of them tried to make allowances for such distortions in their interpretations of the news. As Karl Adams put it: "Their facts are accurate, but the [story] play's the point. You got to correct for that." There seems to be little ground for the fear voiced frequently that media audiences are totally at the mercy of the media when it comes to putting stories into realistic perspectives. Average people, as V.O. Key has reminded us, are no fools.[18] The panelists faulted the media for concentrating on exceptional events without indicating their relative significance, focusing on sensational details, and frequently omitting background information. Experiences with life permit most respondents to put the bulk of stories into a fairly realistic focus or, at least, to recognize that media images are distorted. A precise adjustment is often impossible, however. For example, if stories about nursing homes report mistreatment of aged patients, it is easy to know that not every patient is mistreated in every nursing home. But it may be quite difficult to get a sense of just what percentage of patients are suffering in what percentage of nursing facilities.

Our panelists attempted to fathom the nature of reality through a variety of strategies. These included filling in details, perspectives, and interpretations on the basis of past learning and experience, accepting the information but labelling it as incomplete and reserving judgments, and rejecting the data as too unreliable. Regardless of the success or failure of these tactics in gaining insights into reality, the important point is that our panelists were aware that the media present distorted images of reality and that it was up to them to make the necessary corrections. Many, but by no means all, of these corrections bring media images closer to reality. Generalizations from often limited personal experiences or acceptance of guidance from unreliable sources, may lead to serious misconceptions.

To mention just one example of useful corrections: Murder, the most sensational crime, constituted 0.2% of all crimes recorded in the 1976 police index in Chicago. Nonviolent crimes, like theft and car theft, constituted 47% of all police index crimes. Yet in the *Tribune*, murder constituted 26% of all crime mentions, and theft and car theft constituted a mere 4%. None of our panelists believed that murder was more prevalent than theft. Despite media images, none of them even believed that 25% of all street crimes were murders. But few panelists knew that murders constituted only a fraction of a percent of the crimes reported to the Chicago police and recorded in the official index.

The finding that people do not fully adopt the images and priorities of the media fits more closely into the modulator model of audience effects than into the basic agenda-setting model. According to the modulator model, media effects are modulated by the sensitivity of the audience to particular issues and by the background, demographic characteristics, and experiences of individual audience members. Modulation enhances or diminishes media impact, depending on the salience of specific issues to an individual. Personal experiences are especially influential and almost invariably override media images and evaluations.[19]

The discrepancies between the panelists' perceptions of the world and relevant media information were significant, but so were the similarities. We have already noted that the same characteristics were used by the panelists and the media to evaluate the candidates during the presidential election. Similarly, as Table 4.3 shows, when diary stories were ranked according to the frequency of mention of selected topics, the corresponding data for newspaper and television coverage were quite similar.[20]

TABLE 4.3. Frequency of Selected Topics in Diaries, Press, and TV

| Rank | Topic | Diaries* | Press | TV |
|------|-------|----------|-------|-----|
| 1 | Individual crime | 18.4% | 16.5% | 16.2% |
| 2 | Judiciary | 10.8% | 15.5% | 12.1% |
| 3 | Disasters/accidents | 10.7% | 5.9% | 12.5% |
| 4 | Political gossip | 8.4% | 4.4% | 3.6% |
| 5 | City government | 7.3% | 5.2% | 8.5% |
| 6 | Political terrorism | 5.9% | 5.2% | 8.4% |
| 7 | Education | 5.7% | 7.3% | 7.4% |
| 8 | Corrupt politics | 5.6% | 4.0% | 4.6% |
| 9 | Middle East | 5.2% | 4.9% | 2.9% |
| 10 | Congress | 5.1% | 6.9% | 3.1% |
| 11 | Police/security | 4.5% | 12.7% | 7.8% |
| 12 | State government | 4.5% | 4.8% | 5.6% |
| 13 | Business crimes | 2.9% | 1.7% | 3.8% |
| 14 | Energy policy | 2.5% | 2.7% | 1.8% |
| 15 | Drug offenses | 1.3% | 1.8% | 1.7% |
| 16 | Gun control | 0.3% | 0.5% | 0.2% |

* $N$ = 4,287 for diary, 12,144 for press, and 4,333 for TV mentions.

When social scientists test people's learning of specific information from mass media stories, they often express great disappointment because learning appears to be slim. Perhaps there should be at least a partial sense of elation instead. People are not blindly allowing the media to tell them what to think, or even what to think about. While the media provide the available menu of news from which most choices must be made because personal experience is unavailable, media consumers do make specific choices in line with their personal needs for news. Media consumers also evaluate news in light of past learning and determine how well it squares with reality, as they understand it to be on the basis of a lifetime of socialization.

Despite inattention, substantial forgetting, and limited learning, all our panelists had developed a broad knowledge base drawn to a very large extent from the ample media information available to them. Over time, the media do turn out to be effective providers of most of the information people need, given their desire to learn. Our panelists had learned specific details about the most prominent current news stories and had at least hazy recollections of the rest. They also had general notions about trends and broad patterns of politics, even though the media rarely supplied such analytical information explicitly. This indicates that our panelists, as a group, were able to make generalizations from specific data and to construct their own stereotypical images. What they knew, and the deductions and inferences that sprang from that knowledge, evidently was not limited to what the media supplied. The media are powerful, but not omnipotent, agenda-setters.

The next chapter reports how people make their choices from the news menu that the media supply. We shall look at news selection, news rejection, and memory patterns.

# Notes

1. Robert Putnam, *The Beliefs of Politicians: Ideology, Conflict, and Democracy in Britain and Italy*, New Haven, Yale University Press, 1973, p. 1.

2. The impact of various multiple coding procedures on coding results is discussed in Doris A. Graber, "Hoopla and Horse-Race in 1980 Campaign Coverage: A Closer Look," in Winfred Schulz and Klaus Schoenbach (eds.), *Mass Media and Elections in Democratic Societies*, in press.

3. To save money, the first three months were sampled only, rather than coded in full on a daily basis, with the exception of election news. For this reason, figures for the first three months have been excluded from the data presented here.

4. The NBC local broadcast was expanded to 90 minutes during the last 3 months of the study.

5. Doris A. Graber, *Crime News and the Public*, New York, Praeger, 1980, pp. 32–35. Only 4% of the semi-monthly Z-scores for each topic group reached or exceeded two standard deviations.

6. Leon V. Sigal, *Reporters and Officials: The Organization and Politics of News-making*, Lexington, Mass., D.C. Heath, 1973, p. 66.

7. Both of these areas of news were content-analyzed in detail. For specifics, see pp. 20–22.

8. For example, comparisons of media stories with stories listed in the panelists' diaries showed that the panelists paid substantial attention to stories about the entertainment world that received comparatively little media coverage. At the same time, the panelists paid little regard to stories about the economy, the environment, consumer protection and education, even though these were topics that had received more ample and prominent media coverage and in which the panelists had expressed high interest.

9. For similar findings see, Thomas E. Patterson, *The Mass Media Election: How Americans Choose Their President*, New York, Praeger, 1980.

10. J. David Gopoian (who used CBS News–*New York Times* primary election exit surveys to study 20, 1976 presidential primaries, concluded that "candidate attributes are the most important variables involved in the process of candidate choice"), "Issue Preference and Candidate Choice in Presidential Primaries," *American Journal of Political Science*, 26:3, August 1982, p. 544.

11. For more detailed findings on agenda-setting by the *Tribune*, see David H. Weaver, Doris A. Graber, Maxwell E. McCombs, and Chaim Eyal, *Media Agenda-Setting in a Presidential Election*, New York, Praeger, 1981, pp. 161–193.

12. Arthur H. Miller, Martin P. Wattenberg, and Oksana Malanchuk, "Cognitive Representations of Candidate Assessments," 1982 *American Political Science Association Paper*, p. 15.

13. Patterson's study, as cited in note 9, pp. 134–138, shows the same patterns.

14. Self-appraisals of how much learning has taken place and the objective tests of learning that measured ability to spontaneously recall facts, were correlated significantly for learning from the 1976 presidential debates. The scores were $r = .68$ ($p < .001$) for issue learning and $r = .62$ ($p < .001$) for learning about the candidates.

15. The data demonstrating the lack of relationship are significant at the .01 level. The impact of the debates on the panelists' voting behavior is questionable, at best. Of the 4 panelists who made their final decision after the debates, 3 votes went to Ford, the declared loser of the debate, and 1 went to McCarthy. None of the panelists who had made a pre-debate decision, tentative or firm, changed their decision as a result of the

debates. When asked about debate influence on voting, 14 panelists thought that there had been none.

16. Doris A. Graber and Young Yun Kim, "Why John Q Voter Did Not Learn Much from the 1976 Presidential Debates," in Brent D. Ruben (ed.), *Communication Yearbook 2*, New Brunswick, N.J., Transaction Books, 1978, pp. 407–421.

17. Graber, as cited in note 5, p. 50. Also see, Harold G. Zucker, "The Variable Nature of News Media Influence," in Brent D. Ruben (ed.), *Communication Yearbook 2*, New Brunswick, N.J., Transaction Books, 1978, pp. 225–240.

18. V. O. Key, Jr. (with the assistance of Milton C. Cummings, Jr.), *The Responsible Electorate*, Cambridge, Mass., Harvard University Press, 1965, p. 7.

19. Lutz Erbring, Edie N. Goldenberg, and Arthur H. Miller, "Front-Page News and Real-World Cues: A New Look at Agenda-Setting by the Media," *American Journal of Political Science*, 24:1, February 1980, pp. 16–49. The article also contains a good summary of agenda-setting research.

20. When the significance of the correlations among the items in table 4.3 was tested, 26 out of 48 relationships were significant at the .01 level, 10 were significant at the .05 level, and 12 were not significant at all.

# 5

## Selecting News for Processing and Storing

To cope with the flood of information presented daily by the mass media, people must develop strategies for excluding news and for selecting what they would like to know. This requires efficient ways for monitoring available news, criteria for determining what is wheat and what is chaff, and ways to clear the mind of information that is no longer needed. In this chapter, we shall outline the various steps involved in selecting news for processing and in clearing news from memory. All of the panelists were so adept in these procedures that they performed them automatically, with little conscious effort.

### ATTENTION AROUSAL

The first step in acquiring information for processing and formulating opinions is *attention arousal*.[1] Much of the information available in the average home is unused because it has not aroused attention. As Darlene Rosswell described it, with a somewhat sheepish grin: "My father gets the *Tribune* nearly every day. He brings it in and reads it and all I do is take it out to the garbage." Obviously, having easy access to a newspaper does not assure that it will be read. When Rosswell does read the paper, she looks for the food advertisements, the "help-wanted" notices, obituaries, the movie section, news about weddings ("to see if I know anybody there"), and crime stories, but "I usually skip right over political things." How do people make these types of selections? How do they become consciously aware of certain news stories which are embedded in the stream of information to which they are exposed?[2]

To understand the attention arousal process, one needs to investigate (1) how extensively individuals scan the news; (2) how selective they are in noting information stimuli; (3) the degree of attention they give to stimuli that are detected; and (4) their patterns of acceptance and rejection of information stimuli prior to processing. One also needs to know what kinds of information are likely to attract individuals at any particular time. (The motivations that lead people to seek out specific types of information will be discussed more fully in chapter 6.)

Since newspapers are the richest source for current news for most Americans, I will describe the attention arousal process during newspaper exposure. To check how people select newspaper stories, we asked our panelists on two occasions to run a marking pen alongside those portions of stories which caught their attention. The results revealed interesting news selection patterns that run counter to conventional wisdom. Overall, our analysis showed that our panelists totally ignored 67% of all of the stories in the paper. This probably means that they scanned them so lightly for cues that the scanning was not remembered. The process seems to be akin to watching the fleeting scene from a train window and failing to record most of the images that pass in front of the eye. As psychologists have noted, the ability to scan information without becoming fully aware of it seems to have no fixed limits, although consciousness does.[3]

Of the 33% of the stories that were noticed, our panelists read 18% completely and 15% partially. The range of individual selection behaviors varied from skipping 23% of all stories to skipping 88%. Complete reading of stories ranged from 8% to 36% of all stories and partial reading from 4–47%. Our interview data revealed that partial reading is encouraged by the inverted pyramid style used by newspapers, where the salient facts are presented in the opening paragraphs. Readers know that they can glean the essence of a story without going to the trouble of reading all of it.

When asked how they were alerted to particular stories to which they had paid attention, three types of stimuli were routinely mentioned. One of these is *cuing by the media*. Everything else being equal, the panelists were more likely to say that a story had caught their attention because it appeared on prominent pages of the paper, because it was characterized by prominent headlines or pictures, or because it was given lengthy and often repeated exposure. On television, prominence cues that were noticed included announcement of the story, followed by lengthy treatment early in the show, and the appearance of important people or well-known commentators. These cues were repeatedly mentioned when panelists, asked about reasons for missing stories that interested them, said that these stories were not featured prominently enough.

However, media importance cuing was not nearly as potent as generally believed. We found that high prominence of a story did not necessarily mean that our panelists would rate it as especially important. Conversely, low prominence did not necessarily mean that the story would be considered unimportant. Thus foreign news, despite its far greater prominence in the papers and telecasts, received much less attention than street-crime news which ranked slightly below average in prominence of treatment. More than half of the newspaper stories that were read (53%) came from pages after the first five. An average of only 12% of the stories that caught our panelists' attention came from the front page.

For individuals, this varied from 4–23%. Many front-page stories were left unread. However, the bulk of stories that were read (72%) did come from pages in the first section of the paper.

Pictures and headline size appeared to have limited cuing effects. Half of the available pictures were ignored by our panelists.[4] While larger headlines grabbed attention, smaller ones did not mean that a story would be ignored. Of the stories that were noticed, 41% had headlines extending only across a single column. Another 30% carried two-column-width headlines.[5]

Frequency of mention appeared to have greater impact than prominent display, but it did not ensure attention, even though frequent stories were more likely to be noticed because repetition provides more chances for discovery and absorption. Moreover, frequency patterns tend to be shared among various media outlets, in contrast to prominence patterns. What mattered most of all in attention arousal was the panelists' interest in a particular story. Brief stories, back-page stories and stories with minuscule headlines were routinely noticed if they coincided with the respondent's interests and priorities.[6]

The second type of cuing related to *key words*. Our panelists scanned the newspaper, alert to verbal cues referring to matters of interest to them. Cues were located by scanning story headlines or the opening paragraph of stories. As Craig Kolarz described it:

> I might just read the first paragraph, or look at the headline; maybe a single word catches my eye that might relate to me, I might read it. If I see, say a name, if I saw someone I know or I've read a lot about, I'd read that column.

Kolarz passed over stories if they contained "nothing unusual. You see a story like that and subconsciously you just block it out." The practice of limiting cue searches to headlines varied sharply. On the low end, panelists paid attention to headlines only in 17% of the stories they read. On the high side, it was 82%. The average was 40%. The reasons given for downgrading headlines was inability to adequately judge story content from them.

Finally, our panelists paid attention to cues from their *social environment*. When they sensed that a topic had become the focus of attention for conversation among their friends or associates, when it seemed to arouse a lot of public controversy, or when one of their contacts persisted in mentioning the topic, they were apt to search for relevant information. Tugwell Quentin, for example, explained that he first became alerted to stories about the Vietnam war because of "the rhetoric of other people." Deidre Sandelius commented: "When people start trying, to me, to ram a viewpoint home or to proselytize or anything like that, I start taking notice." Kolarz paid attention to corruption stories about a senator which he labelled as "dull" because "it was every day in every news, continually, so you can't help noticing it." Since bizarre stories make good topics for conversations, panelists frequently mentioned recalling a story simply because it was weird.

On the whole, information scanning is not done very carefully and systematically. With much to scan, much gets missed, even when it was information that panelists had declared to be of substantial interest to them. When asked about missing specific stories, nearly half of the misses were attributed to casual inattention. But since the motivation to be informed about news was not very powerful, compared to other motivations, the fact that many stories were missed was taken very calmly. We rarely encountered expressions of deep chagrin about missing particular stories.

If stories likely to be of interest were routinely found in specific sections of the paper, many panelists looked at these sections first or even exclusively. This simplified their search procedures. Of the stories which caught our panelists' attention, less than half (43%) could be classified as news about government and politicians, with 1976 election stories rating as the most popular choice (11%). Thirty-one percent of the selected stories dealt with social problems, with street crime (8%) as the most attention-getting subject and 16% concerned human interest topics, with half of them devoted to gossip about well-known persons in all walks of life. Finally, 11% of all stories selected for attention dealt with a variety of economic themes.

Reading a news story or watching one on television does not necessarily arouse sufficient attention to lead to information processing and the ability to recall the story.[7] Panelists frequently mentioned during interviews that they had read or watched news stories without really paying attention to them. Consequently they were left with no recollection of what had been read or viewed, even within minutes of the conclusion of reading or viewing.

Why do people go through the motions of monitoring news stories when they gain nothing from the process? Some said that they did it merely as a matter of habit or from a sense of obligation that news monitoring is required from responsible citizens. Others alleged that their purpose was to look for cues to specific types of information that they wanted to monitor. To borrow a term from Harold Lasswell, this is the personal surveillance function.[8] The panelists scanned information to make sure that it contained nothing of predetermined importance to them. If nothing was found, their personalized orientation to the news was apparent from the common remark that "there was nothing in the news today."

If the bulk of information presented by the mass media never registers in people's consciousness, one piece of the puzzle of great ignorance in the midst of plentiful information falls into place. Much of the available information is ignored from the start. When we sum the stories that are read or viewed without recall, and add to this the stories that are quickly forgotten, only a fraction of the information supply becomes part of the knowledge base.

## INFORMATION SELECTION

The attention arousal test provided data about information selection from an average array of news stories. We anticipated that selection would be richer in quantity and quality when the panelists were asked about their attention to an array of prominently featured news stories. This was, indeed, the case. To test recall of such stories, we selected 275 news stories over the course of the year that dealt with a wide range of important and amply-publicized national, local, and international matters. The subjects covered by these stories reflected the topical diversity of the average newspaper and newscast. Our panelists were asked about these stories while the stories were either current or very slightly dated. At most, no more than 30 days had elapsed since the story had received media coverage.

We found that, overall, 29% of the replies we received about these stories indicated that the story could not be retrieved from memory. Either it had not been noticed at all, it had been forgotten, or recall procedures had failed to recapture it. Another 48% of the answers indicated that panelists knew about the story, but recalled it only vaguely or could provide only a minimal number of facts about it. For 23% of the stories, knowledge was ample so that four or more statements of facts or opinions could be recounted. There were wide variations among individuals in ability to provide information about these stories. But even at best, losses of information included in these media stories were substantial.

We asked our panelists to name all sources from which they remembered receiving the story. (All of the test stories had been covered by print as well as electronic media.) Although the majority of panelists had rated television as their most common news source, they named newspapers 48% of the time in response to questions about sources of specific stories. Television came next, constituting 27% of the replies, followed by radio (9%), conversation (8%), news magazines and weekly papers (6%), and other media, such as books and pamphlets (2%). These data, presented in Table 5.1, provide strong support for the view that newspapers, even in the age of television, remain the chief source of remembered information.[9] Newspapers must, therefore, be considered an important factor in shaping the political images of American mass media audiences. In fact, their importance may well surpass television, especially for the better educated, when the full array of topics is considered to which mass media audiences pay attention.[10]

The impression that newspaper stories provide media audiences with more information about various topics than does television news was heightened by the fact that newspapers were cited as an even larger source of information for diary stories. But the most interesting aspect about the data presented in Table

TABLE 5.1. Information Sources for Interview and Diary Stories

| Source | Interview* | Diary |
|---|---|---|
| Newspapers | 48% | 57% |
| Television | 27% | 30% |
| Radio | 9% | 6% |
| Conversation | 8% | 3% |
| News magazines/weeklies | 6% | 3% |
| Other | 2% | 1% |

* $N = 1,568$ for interview. $N = 10,121$ for diary.

5.1 concerns the importance of interpersonal communication. Conversation turned out to be a fairly rare source for memorable information. Conventional wisdom has held to the view that interpersonal information transmission is especially effective. The finding that conversation contributed little to the store of recalled information was all the more surprising because our panelists indicated that they had discussed two-thirds of the important stories that they recalled with other people.[11] The answer to the puzzle, gleaned from the interview transcripts, was that most discussions involved information already known to the discussion partners. The discussion may have added details and may have structured information processing, but it did not provide the bulk of story information.

## Reasons for Information Acceptance

When people are asked why they paid attention to and absorbed particular information, what reasons do they give? To answer this question, we asked our panelists to tell us extemporaneously their reasons for knowing information produced in response to general interview questions and to interview questions about recent news stories. We also asked them to report reasons in their diaries, either by checking off a list of ten choices derived from pretest data, or by writing out their own reasons. The results for interview news stories and diary questions are presented in Table 5.2.

The data in the table indicate that the primary reason for paying attention to news stories, according to our panelists' self-assessment, was personal pleasure. When we combine the categories of general interest in a story with human interest appeals and various personal gratifications, 61% of the interview news stories and 73% of the diary stories were remembered because they satisfied personal life needs. The information served no work-life or civic-life purposes. Societal significance of the story was thus a comparatively minor attraction, as was its usefulness for one's job.

A check of the substance of stories recorded in the diaries supported the accuracy of this self-assessment. The heaviest emphasis was on stories containing human interest elements (such as stories about crimes and accidents) and stories relevant to personal life-style (such as stories about health care, sports, entertainment,

TABLE 5.2. Reasons for Processing News Stories

| Source | Interview* | Diary |
| --- | --- | --- |
| Societal importance | 19% | 22% |
| Interesting story | 15% | 32% |
| Job relevance | 12% | 2% |
| Personal relevance | 26% | 19% |
| Emotional appeal | 20% | 22% |
| Chance reasons | 1% | 2% |
| Miscellaneous | 7% | 1% |

* $N = 453$ for interview. $N = 15,453$ for diary.

and assorted celebrities). Table 5.3 records the proportion of attention devoted in the diaries to 14 selected topics. The table is arranged by interest–access groups to show how interest in current affairs and time available for news consumption affects news attention patterns.

The table clearly indicates that people who lack interest in politics pay less attention to political stories and correspondingly more attention to human interest information. This trend is particularly marked in the minimal interest shown by members of the low-interest, low-access group for news about Congress and about energy matters and in their inordinately great interest for news about street crime and accidents. Another interesting fact apparent from the table is that the large number of stories about the Middle East is reflected only in the diaries of the high-interest, high-access group. The appeal of foreign news appears to be limited to a very select group.

Despite the panelists' keen appetite for human interest topics, table 5.3 shows that they managed to select a substantial number of politically significant news stories. Information about Congress, state government, city government, the court system, the Middle East, education, and energy represented from 30–54% of the diary entries. Of course, many of these stories contained substantial human interest elements, especially in their lead-in paragraphs. Newspeople have learned to snare the average reader's interest by giving most stories a personal touch.

As mentioned earlier, the panelists' attention to news was good enough so that they were familiar, to some degree, with 71% of the prominently featured news stories about which we asked them. A number of these stories had personal angles for them, too, like a presidential speech which announced social security tax increases or a local story specifying cut backs in public transportation services. But the knowledge rates are impressive nonetheless.

## Reasons for Information Rejection

Beyond searches restricted to locating selected stories of interest and beyond inadvertently missing stories, people also deliberately exclude information from consideration. This happens when people sense that the information is undesirable and then fail to pay attention to details beyond the initial cues or fail to process the information after it has been noted. Psychological research indicates that it requires little effort to block unwanted information.[12]

What kinds of reasons do people give for rejecting information? There are many, ranging from the individual and her or his life style, to the nature of the story or the mode of its presentation. Table 5.4 presents the picture based on reasons given for neglecting some of the prominent stories included in the interview story tests. The first column gives percentages for all reasons, the second column omits the "missed" category.

The most common reason for failing to pay attention was the excuse, "I missed that one," without giving any apparent reason other than haphazard

TABLE 5.3. Average Diary Mention of Selected Story Topics

| Group | Congress* | State | City | Cops | Court | Mideast | Corruption | Terrorism | Crime | Accident | Education | Energy | Business | Gossip |
|---|---|---|---|---|---|---|---|---|---|---|---|---|---|---|
| 1 | 7.6 | 5.1 | 7.5 | 5.4 | 12.1 | 10.2 | 5.6 | 4.2 | 12.3 | 7.7 | 5.8 | 5.5 | 3.2 | 6.9 |
| 2 | 3.5 | 5.4 | 10.7 | 3.3 | 10.3 | 2.9 | 4.1 | 6.9 | 20.0 | 10.5 | 6.9 | 1.8 | 2.7 | 10.2 |
| 3 | 2.8 | 4.9 | 7.0 | 3.0 | 14.1 | 4.9 | 5.4 | 7.8 | 23.2 | 10.7 | 3.5 | 2.9 | 1.7 | 7.7 |
| 4 | 1.5 | 3.1 | 5.8 | 3.4 | 9.2 | 2.3 | 4.5 | 7.2 | 28.0 | 17.0 | 6.0 | 1.9 | 2.2 | 6.9 |

* The figures represent percentage of all diary stories in this grouping devoted to each topic. The abbreviations, in order, refer to news about Congress, state government, city government, police, court system, Middle East, corruption, terrorism, street crime, accidents, education, energy, business crime, political gossip. $N = 5{,}073$ stories.

TABLE 5.4. Reasons for Rejecting News Stories

| Reasons | All* | Selected |
|---|---|---|
| Missed | 47% | — |
| Too busy | 6% | 12% |
| No interest | 28% | 53% |
| Redundant/boring | 2% | 3% |
| Doubt media | 3% | 6% |
| Doubt story | 1% | 2% |
| Too remote | 10% | 18% |
| Too complex | 3% | 5% |

* $N = 1,493$ for all. $N = 793$ for selected.

scanning. Excluding this inadvertent behavior, what are the major conscious reasons for rejecting information? The biggest category is "no interest." The interview protocols indicate that this category contains more than merely stories that fail to give personal pleasure or satisfy job related or civic needs.

Roughly 15% of the stories labelled as "no interest" were excluded because they contained disturbing information. For instance, Deidre Sandelius shut out information about people she intensely disliked. She did not seem to be aware of this fact, but it became clear from an analysis of her full responses. For instance, when she was asked about reasons for expressing disinterest in a story about Chicago's Cardinal Cody, she replied: "I completely turn myself off about Cody. I do not like the man. I see an article about Cody, and I usually don't read it. . . . I know it's going to make me angry to read it."

People also turn off stories about domestic and international situations that disturb them greatly, but that seem beyond their control or the control of their political leaders. Again, this avoidance tactic, which was involved in roughly 5% of the "no interest" expressions, was never voiced explicitly. Sandra Ornstein, for instance, declared disinterest for all stories about Israel, although she is Jewish and concerned about Mideastern politics. When pressed for reasons, she acknowledged: "I can't allow myself to get upset about these things. I have no control over them. If it's something you can do something about, fine. But if there's nothing, then forget it."

Dissonance avoidance is another, relatively minor reason for claiming that information lacks interest. For example, Craig Kolarz told us that he did not pay attention to Mideast news "because I tend to be more of an isolationist type . . . I feel that the United States is spread out too thin in too many areas, and they're sticking their nose into too much stuff that they don't belong in." However, dissonance is not necessarily a reason for rejecting information.[13] All our panelists were willing to pay attention to some dissonant messages.

The next largest rejection category beyond "no interest" involved information that was either too remote or too complicated. Many stories dealing with foreign affairs fell into both of these categories. Several panelists, especially those with limited education, rejected stories about distant places automatically and claimed routinely that these stories were too complex. Asked about an assassination attempt on the life of African president Idi Amin, Elaine Mullins chided the interviewer: "How can you expect me to remember that? I couldn't even pronounce the name."

Several panelists argued that the United States should concentrate its efforts at home and rejected foreign stories as an unpleasant reminder of ill-considered meddling abroad. Darlene Rosswell confessed that she was not interested in a story about a Soviet satellite: "All I care about is ours flying around." Then she added: "Besides, I didn't pay attention to that story because it just disgusts me as to how much money goes into all of that."

All of our panelists preferred simple stories and stories which readily fit into situations for which they had appropriate conceptual schemas available for in-formation processing. This may be called the "aha" or "I thought so" syndrome. Faced with the need to process complex and unfamiliar information, respondents frequently decided to forego the challenge. Sandelius, for instance, refused to deal with policy statements made by various presidential candidates because she felt confused by them. "One was saying, 'I'm gonna raise taxes,' and the other one's saying, 'I'm gonna lower taxes.' I mean I guess I want everything clearcut. I haven't got the time right now to really sit down and sift through these things that are a hair apart in difference." Then she concluded: "If I just can't follow it, I turn it off." Since much political information is contradictory and confusing, this was a much-used rejection category.[14]

Eight percent of the stories were rejected because of skepticism about the credibility of their source. Stories reporting politicians' messages, in particular, fell into this category. For example, Robert Creighton, an avid consumer of political news, was typical of the many panelists who ignored presidential messages. To him, such messages were "mostly hogwash" and, therefore, not worthy of attention. Karl Adams reflected the wide-spread cynicism about campaign stories when he said that he wanted candidates to take stands on issues "instead of just running around in circles and giving us all this crap. I'd like them to say exactly what they feel and exactly what they think they would do, or what they know they would do now with the information that they have. I would like truth out of them. I can't stand wishy-washy people." Since he figured that he could not get this type of information, he refused to pay attention to the candidates' rhetoric during the primaries. Other respondents routinely rejected stories carrying the names of specific news commentators. Several attributed their disregard for these columnists to specific incidents in which the respondents' personal experiences contradicted the media account.

Finally, 15% of the stories were rejected for what can be characterized as reasons of economy. Heavy family or job-related obligations, worries that preempt thinking and produce psychic exhaustion, heavy leisure-time commitments, and similar strains on time budgets reduce people's inclination to cope with substantial portions of the information available to them.[15] Therefore, they cut out stories where the overall theme is redundant ("no need to read about foreign visitors, they all come to get money") or repetitive stories on the same theme. Helga Holmquist ignored a story about a bombing in Tel Aviv, saying: "That's the kind of stuff I pay attention to only when it first happens . . . but after a while, it gets pretty tiresome." David Utley alleged that accessible information should not be internalized. "I seldom remember names. I make no attempt. I make no attempt to remember things such as telephone numbers. Anything that's on paper, why bother? I don't want that mind of mine cluttered with anything I don't need."

Other tactics for economizing on information processing efforts consist of ignoring a breaking story until it is complete so that only the end result needs to be assimilated or skipping content randomly. Tugwell Quentin, for instance, ignored most stories about the primaries. "I prefer to make my judgments after some of the silt has settled when I know who remains in the race. I haven't tried to absorb scores of people in the campaign. I just can't do it. I prefer to wait and see what kind of person is left." When various economizing tactics prove insufficient to cope with the overload of information, as invariably happens, days and even weeks may pass with no attention to news. People complain that they simply have been too busy, too tired or too ill to keep up. Once a particular time crunch has passed, people rarely bother to catch up with missed information.

The overall impression one gains from examining all the reasons for story acceptance or rejection is that people want to pay attention to much of the current news. However, they assign a low priority to news consumption as compared with other activities. In fact, news consumption, particularly when electronic media are involved, is often paired with other activities. This combination usually sharply restricts the ability to absorb and remember information. When people pay attention to news, stories are processed if they are interesting enough to be remembered, if they are simple to understand, and if they are believable. The story's general civic significance is a relatively minor matter, though not totally unimportant.

Whether a story will be deemed interesting depends partly on story substance and form and partly on timing and context. For example, election stories were found more interesting and were noted at a steeply higher rate (60% compared to 40%) if they were presented at intense moments of the campaign rather than at interludes. A geographic principle is also at work. The further from the United States and personal concerns the news is removed, the less attention it receives. Cesar Ippolito put it this way:

> The things I tend to notice most happen at home. The farther you get away from the American borders, the less I tend to notice. Besides, if I don't have a relation to something, if I'm not personally interested in it, I don't want to waste my time on it.

## INFORMATION DECAY AND FORGETTING

There are several basic causes for failure to recollect a specific piece of information.[16] One is failure to become *aware of the information* for the reasons that have already been outlined. A second is failure to *commit the information to long-term memory*. Much news is never assimilated into long-term memory because too many stories are presented too quickly. Rapid-fire presentation allows no time for processing the information for long-term memory storage. A third cause of forgetting is *decay of long term memory*. Over time, memories fade. Finally, there is an inability to retrieve information because *access to the appropriate storage point in memory* has been lost. We will briefly discuss the latter two causes of forgetting: information decay and problems in reaching stored information.

Knowledge about the forgetting process is still quite limited; more so than understanding of memory acquisition. Forgetting appears to be a gradual process with a period of decay of information preceding the ultimate total loss. Psychobiologists believe that memory has a physiological basis. It is established when electrical charges move along a chain of nerve cells in the human brain and develop temporary pathways, marked by chemical traces. When short-term memory gives way to long-term memory, protoplasmic changes in the brain make these temporary pathways more permanent. Forgetting involves a gradual reversal of the process as pathways fade out or are superseded by subsequent memories.[17] Forgetting may be hastened by an individual's conscious attempts to expunge undesired memories. It may be delayed or stopped by the desire to retain memories and by repeated mental rehearsals.

Memory of specific events seems to decay faster than memory of attitudes distilled from these events. However, repetition of previously remembered information may reverse the decay process and may actually result in deepening and enriching memory.[18] For example, the presidential debates in 1976 served as a rehearsal for previously-known election information that had begun to slip from memory. The debates refreshed this knowledge when it was particularly useful. Similarly, immediately after an interview, topics that had been rehearsed at the interviews were more likely to appear in the diaries.[19] But this effect dissipated quickly because the panelists' memories were desensitized by exposure to large amounts of information. Apparently, information overloads do not only prevent storage of new information; they also interfere with memorization of recently acquired information.[20]

The ability to retrieve information from memory seems to be more limited than the ability to store it. Psychologists believe that the capacity to recall information is tied to the availability and accessibility of appropriate mnemonic devices or memory traces left by prior perceptions.[21] Memory fails when the pathways leading to the stored information are blocked or cannot be found. This may happen because perceptions were only fleetingly imprinted and therefore did not leave an initial memory trace. As mentioned, this seems to be the fate of most news stories, especially those brief snippets of news presented in rapid succession on television or radio.

The desire to remember plays a role, too. Forgetting may also occur because the associations connected with a particular memory have not been replicated.[22] In the process of incorporating information into long-term memory, people transform the information to make it part of their existing knowledge structures and to cue it for future retrieveal. If the appropriate cues fail to be activated, the information cannot be retrieved.[23]

Memory is thus like a locked treasure house that can be opened only with the right keys. When access is gained, it may be solely to limited bits of information. This depends on the circumstances and the kinds of cues that are supplied. The importance of using the right cues becomes apparent when people cannot recall information in a particular setting, but are able to bring it forward when the cues are changed. Whether or not people recall news stories, and the kinds of features they report from them depends very much on the way questions are asked (see chapter 7). If the thrust of questions does not match the memory patterns, answers may not be forthcoming even though the information is stored in memory. Unfortunately, many of the questions asked in conventional survey research do not correspond to the manner in which information is ordinarily stored by most people. Their answers consequently are impoverished or are totally unavailable.[24]

We tested the long-range memory capabilities of our panelists by asking each to recall several stories that had appeared in the news 3 to 9 months earlier. For maximum recall, questions were structured to match the processing patterns of each panelist. On the basis of 45 stories presented to each respondent after delays ranging from 2 to 9 months, we concluded that the ability to recall news stories fades gradually and very substantially over time. This is true even for stories that received extended news coverage over long periods. Most panelists in the "low interest" groups could not recall any details at all about stories that had not been mentioned in the news for more than three months.

John Sprague has pointed out that continuous reinforcement, which is a feature of election coverage, "teaches rapidly but provides poor protection against extinction. Take away the campaign and deterioration may be anticipated."[25] Our findings bear out this observation. Of the election stories, 70% were remembered to varying degrees for roughly 60 days, with panelists recalling substantial amounts of information for 12–18% of the stories. Beyond the 60-day span, memory rates dropped rapidly and details vanished, possibly because of a lack of desire to remember. As Adams remarked about his handling of election stories: "My basic pattern is to read 'em and forget 'em unless I have to remember them for some other purpose. To remember them for remembering's sake—no." Our research produced no evidence that basic schemas about the political world are forgotten, however. This may be due to more profound learning of basic concepts compared to particular incidents, or it may occur because basic schemas are activated frequently and these rehearsals deepen memories.

Panelists in the high-interest group could recall selected stories almost as well after a lapse of three months, and occasionally even after nine months, as when these stories were only a few weeks old. But the array of stories for which this was true was limited. Most of these well-remembered stories involved major personal concerns. Recall of "a lot" of facts and specific, rather than general, information, was twice as common for stories that the panelists remembered on their own than for stories first mentioned by the interviewer. This suggests that memory capabilities are put to full use only selectively.

We also encountered "flashbulb" memories among our panelists. These are "particularly vivid, detailed memories of some personal experience" or a dramatic public event such as the assassination of President John F. Kennedy or the moonwalk of the astronauts.[26] Such memories appear to be a permanent part of the panelists' store of information. Most of the events remembered from childhood fall into this category. The existence of such seemingly indelible detailed memories of major events suggests that there is considerable latitude in the permanence of memories.[27]

Besides differences related to the degree of interest in news stories, memory data also reflect differences in life-style linked to education, age, and gender. Women generally feel little social pressure to retain information and, therefore, show higher forgetting rates than men. Women under age 40 had totally forgotten an average of 37% of all stories for which we tested recall, compared to 26% for their male contemporaries. Older people, more experienced and wiser in the ways of the world, remembered more about various stories than did younger people of the same sex. Older women had forgotten 27% of all test stories compared to 17% for older men. Within age and sex groups, better-educated panelists tended to have more information available for recall than did most of the panelists with more limited education.

On a scale ranging from no facts recalled from a story—but with knowledge that such a story was reported—to three or more facts recalled, younger women rated an average of only 1 fact remembered per story, compared to 1.4 facts for younger men. Older women recalled 1.2 facts per story and older men scored 1.9 facts. Older men thus retained almost twice as many facts per story as younger women. Furthermore, women recalled fewer statistics and had slightly less information about specifics of actual and proposed policies. In recall tests of stories about the positions that the presidential candidates had taken on unemployment and inflation, women remembered statistics for 0.6% of the stories compared to 2.1% for the men. Women remembered specific policy proposals in connection with 4.4% of the stories to which they had paid attention compared to the men's 5.4%. Women also needed more repeated exposures to stories before they remembered them. These differences seem closely tied to the fact that most women, unlike men, saw no particular reason for committing media information to memory. Whenever a particular need arose, they did learn on a scale comparable to men. However, when women were questioned about forgotten information, they gave the same chief reason as men—the information lacked interest. They did not say that they forgot the information because it was unnecessary for their life-styles.

It was also apparent that men internalized stories better than women when we asked the panelists for reactions to stories. Younger women showed the highest "no reaction" rates (48% of all stories) followed by older women (41%), and younger men (39%). Men over age 40 gave "no reaction" responses to only 22% of all stories. These figures point to the fact, corroborated by other studies, that the cognitive maps of males and of older people are richer in detail about current happenings than those of females and younger people. Contrary to political folklore, older people can retrieve these facts better than younger people, although this ability diminishes in the highest age ranges.

The extent of fact retention varied, depending on the nature of the story. Looking at retention patterns for 14 topics, each representing approximately 10 generally well-remembered test stories, none of the young women reached a mean of 2 facts per topic. Of the older women, 3 reached the 2-facts mean, for 1, 2, and 5 of the 14 topics respectively. Among younger men, 2 reached the 2-facts mean. One reached it for all 16 topics, the other for just 1. All of the older men reached the 2-facts mean, with 2 of them reaching the mean for 4 topics, and 3 scoring on 9, 10, and 13 topics, respectively.

In table 5.5, data on average recall of stories about these 14 topics have been grouped using interest/access criteria again. As held true in other contexts, those panelists who were most interested in current news and had highest exposure also recalled the most facts, while those at the opposite end of the scale recalled the least. Panelists in the two middle groups, representing high-interest, low-access and low-interest, high-access combinations scored in the middle range. Panelists were given a score of 1 if they recalled no details about a particular story. Mention of 1 fact rated 2 points, mention of 2 facts yielded a 3-point rating, and mention of 3 or more facts was scored as 4 points.

The highest average score shown in Table 5.5 is 3.6 points for stories about energy issues. The lowest score is 1.6 for stories about Congress, state government, and the police. The interview protocols indicate that low recall of a particular topic was generally associated with its intrinsic unattractiveness to our panelists or with saturation boredom. The latter means that media audiences, who are not vitally interested in a topic, tire rather quickly of repeat exposures even when new details are disclosed. Media audiences, therefore, make little attempt to commit these new facts to memory. For stories of high interest, the saturation point comes much later. The fatigue factor may temporarily or permanently insulate people from entire story categories, such as disaster stories or energy stories or even election stories.

An example of a story embodying more than three facts follows. It demonstrates recall at its best. The story concerns a strike by the Teamsters' Union. Karl Adams reported it this way:

> I think they held a meeting in Chicago. I'm pretty sure they got a pretty big wage increase out of it. And I remember there was a lot of dissension between independent drivers and union drivers about it. I think there was even some violence between the two groups. I think they struck for like three days and it was getting just to the point where inventories were growing short. If they hadn't settled, things would have gotten worse.

Table 5.6 presents the percentage of stories in various topic categories for which the panelists had no recall at all. Again, the table is divided into the four interest/access categories. The basic forgetting patterns in the table run along expected lines with group 1 forgetting the least and group 4 forgetting the most. The two middle groups, overall, are close in their forgetting rates. However,

TABLE 5.5. Average Number of Facts Recalled for Selected Topics

| Group | Congress* | State | City | Cops | Court | Mideast | Corruption | Terrorism | Crime | Accident | Education | Energy | Business | Gossip |
|---|---|---|---|---|---|---|---|---|---|---|---|---|---|---|
| 1 | 3.1 | 2.3 | 3.2 | 3.3 | 3.0 | 3.2 | 3.1 | 2.9 | 2.9 | 3.2 | 2.8 | 3.6 | 2.6 | 3.4 |
| 2 | 2.0 | 1.7 | 2.4 | 2.1 | 2.6 | 1.9 | 2.2 | 2.3 | 2.3 | 2.3 | 2.1 | 2.4 | 2.0 | 3.0 |
| 3 | 1.8 | 2.1 | 2.3 | 1.8 | 2.2 | 1.9 | 2.2 | 2.3 | 2.5 | 2.7 | 2.1 | 2.3 | 2.2 | 3.0 |
| 4 | 1.6 | 1.6 | 1.9 | 1.6 | 1.9 | 1.8 | 1.8 | 2.0 | 2.3 | 2.2 | 1.9 | 2.1 | 1.7 | 2.4 |

* Point values: 1 = none; 2 = a little (one fact); 3 = some (two facts); 4 = a lot (three or more facts); the abbreviations, in order, refer to news about Congress, state government, city government, police, court system, Middle East, corruption, terrorism, street crime, accidents, education, energy, business crime, political gossip. N = 2, 180 stories.

TABLE 5.6. Average Forgetting Rates for Selected Topics

| Group | Congress* | State | City | Cops | Court | Mideast | Corruption | Terrorism | Crime | Accident | Education | Energy | Business | Gossip |
|---|---|---|---|---|---|---|---|---|---|---|---|---|---|---|
| 1 | 17.6 | 27.0 | 6.6 | 0.0 | 24.0 | 0.0 | 18.4 | 14.8 | 17.6 | 12.0 | 19.8 | 0.0 | 25.0 | 0.0 |
| 2 | 59.6 | 66.6 | 14.8 | 37.4 | 33.6 | 55.2 | 34.0 | 24.6 | 32.2 | 17.0 | 37.6 | 0.0 | 55.0 | 4.0 |
| 3 | 65.2 | 46.0 | 27.0 | 42.4 | 20.6 | 41.4 | 22.2 | 26.0 | 19.6 | 8.4 | 31.6 | 16.8 | 28.4 | 6.2 |
| 4 | 56.5 | 63.3 | 49.3 | 58.0 | 37.6 | 46.2 | 64.3 | 32.3 | 27.5 | 24.3 | 48.3 | 19.3 | 55.3 | 22.3 |

* The figures represent percentage of all interview stories in this grouping devoted to each topic. The abbreviations, in order, refer to news about Congress, state government, city government, police, court system, Middle East, corruption, terrorism, street crime, accidents, education, energy, business crime, political gossip. N = 5,521 stories.

there are significant variations in scores for individual topics that can be explained by idiosyncracies of particular individuals in these groups. For instance, Helga Holmquist boosted the score for forgetting state news in group 3 by remembering no state stories at all, while Betty Nystrom kept the score low for group 4 by remembering every state news story. Overall, group 3 had slightly lower forgetting scores than group 2 which suggests that passive learning may be involved. People who are exposed to large amounts of news will remember many stories despite lack of interest because mere exposure produces learning. By contrast, people who are interested but lack exposure are likely to miss many stories entirely, making recall impossible.

## THE MORAL OF THE STORY

What do the data reported in this chapter tell us about the way our panelists selected news for processing? They tells us that people do not take the selection process very seriously, despite frequent lip service to its importance. The panelists did have a set of criteria for selecting and rejecting information, but they did not scan the news carefully enough to apply these criteria systematically. Even though the criteria excluded large amounts of available information from consideration, and even though they tilted toward selection of nonpolitical news, most of our panelists absorbed sufficient information to be aware of a large number of important political and nonpolitical current issues.

The ability to retain stories and retrieve them varied widely. Interest in news appeared to be the chief factor explaining above average memory capabilities in general and for remembering particular stories. But, at best, memory for news stories was quite limited when it came to retention of detail. For the most part, recall was hazy and incomplete. The number of remembered facts was small compared to the number of facts available for recall. However, this did not necessarily mean that the forgotten information had lost all usefulness. As discussed more fully in chapter 7, news stories are streamlined and often reduced to their general meaning in the process of becoming incorporated into established thought patterns. The story as such can then be forgotten, but its meaning is retained as part of a general schema stored in memory.

Our findings about the casualness of the news selection process and the defects of memory are thus no grounds for pessimism about people's capabilities and inclinations to keep informed about current affairs. Rather, the findings indicate that people know how to cope with information overload, that they balance a healthy respect for their own pleasures with moderate willingness to perform their civic duties, and that they have learned to extract essential kernels of information from news stories while discarding much of the chaff.

How do the reasons people give for selecting or rejecting news for processing square with widely accepted theories about information acquisition? The next chapter provides some answers.

## Notes

1. Roy Lachman, Janet L. Lachman, and Earl C. Butterfield, *Cognitive Psychology and Information Processing: An Introduction*, Hillsdale, N.J., Lawrence Erlbaum, 1979, p. 200.

2. For a fuller discussion of these questions, see Geoffrey Underwood (ed.), *Strategies of Information Processing*, New York, Academic Press, 1978, pp. 235–266.

3. Lachman et al., as cited in note 1, p. 200.

4. The effects of photographs on information processing are discussed in Peter B. Warr and Christopher Knapper, *The Perception of People and Events*, New York, Wiley, 1968, pp. 296–318.

5. The impact of headlines on information processing is discussed in Warr and Knapper, as cited in note 4, pp. 290–295.

6. Interestingly, frequency and prominence were not significantly correlated.

7. Underwood, as cited in note 2, p. 236. W. Lance Bennett, "Perception and Cognition: An Information-Processing Framework for Politics," in Samuel L. Long (ed.), *The Handbook of Political Behavior*, vol. 1, New York, Plenum Press, 1981, p. 83, distinguishes between *perception* that "involves the selection and transmission of information," and *cognition* that "involves the subsequent coding and use of perceived information."

8. Harold D. Lasswell, "The Structure and Function of Communication in Society," in Wilbur Schramm (ed.), *Mass Communications*, Urbana, University of Illinois Press, 1949, p. 103.

9. The effect of esteem for a newspaper on information processing is discussed by Warr and Knapper, as cited in note 4, pp. 324–328.

10. The respective roles of newspapers and television in setting the agenda for public thinking about political issues is discussed fully in David H. Weaver, Doris A. Graber, Maxwell E. McCombs, and Chaim Eyal, *Media Agenda-Setting in a Presidential Election*, New York, Praeger, 1981. See also Peter Clarke and Eric Fredin, "Newspapers, Television and Political Reasoning." *Public Opinion Quarterly*, 42, Summer 1978, pp. 143–160; and Lee B. Becker, Idowu Sobowale, and William E. Casey, "Newspaper and Television Dependencies: Their Effects on Evaluations of Public Officials," *Journal of Broadcasting*, 23, Fall 1979, pp. 465–475.

11. Of the prominent news stories, 38% had been discussed with friends, 35% with fellow workers, 19% with family members, and 8% with miscellaneous contacts. For diary stories, which involved a much heavier emphasis on human interest materials, the discussion partners were 58% friends, 28% family members, and 14% fellow workers.

12. Lachman et al., as cited in note 1, p. 198.

13. A variety of studies have found low or nonsignificant relationships between recall of message arguments and attitudinal acceptance of the advocated message. Richard M. Perloff and Timothy C. Brock, "And Thinking Makes it So: Cognitive Responses in Persuasion," in Michael E. Roloff and Gerald R. Miller (eds.), *Persuasion: New Directions in Theory and Research*, Beverly Hills, Sage, 1980, p. 75.

14. Robert E. Lane (*Political Ideology: Why the American Common Man Believes What He Does*, New York, Free Press, 1962) reports that his panelists also found much of the political information confusing. See pp. 27–35.

15. As Lane, cited in note 14, put it: "The problem is, simply, the capacity of the mind to receive and deal with a wide variety of stimuli, most of which require some kind

of response." Lane cites Sigmund Freud to the effect that "protection against stimuli is an almost more important function for the living organism than *reception* of stimuli."

16. Brief reviews of recent research on various aspects of the memory process can be found in John F. Kihlstrom, "On Personality and Memory," in Nancy Cantor and John F. Kihlstrom (eds.), *Personality, Cognition, and Social Interaction*, Hillsdale, N.J., Lawrence Erlbaum, 1981, pp. 123–152; John H. Lingle and Thomas M. Ostrom, "Principles of Memory and Cognition in Attitude Formation," in Richard E. Petty, Thomas M. Ostrom, and Timothy C. Brock (eds.), *Cognitive Responses in Persuasion*, Hillsdale, N.J., Lawrence Erlbaum, 1981, pp. 399–420; Reid Hastie, "Schematic Principles in Human Memory," in E. Tory Higgins, C. Peter Herman, and Mark P. Zanna (eds.), *Social Cognition: The Ontario Symposium*, vol. 1, Hillsdale, N.J., Lawrence Erlbaum, 1981, pp. 39–88.

17. Thomas S. Brown and Patricia Wallace, *Physiological Psychology*, New York, Academic Press, 1980, pp. 450–455. Also see, Steven A. Peterson, "Neurophysiology and Rationality in Political Thinking," *American Political Science Association Paper*, 1982.

18. Lachman et al., as cited in note 1, p. 238.

19. Correlations were significant at the .001 level.

20. For a discussion of interference with memorization, see Bennett, as cited in note 7, p. 130.

21. Irving Rock and John Ceraso, "Toward a Cognitive Theory of Associative Learning," in Constance Scheerer (ed.), *Cognition: Theory, Research, Promise*. New York, Harper & Row, 1964, p. 135.

22. Solomon E. Asch, "The Process of Free Recall," in Constance Scheerer (ed.), *Cognition: Theory, Research, Promise*, New York, Harper and Row, 1964, pp. 84–87. Also see Hubert A. Zielske, "The Remembering and Forgetting of Advertising," *Journal of Marketing*, 23, 1959, pp. 239–243.

23. Bennett, as cited in note 7, p. 131.

24. Ibid. p. 132.

25. John Sprague, "Is There a Micro Theory Consistent with Contextual Analysis?," in Elinor Ostrom (ed.), *Strategies of Political Inquiry*, Beverly Hills, Sage, 1982, p. 115. Also see Zielske, as cited in note 22, p. 240.

26. John F. Kihlstrom, as cited in Note 16, p. 140.

27. See also Bennett, as cited in note 7, p. 131.

# 6

# To Learn or Not to Learn: Incentives and Disincentives

## THE TRANSACTIONAL MODEL

How do people determine to which news stories they wish to pay attention? We have already discussed their methods of skimming and their overall goals in selecting news. What are the factors that make news interesting and personally satisfying and what are the factors that cause the opposite reaction? In short, what are the incentives for learning and what are the disincentives?

The incentives to learn or not to learn from media messages hinge on three factors. They are (1) *the nature* of the media message, (2) *the concerns* of the audience, and (3) *the context* in which the audience finds itself at the time the message comes to its attention. Because of the interaction of these three elements, communications scholars talk about a ''transactional'' model of communications effects. As Figure 6.1 shows, this model is based on the idea that communication effects represent an interaction or transaction among message factors, audience factors, and context factors. Examination of just one or two of these factors will therefore be insufficient to account for the nature of the effects. All three factors must be jointly considered.

While transactional models are currently the most widely accepted models of media effects, the "hypodermic" models that preceded them retain a hold on popular fancy.[1] Many people still believe that media messages reach their target audiences without fail and that these audiences, for the most part, attach to them the meanings intended by the reporter. It follows that a study of message factors is the key to understanding media effects. The experiences of our panelists demonstrate of course, that there is very little truth to such a conception.

We have already indicated that several other models that have been developed

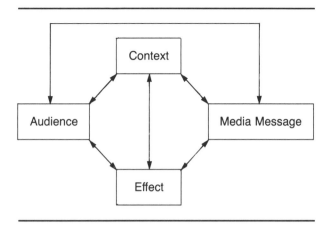

FIGURE 6.1. A transactional model of communications effects.

to explain mass media impact also do not square with our findings. The "two-step" or "social influence" model and the "diffusion" model are examples.[2] Proponents of these models argue that the impact of the mass media is largely indirect. People absorb mass media information from opinion leaders who have been in direct contact with the media, in a two-step or multi-step process. During information transmission, these opinion leaders put their imprint on media information by relaying it from their own perspectives. Accordingly, study of opinion leaders and channels of message diffusion are of primary importance. As discussed in chapter 3, with few exceptions, our panelists received their mass media information directly. When they engaged in conversations with others, or listened to others, they learned little new. Rather, most conversations revolved around matters that had been transmitted by media stories directly to each conversation partner. While all panelists occasionally reported receiving media information second- or third-hand, the prevailing mode for learning about current news was direct contact with the media.[3]

Since the transactional model best fits our data, we shall use it to structure the discussion in this chapter. Accordingly, we shall first examine message factors that provided incentives or disincentives for learning. Then, we shall check how well various theories about motivations to learn from mass media information explain our panelists' learning behavior. Finally, we will look at various aspects of the context in which learning occurred to assess their impact. Some of these factors have already been sketched out briefly in chapter 3 (The reader is urged to review in particular the discussion there of psychosocial settings.) The contextual factors selected for closer examination in this chapter are the ones that communications researchers have found to be particularly salient for learning. These contextual factors include life-style, political socialization, prior knowledge acquisition, interest in news, and credibility factors.

## MESSAGE FACTORS

### Substance and Format

Both the substance of messages and their formats of presentation affect the ease and quality of learning. We shall use data about learning from the presidential debates as illustrations because we asked the panelists about the attractiveness of the messages conveyed by the debates. Why did the 4-stage, 5½-hour-long television spectacular produce only limited political learning when it was amply publicized by all the mass media and when each debate was watched by an average of 85 million Americans? The answer is threefold: (1) Debate effects were reduced because our panelists had been saturated with election news prior to the debates so that debate information was redundant. (2) The effects were further diminished because much of the information disseminated in the debates lacked interest for the panelists who were not eager to delve into the intricacies of various public policy issues. (3) The debates missed their mark because the audience found the format unattractive.

Specifically, a number of respondents stated explicitly that the debates contained nothing new and, therefore, like much of the news, were boring. Most people, most of the time, simply cannot get very excited about election rhetoric that sounds like a broken record played over and over again throughout a campaign that drags on for many months and sometimes even years. A direct question about whether the first debate was interesting elicited 6 comments that it was highly interesting, 14 comments that it was somewhat interesting, and 1 comment that it was boring. Several panelists, disappointed with the first debate, decided to skip later ones. The second debate received even less favorable ratings. Only 2 panelists thought it was highly interesting, 6 found it boring, and 3 had paid so little attention that they did not know. The remaining 10 thought that the debate was moderately interesting.

When people were asked in open-ended questions why they had missed large portions of each debate, judgments became much harsher. People called major portions of the debates dull, repetitive, stale, hard to follow, and the like. Several panelists claimed that they fell asleep while watching. Others had become distracted. Deidre Sandelius, for instance, said that when the discussion bored her, "I concentrate on watching them. I enjoy sitting there and watching them and trying to figure out what's going through their heads as they're talking." It was no wonder that she remembered next to nothing about what was said.

Panelists who had been highly interested in election news all along indicated that all the information made available by the debates had been covered repeatedly by past media stories. They were right. After more than a year of coverage of the campaign, it was highly unlikely that much significant new information could be uncovered during the closing weeks of the contest. We also were able to tell from pre-debate interviews and diary analyses that our respondents were indeed aware of the issues discussed in the debates. We knew that they had already formed fairly firm conceptions about the personalities and qualifications of the candidates and their stands on those policy issues that were of particular concern to individual panelists. The debates rehearsed many issues. Awareness of some of these issues may have been in a stage of decay. But when they were mentioned again, the memories revived and the issues seemed stale.

The emphasis in the debates on public policy issues was not to the panelists' liking. As mentioned in chapter 4, despite lip service to the importance of judging candidates on their issue stands, most people are primarily interested in the candidates' personal qualities. Some panelists wanted to know things about the candidates that were not likely to come to the fore. Max Jackman, for instance, was eager to fathom "what goes on in Carter's head on the subject of evangelism." Such matters were not likely to be discussed in debates devoted to the airing of public policy issues, nor in most routine news stories. Some panelists were interested in more speculations about the candidates' future performance. Others complained that there was already too much talk about the future that was impossible to evaluate. These panelists said that they ignored such speculations because they were a waste of time.

Several panelists complained that the facts that they really wanted to know were usually ignored by news stories. But when pressed to be specific about their needs and desires, they often mentioned information that was available, but that they had missed. To illustrate the point, Darlene Rosswell contended that

> they [the media] show Senate meetings or Congressmen, and they show one arguing with the Speaker of the House, and this one's arguing about that. And then they cut it off. And they give you one point—that so and so was arguing about something. But they don't go into the fact that the reason for this meeting was for a totally different subject . . . I really don't care about the heated conversation. I just would like to know, you know, how they came out, or what happened with the main reason for the meeting, or things like that.

When we checked the news broadcast that had prompted this comment, we found that the main thrust of the congressional discussion had been clearly delineated. Rosswell, distracted by the animated verbal battle on the screen, had simply missed the explanatory commentary.

The issues involved in many news stories, like the debates, are highly complex. This makes it almost inevitable that most people will find them difficult to comprehend and therefore dull. Are wage and price controls necessary to stop inflation? Are tax cuts possible without budget cuts? Is zero-based budgeting sound? Did the Ford vetoes signify that he was unable to lead Congress, or did they indicate that Congress was irresponsible and cantankerous? Can human rights be protected without undue intervention in the affairs of foreign countries? These were some of the highly complex and controversial questions that listeners were asked to judge during the presidential debates, amid cleverly phrased claims and counterclaims by the candidates.

Both candidates cited a wide array of confusing facts and statistics and made skillful use of emotion-laden abstractions that could not possibly be checked for accuracy. Carter, for instance, claimed that the United States, under Ford's leadership, was short on morality, leadership, compassion for human rights, and short on respect by its own people and the world. What yardsticks could the audience use to test the veracity of these kinds of claims? Karl Adams, a very astute observer of politics, reflected the confusion.

> The more things I read and hear about the campaign, the more unsure I am exactly about what the many different candidates would do. Things keep popping up in the paper that completely change my thoughts . . . You don't know what to believe. Maybe it's all true; some of it is true. Why did they write that? It just causes doubts and it makes you unsure of where exactly to draw the line between these people.

While the issues in the presidential debates were complex, the time alloted for discussion was totally inadequate, although it was far more ample than is customary in ordinary newscasts. The format called for a 3-minute reply to the initial question (2 1/2 minutes in the third debate) and 2 minutes for a follow-up. Then there were 2 minutes for rebuttal. Closing statements were limited to 3 minutes each. Candidates could not possibly explain the issues, state their positions, and delineate the consequences of various alternatives within these time constraints. So they chose, instead, to use their answers as a springboard to convey impressions about their personal competence, erudition, poise, and credibility. Subsequent media stories did little to clear up what points the debates had left unanswered. These stories stressed who had won and lost, but shed little light on the meaning of what the candidates had said and on the merits of the various and sundry claims.

A number of panelists complained about the unattractiveness of the debate format. They thought it was akin to parallel press conferences, rather than true debates where candidates would interact directly with each other. They also thought that the whole affair was staged carefully to manipulate the media audience. The impression that the debates were rehearsed and phoney was enhanced by media reports about the briefings that the candidates had received to "program" them to set answers. The *Tribune*, for example, carried a story of Ford sparring with a mock panel over a 3-day period. It also described the careful tests of cameras, clothing, and make-up. This air of watching a "show" rather than reality, and the resentment against being manipulated, probably reduced impact.

One may ask why people watch at all when they believe that there is little new to be learned, that the subject matter lacks interest, and that they find the format unattractive? The answer is that they watch partly out of a sense of obligation, partly because they want to avoid missing something of importance, and partly because media attention is a habit that one pursues, regardless of the gratification it brings at any particular time. Donald Burton said it well.

> You pay attention to the primaries because they are the only news going on at the time; and I think they're blown way out of proportion by the press. . . . I don't like it, but that's the only game in town when they're going on.

The things said thus far about the presidential debates hold true of news in general. The disincentives for learning are substantial. On a daily basis, much of the news consists of new, yet repetitive scenes in old political dramas. Much of it seems staged—pseudoevents created by publicity-hungry individuals or news-hungry reporters. There is a good deal of overlap between television news and newspaper stories and between earlier and later versions of daily television programs. Switching the television or radio dial helps little in trying to escape from repetition. Many topics covered by the news, while important, are too complex and too boring for the audience. People know that they should be interested, but interest cannot be turned on and off at will.

Our panelists also grumbled frequently about the oversimplified treatment of all news, including election news, on television. Yet when the debates and other special news programs and newspaper features presented a small opportunity for more extensive exposure to issues, they were unwilling to seize it. For the most part, the panelists would not read and study carefully the more extensive versions of election and other news in newspapers and news magazines. Masses of specific facts and statistics were uniformly characterized as dull, confusing, and unduly detailed. Such attitudes present a catch-22 situation. If more detail and specificity is resented, how else can the demand for greater depth be satisfied?

As John Kessel has pointed out, richness of media information is no guarantee of richness of learning. "How closely a citizen monitors his or her information appears to be more important than how rich a given information source is."[4] Most citizens are not willing to monitor the news closely, given current news formats and given their social contexts. Even if information could be presented in formats that would please every member of the audience far better than is the case today, it is unlikely that news consumption would rise radically. It would require a major change in motivation to attend to news to bring about substantial change.

## Obtrusive and Unobtrusive Issues

Redundant news is rejected not only because repetition is boring and because it wastes time. It is also rejected because of the practice of reaching closure. When closure has occurred, redundant news stories may either be ignored entirely or the lessons that they teach may be ignored. What is closure? In an old television series, comedian William Bendix would cut off further argument by saying "Stop it, my head is made up." In the same fashion, our panelists, after being exposed to a substantial number of stories or experiences on a given subject, reached closure. Their heads were made up and they wanted no further information to disturb the images that they had formed.

The closure phenomenon has been observed in a number of studies of media impact. They have produced evidence that media audiences follow media cues about the importance of issues only for selected issues. The difference between issue areas in which media cues are accepted and issue areas in which they are ignored lies in the audience's familiarity with various topics. If the audience is familiar with the topic, either through personal experience or through prolonged exposure by the media, or a combination of both, the issue becomes "obtrusive." For such obtrusive issues, media audiences become "obstinate," as Raymond Bauer characterized them in 1964.[5] They have formed their own judgments and cling to them, regardless of media attention or inattention to these topics and regardless of the thrust of more recent media stories.[6] In fact, such media stories stand a good chance of being ignored entirely.

In 1976, economic issues such as unemployment, taxes, inflation, and the general economy appeared to be obtrusive issues.[7] The panelists held definite views about these issues, irrespective of media coverage. The reasons were obvious. It was a period of moderate recession, considerable unemployment, and constant worry over high taxes and inflation. Because these were matters of daily concern to our panelists, they had formed distinct impressions about these issues. Other issues, such as race relations, energy problems, and foreign affairs touched their lives far more intermittently in 1976. Their ideas about the significance of these issues, therefore were on the whole less firmly established so that media guidance was more likely to be accepted.

To test these findings statistically, we ascertained the level of association between the topics that the media had pictured as most significant and the topics that our panelists had labelled as most important. We found high positive correlations with the unobtrusive issues and low and mostly negative correlations with the obtrusive issues.[8] This substantiated that the influence of media stories on our panelists' thinking was much greater for the unobtrusive than the obtrusive stories.

The differences between obtrusive and unobtrusive issues were also reflected in the diaries. Unobtrusive issues were reported on the basis of media coverage. Obtrusive issues, on the other hand, were more likely to be reported on the basis of personal experiences and earlier judgments. For these issues, panelists were more likely to say that the media were wrong and to express explicitly contrary opinions.

Issues may become obtrusive even when there has been no recent media coverage, yet the topic is the subject of frequent discussions. For instance, most of our panelists had firm opinions about environmental problems and the plight of senior citizens at a time when the media were silent about these concerns. A comparison of the images of persons and events presented by news stories with the panelists' images of these persons and events also showed greater correspondence when unobtrusive issues were concerned. For obtrusive issues, there were marked divergencies. The differences in the realm of crime news, discussed in chapter 4, are examples.

Unobtrusive issues may become obtrusive temporarily or permanently as a result of media coverage or personal experiences. Obtrusiveness thus is not a constant attribute of specific issues. It varies with the social context and the times.

An example is presented by media coverage of various issues in connection with the 1976 election. During the primaries, before the panelists had become fully familiar with election issues, the distinction between obtrusive and unobtrusive issues was clear. The panelists shared media assessments of the importance of various issues for the unobtrusive issues, but not for the obtrusive ones. But as people became more familiar with all of the issues because of the heavy media coverage of the election and the emphasis on election-related news in personal conversations, the distinction between unobtrusive and obtrusive issues faded. All issues discussed in connection with the election had become obtrusive. With their minds made up, learning from the media and the significance of media influence, declined for all the panelists.[9]

It is, therefore, obvious that the subject matter of stories and their timing affect the degree of influence they have on the media audience. Attention to media stories and learning from such stories diminishes when the subject matter becomes familiar through exposure to prior stories or through personal experiences. There seems to be an ill-defined line between the point where repetition increases the chances that a story will be noted and ample detail absorbed and where repetition produces saturation boredom and makes issues obtrusive. By contrast, personal experience with a topic clearly robs media stories of their influence.

## MOTIVATIONS FOR LEARNING

Why do people take an interest in some stories and reject others? We now turn to major theories about motivations for information selection and rejection. Three theories that will be examined briefly here are *uses* and *gratifications* theories, *cognitive balance* theories, and *agenda-setting* theories. All of them predict media usage considerably better than is possible from demographic factors such as gender, age, or education.[10] Since these theories are interrelated, it is not surprising that our findings are, at least partly, in accord with all of them.

### Uses and Gratifications Theories

According to uses and gratifications theories, people pay attention to information that is useful for them in their daily pursuits or that provides psychological gratifications.[11] The latter may range from simple desires for diversion to more complex needs such as overcoming loneliness or coping with feelings of hostility.[12] For example, people pay attention to stories that help them in making business or political decisions, such as investing in a home or casting a vote. They use the media to have material for small talk with others, to occupy their empty time, or to gain a sense of security and social adequacy from knowing what is happening.

The specific uses that people want to make of media stories and the specific gratifications that they derive vary, of course, among people and over time. Current life-style and the interests and needs it creates are important, along with psychological predispositions and past experiences.

Max Jackman, for instance, who watched practically no television news when his work kept him away from home in the evening, became an avid watcher when he changed to a daytime work shift. But when he experienced marital difficulties in the fall of 1976 and spent his evenings at a local bar, conversation with other bar flies replaced the media as a way to gratify his needs for information. Betty Nystrom paid close attention to local political stories while she was a low-level party official; she stopped when she relinquished these duties. Sandra Ornstein varied her attention to media offerings depending on her assessment of the news tastes of prospective visitors whom she hoped to entertain with sprightly conversation.

The specific stories which may fill a particular need vary as well. For instance, the person who wants excitement may satisfy this urge either by watching a thrilling football game, paying attention to the exploits of astronauts, or observing a terrorist incident depicted on television in a blow-by-blow account. People who want nothing more than to ward off boredom may turn on the television set without caring about tuning to a specific program. Any program, regardless of its nature, may fulfill their purpose. In fact, so many people choose "television watching," per se, as a leisure-time activity that television program planners go to great pains to attract an audience to a particular station early in the prime viewing periods. Once the set is tuned to a particular station, it is highly unlikely that an undiscriminating audience will change channels. Hence, the station is assured of a steady following throughout the entire viewing period.

Researchers interested in fleshing out uses and gratifications theories have tried to discover why people turn to the media, rather than elsewhere, as a potential source of gratification for various needs. Researchers have also wondered how well the media gratify specific audience needs. Thus far, the findings remain slim.[13] Our study seems to indicate that media use patterns originate from social forces within a particular cultural environment. They are learned early, when children are taught the elements of good citizenship in grade school and high school and when they copy parental and peer behavior.

From these models, as well as from overt teaching, children learn that they should be informed about current happenings and that the media provide one comparatively easy and culturally approved way to meet their diverse information needs. However, keeping informed about current affairs is an activity that ranks comparatively low in life's pursuits. Hence, it often yields to higher priority activities.

Children also learn that media, particularly television, are sources of entertainment and companionship. Television watching is a reward that one earns by being "good" or refraining from being "bad." As familiarity with various media increases, the probability of gaining the desired information or entertainment gratifications increases as well. In fact, the mere usage of mass media carries its own rewards since it is a culturally approved activity.[14]

As reported earlier (chapter 5), for the majority of our panelists, psychological gratifications were the major reasons for selecting stories. That is why they paid a lot of attention to news containing human interest elements, such as stories about crimes and accidents and stories relevant to personal life-style, including health care, sports, entertainment, and gossip about assorted celebrities. This finding is compatible with William Stephenson's "play theory" of mass media use. Stephenson contends that people use the mass media primarily for recreation.[15]

The panelists' interview protocols and diaries also provided evidence for other gratifications. Some stories were selected because they were relevant to the respondent's job or satisfied the need to act as a "good citizen" interested in important public affairs. Our panelists also derived gratification from reducing their uncertainty about matters related to pending decisions. Campaign information just prior to an election fell into that category. So did information about the weather, about the stockmarket, and about conditions in areas where panelists expected to travel.

On the whole, there was not much political information that stimulated our panelists' urge for reduction in uncertainty. Since they were only mildly interested in politics, they did not anticipate many gratifications from political news stories other than a sense of being a "good citizen." They rarely expressed pure curiosity for political information, even though there were other knowledge areas where they sought information simply for the sake of knowing. When asked if they ever watched election information for the sheer excitement, most said "no."

However, people do not invariably derive gratifications from their media use or the gratifications obtained may be different from those that were expected. Our panelists repeatedly expressed disappointment with media stories that did not give them the information or relaxation they needed or wanted or that were presented in formats they disliked. Watching the debates was a case in point. The debates did not supply the information that most panelists hoped to receive, although they gave unexpected insights about the candidates' ability to perform in front of the cameras. When anticipated gratifications from attending to particular information did not materialize, our panelists were quite willing to abandon unsatisfactory stories. This is further support for the notion that gratifications are an important motivating force for seeking information. While such disappointments with media offerings may temporarily discourage media use, the effect is ordinarily short-lived. Our panelists' media use patterns were so well integrated into their life style patterns—almost like eating, drinking, and sleeping—that return to accustomed behavior was swift.[16]

Moreover, all panelists were aware of the problems newspeople face in presenting ample news in a serious, yet appealing manner. They were, therefore, quite tolerant and forgiving of media shortcomings. As Helga Holmquist put it: "The media still are private enterprise. They're money-making propositions in the United States. They are going to act accordingly. And that's alright with me."

How can we be sure that the motivations just described actually are the ones that produced the news attention behavior exhibited by our panelists? As with other mental functions, our evidence is indirect. It rests partly on self-reports, partly on inferences from what the panelists said in various contexts, and partly on what they did in terms of story selection and attention to specific story features.

We asked many general questions about our panelists' attitudes towards the media and their satisfaction with media performance in general. We also asked for their assessment of the quality of coverage of specific stories. What kinds of information did they find most and least helpful and for what purposes? Which news stories had been discussed with others and who were the discussion partners? We requested that our panelists note in their diaries why they had selected the stories that they were reporting. Whenever we asked about specific news stories, we inquired why the panelists had paid attention to that particular story. If a panelist did not recall the story, we asked why the story had been skipped. In this way, we gathered a large number of responses about what pleased and displeased the panelists about media coverage and the benefits they derived or failed to derive.

From the patterns that emerged, we developed predictions about the kinds of stories and story details to which the panelists were likely to pay attention, given their expressed choice criteria. We checked the accuracy of these predictions in later interviews. When most predictions proved reasonably accurate, we considered this as confirmation that our appraisal of gratifications sought by various panelists had been accurate. Further confirmation of the validity of our conclusions came from other studies that reported various types of information that different population groups had absorbed from the mass media. These studies, like our investigation, revealed a close correspondence between various life-styles and media use patterns.[17]

## Cognitive Balance Theories

A second set of theories that attempts to explain people's interactions with the news are cognitive balance theories. According to such theories, people avoid information that conflicts with knowledge, attitudes, and feelings that they already possess or that is disturbing or threatening to them in other ways. They seek out information that is reassuring and congruent with their beliefs.[18] Uses and gratifications theories can also account for this phenomenon by arguing that dissonant or threatening information brings no gratifications because it is psychologically disturbing.

Like other tests of cognitive balance theories, our research indicates that the phenomenon does occur, but it is limited. The panelists frequently rejected information that they found annoying or disturbing, when headlines allowed them to identify it readily. But this was by no means a consistent practice. Furthermore, once opinions had become entrenched, as happens when issues become obtrusive, people tended to limit or exclude further information, supportive as well as contradictory. The exclusion of contradictory information under these circumstances explains the considerable stability in a variety of beliefs and conceptions in the face of conflicting media stories. But there are also many instances when people did pay attention to major changes in information and adjusted their beliefs accordingly. While our panelists were reluctant to change their well-established views, all of them did so on occasion.

Encountering dissonant views and yielding to them did not appear to be unduly painful. Whenever the panelists called attention on their own to major changes in beliefs, they did so without expressions of regret or apparent embarrassment. However, when the interviewer pointed out unacknowledged changes or dissonance between media information and the panelists' views, most panel members showed signs of embarrassment and tried to rationalize the changes. When asked about this, several panelists attributed their feelings to strong cultural pressures to be consistent and steadfast, except when changes were made consciously to correct errors or adjust to changed conditions. The pain of dissonance became acute only when it was exposed to the gaze of others.

Lack of selectivity may be due, in part, to the inability to shut out unwanted information. It is particularly difficult to shut out discordant information presented in television and radio news because one never knows when it will appear. By the time one realizes that a particular bit of news is disagreeable, it has already been presented in full. Similar problems make it difficult to reject discordant information from other sources. To appraise how well new information conforms with internalized views, one must familiarize oneself with the new information in order to compare it carefully to established views. By the time this is done, the discordant information has become at least partly familiar. Much discordant information is also accepted because viewers or readers never scrutinize it carefully to see whether it matches their preconceptions. Hence they are unaware that the information is actually discordant.

The main barrier to systematic selectivity is the casualness of the news selection and rejection process. Except for a few professionals on the panel who read specialized journals, our panelists selected information primarily on an opportunity basis. They read the newspapers and magazines that were within convenient physical reach, looking for whatever pleasing stories might be presented on a certain day. Searches for specific preselected stories were rare. Similarly, once the television set was turned on to a particular channel, many panelists shunned the effort of turning the dial, except to tune into a few favorite programs each week.

While exposure was generally haphazard and information selection and rejection were based on relatively simple-minded criteria, information processing was a different matter. Here rigorous selection and information transformation rules enter the picture (see chapter 7). In fact, much processing ultimately leads to total or partial rejection of information. Therefore, it is at the information-processing stage, rather than during initial selection, that cognitive balance considerations appear to have their greatest effect.

## Agenda-Setting Theories

Finally, our findings about the incentives that prompt attention to news stories and produce learning correspond to the general framework of agenda-setting theories. According to these theories, media audiences accept guidance from the media of their choice in determining what information is most important and worthy of attention. These cues come in the form of frequent attention to particular topics and prominent display of selected stories. Like cognitive balance theories, agenda-setting theories explain important behavior patterns, but (as noted in chapter 5) there are also major exceptions to these patterns.

Our panelists definitely were influenced by the many cues to the importance of stories that the media supplied. The panelists often told us that they paid attention to various events only because the media had featured the information. "I watched it because the TV was on," was a common remark. They were more likely to encounter and to expose themselves to frequently occurring stories, at least until saturation boredom had set in. Most considered frequency of coverage as an indication that newspeople deemed the story important. The panelists also showed some preference for front-page and front-section stories, for big headlines, and for spreads with pictures. But, as pointed out before, prominent display did not guarantee attention, nor did lack of prominence assure that the story would be missed or ignored.

Barring reasons to disagree, most panelists were willing to adopt media judgments about the newsworthiness and importance of stories in general and about the relevance of various story segments for assessing the situation in question. Cesar Ippolito, for example, felt that his lack of regard for Sargent Shriver was a product of the newspaper stories he had read. He attributed Shriver's quitting the presidential race to media coverage.

> I think it's a product of the way the media treats him. I'm afraid I'm very much influenced that way. They never really got to the fact of what the hell he's all about, just the fact that he was trying to ride the Kennedy coattails and he was a lightweight. I never gave the guy an even break. They never gave him one, and therefore I never gave him one.

Media cues about the importance of stories lose their potency as guides to what people will read or watch or think about when conflicting pressures arise from other facets of the individual's life. Again, the picture fits in well with uses and gratifications theories. Everything else being equal, people are willing to follow media cues. It is the path of least resistance that saves one the trouble of independent thinking and is, therefore, attractive.

Media agenda setting, to the degree that it does take place, is a powerful force in determining which problems are taken seriously and in providing the context within which policies and individuals will be judged. But when media information seems no longer useful because individuals already have made up their minds about a given issue, when the information is psychologically disturbing, or when the media give scanty, undistinguished coverage to a matter of particular concern to individuals, people are likely to ignore media cues.

Similarly, when people have doubts about the arguments presented by a media story and, especially, when they are able to argue against it, the story loses its persuasiveness. Shanto Iyengar, Mark D. Peters, and Donald Kinder contend that this means that: "Those with little political information to begin with are most vulnerable to agenda setting. The well-informed resist agenda setting through effective counterarguing, a maneuver not so available to the less informed."[19] However, the well-informed may even the score by exposing themselves to a lot more media information than the poorly-informed, provided that much of this information is unobtrusive. On balance, it is, therefore, hard to predict whether the well-informed or the poorly-informed are most influenced by media agendas.

## CONTEXTUAL FACTORS

A number of contextual factors also provide incentives or disincentives for paying attention to the mass media and learning from them. They include differential socialization, different life experiences, and different needs for various types of information. Likewise, they encompass such attitudinal factors as interest in news, trust or distrust of news sources, and trust or distrust between the sender and the receiver of a message. If the panelists were cynical about the credibility of politicians in general, or about the credibility of reporters, or if they thought their views clashed with the interpretations provided by the story, this cynicism often led to minimal attention and learning.

## The Impact of Life-style and Political Socialization

Political socialization has a profound impact on media use because it teaches children what they should learn about their environment and how they should go about learning. Children are taught how to reason, how to see patterns, how to discern relationships, and how to evaluate. These cognitive skills are bound to affect the way they process the news. Children are also taught the value of media use and the kinds of uses and gratifications that they can expect to obtain from mass media.

As indicated earlier, these lessons ordinarily last a lifetime. Patterns observed and practiced during childhood persist if current life-styles permit it. Panelists who reported ample media use by their parents and peers and who indicated that they were taught that citizens' interest in politics was important, carried those habits forward into adulthood. In some instances, there was a switch of medium in the wake of new electronic technologies. For half the panel members, this meant that television, which had been available to them in childhood, became an important medium in their adult years. Very few panelists reported that their parents had used electronic media extensively. Panelists whose current life-style made media use more difficult than in the past usually retained their original norms of how they ought to behave. They expressed strong and frequent regret about their inability to continue in the desired patterns.[20]

Our study indicates that childhood socialization perpetuates age, gender, and socioeconomic stereotypes. The panelists were fully aware that expectations differ along demographic lines when it came to the use of various media, the subjects to be learned, the breadth of information to be gleaned, and the appropriateness of engaging in political conversations. Such expectations tended to become self-fulfilling prophecies. According to these social cues, careful newspaper reading is a norm to be followed primarily by adult males. Less is expected from women and nearly nothing is expected from children. Children's serious interest in current affairs generally is not anticipated until they reach high school. Less interest is expected from low socioeconomic groups than from those with greater means and generally better education.

The socialization distinctions that were particularly noticeable for our panelists were those between men and women. Men traced their greater attention to politics back to childhood. Half the men, compared to one-third of the women, reported that they were encouraged as young adults to take a substantial interest in politics. And so they did. Compared to women, men recalled more than twice as many specific political incidents from their childhood years, covering a much wider issue spectrum. This was particularly true of younger men. Wars and elections were remembered by both sexes, but beyond these topics, women's recall tended to concern local issues and general economic concerns, while men apparently had paid attention to and remembered a broad spectrum of national and international happenings.

Men also reported using media more during adolescence than did women, even though access to media was equally convenient for boys and girls. Women and men both told us that, compared to their fathers, their mothers had made little use of mass media for political information. Men seemed to copy their fathers, while women followed in their mothers' footsteps. When it came to political conversations, mothers were remembered as remaining on the sidelines or participating less vigorously than fathers. In social gatherings, political discussions were largely a male preserve.

Women, thus, had role models who read less than men, rarely discussed politics, and had only a fleeting interest in political news. Most women described themselves as conforming to this role model. In our panel, none of the women expressed high current interest in politics, but 1 of 4 older men and 3 of 7 younger men did. Women reported less discussion of politics with family and outsiders than did men. While women reported regular use of daily papers and television slightly more often than men, men used newspapers substantially more for politics.[21] Of the 11 men, 5 said that they read newspapers systematically, without skipping around; none of the women did. The men, continuing patterns witnessed and encouraged in childhood, used richer sources and used them more systematically than women.

Even when women's life-styles led them to increased media use and attention to a wider range of topics, as shown by the various tests employed in this study, they still stereotyped themselves in the traditional ways. Compared to men, they described themselves as having far greater interest in human interest stories, crimes, accidents, and features relating to the home and garden. In fact, the interests of men and women for these topics were quite similar, as judged by news attention scores. Likewise, women claimed to have slimmer interest in international politics, and in national, state, and local politics than was warranted by their story recall scores and diary entries.[22] Women did show substantially lower rates than men when it came to taking a lead in political discussions or participating in them.

Women's views on the merits of public policies and their attention to economic issues, such as inflation, taxes, government spending, and unemployment did not differ materially from their male counterparts in similar age groups.[23] Their attention to foreign affairs and defense issues was only slightly behind male patterns, and their attention to welfare issues, education, health care, and crime was only slightly ahead. Most of the differences were below a .05 significance level. The claimed differences obviously conformed to the stereotypical views of differences between men's and women's concerns that the panelists had learned in childhood.

Community patterns were important as well—particularly for panelists raised in small communities—in shaping news attention and learning behaviors. There appear to be strong social pressures in many small Midwestern communities to be interested in and informed about certain aspects of life. These pressures extend to entertainment as well as news programs, and to the use of specific media for specific offerings.[24] While some of these pressures subside when people move away from their home towns, residual effects persist. They come to the fore mainly when people express ideal norms of behavior that should guide all citizens.

Early socialization also seems to establish rankings of importance for various aspects of life. If politics is ranked highly, information needs are created accordingly. If the media are viewed primarily as a form of diversion, to be used during leisure hours, use patterns emphasize entertainment. However, these rankings may change if the expectations of the surrounding society change substantially. We found that panelists who changed their life styles in major ways altered their media use patterns so that they would fit better into the new setting. Betty Nystrom, for instance, reported that she felt pressured to stop indulging her interest in New York politics by reading East Coast newspapers. After moving to the Midwest, she found that her co-workers were unreceptive to the stories she told. Conversely, she could not readily join into many of their conversations until she switched to the local press and concentrated on problems that interested her new colleagues. Social pressures linked to life-style thus seem to outweigh the effects of prior socialization. The force of the past is great, but it is no match for strong, countervailing current pressures.

## Prior Learning

Just as attitudes towards media use are developed early in life, so people develop a fund of general information throughout their lifetime, starting in childhood. Social, political, and economic conditions determine the nature of information available for learning. New information drawn from one's environment is integrated into one's existing fund of information. Regardless of whether the new information changes old beliefs, reinforces them, or is rejected because the receiver is unwilling to reopen her or his thinking on a particular subject, the presence of the old information has an impact on the uses made of the new.[25]

For most news stories, the impact of prior information is profound. It affects the perspective from which the story is viewed and the kinds of details that will be absorbed. As pointed out earlier, regularities in news patterns guarantee that the scenarios presented in most news stories remain familiar. The actors involved in a newly reported situation may be new faces, and the details of the scenario may vary somewhat. But, basically, it is the same old drama or comedy with readily predictable outcomes. If people remember it (forgetting rates are high), they process it accordingly, either rejecting it as redundant information or remembering it as one more example of a familiar occurrence.[26]

If the news story is about an ongoing event in which the reader or viewer has taken an interest, information already absorbed may determine what additional information is internalized. For instance, many of our panelists ignored stories about events in progress if they had not paid attention to the initial reports. They felt that they could not completely comprehend a sequence of events without full exposure to the initial information. By contrast, people whose interest had been piqued by initial reports often looked eagerly for follow-up stories, as long as the stories provided substantial amounts of new information. Once the stories had little more to add, saturation boredom set in. These findings support the journalistic folk wisdom that interest in a story can rarely be maintained for more than three weeks.

There is much research evidence that people who have acquired a large fund of information are likely to learn more from current news than people who lack such knowledge. This is the "knowledge-gap" phenomenon that makes the knowledge-rich richer and leaves the knowledge-poor poor.[27] The explanation is simple. Knowledge creates interest because people like to hear additional information about matters that they deem worthy of committing to memory. The person interested in ten policy areas who is following all relevant new developments in these areas is likely to pick up more news than the person who is only interested in one policy area.

Converse describes graphically the advantages enjoyed by the knowledgeable:

If an informed observer hears a surprising policy statement in the news by the secretary of defense, he may prick up his ears and pay close attention. He relates this information to what he knows of recent policy, what he knows of the secretary's relationship to the president, what he knows of past positions the secretary may have taken, and the like, since he is intensely interested to detect even small reorientations of national policy. In short, he automatically imports enormous amounts of prior information that lends the new statement high interest. The poorly informed person, hearing the same statement, finds it as dull as the rest of the political news. He only dimly understands the role of the secretary of defense and has no vivid image grounded in past information as to the inclinations of the current incumbent. His awareness of current policy is suffiiently gross that he has no expectation of detecting nuances of change. So the whole statement is confronted with next to no past information at all, hence it is just more political blather: in five minutes he probably will not remember that he heard such a statement, much less be able to reconstruct what was said. This means in turn that four months later, when confronted by another statement by the secretary of defense, he will bring as little to it as he did before and hence forget it with equal rapidity. . . . In short, with respect to politics the richness and meaning of new information depends vitally on the amount of past information one brings to the new message. So does retention of the information over time.[28]

Statistical tests of learning of new information during the election confirmed that our panelists who knew more initially tended to learn more as long as there were new things to be learned. A comparison of learning scores of panelists high and low on prior knowledge ratings showed significant correlations between high prior knowledge and high learning rates.[29] Since news stories generally cover several knowledge areas, people who pay attention to them are apt to learn about more than one area. For example, learning about issues and candidates was highly correlated. During the presidential debates, panelists who learned most about issues also learned most about candidates.[30] In the same manner, learning about the two candidates was closely related. Those who learned more about Ford also learned more about Carter.[31]

Despite the fact that those who knew more ordinarily learned more, we found that knowledge acquisition often reached a plateau in specific areas where coverage had been prolonged. At that point, there was little left to learn. Whenever the plateau was reached, our most knowledgeable panelists reported the least new learning about events and showed the lowest increments in learning scores, while displaying high levels of knowledge. The reason was that they already knew a lot, often were able to make correct inferences or guesses about likely new developments, and had greater than average ability in retrieving facts from memory. The effects of prior learning on new knowledge acquisition cut both ways: They stimulate learning until a saturation point is reached and then, they suppress it.

## Interest in News

Among the psychological predispositions that affect learning from the media, interest turned out to be paramount. People who are interested in media information because it provide them with ample gratifications are likely to learn more than those who express little interest. When interest levels fluctuate, because of the march of public or private events, attention to media stories and learning rates fluctuates correspondingly. For instance, early in 1976, our panelists expressed most interest in information about domestic economic and social problems. Correspondingly, they devoted much attention to stories about these issues. The interest focus shifted to foreign affairs in May when unrest and fighting in the Middle East increased and when NATO issued a warning about rising Soviet military strength in central Europe. Media use patterns followed suit.

With respect to election news, there was a sharp rise of 3.5% in interest scores during the Illinois primaries in March, followed by a steady decline back to January levels, and an upswing in late June as the Democratic convention drew near. To confirm the accuracy of self-reports about corresponding fluctuations in media use, we also checked the percentage of diary stories dealing with the election, the levels of recall for election-related stories, and the frequency with which certain topics were mentioned as the subject of conversation. The self-reports about interest levels and related media use proved accurate.[32]

We also tested the relationship between interest and learning about the election. Interested people invariably learned more. During the presidential debates, for example, the highest learning was scored by panelists who were very interested in the event because their life-style had made it difficult for them to make full use of media information up to that point. The average number of facts learned about the candidates' qualities was 5.0 for the high-interest groups and 3.5 for the low-interest panelists.[33] On issue learning, the high-interest groups learned most, with an average of 3.7 facts reported. The low-interest groups scored 0.7.[34]

Interest in news seems to encourage people to focus attention on specific aspects of stories, which are then learned. By contrast, panelists whose interest was low also were unable to focus their attention. Since they did not know what information they wanted, their learning was passive and haphazard rather than active. Consequently, they learned little, even when they spent considerable time watching the debates on television and felt that they needed more information. Many of them conceded that their lack of motivation to learn would prevent them from learning even if more information became available in a format and at a time ideally suited to their tastes. As Sven Peterson put it when he tried to explain why he had not paid attention to news stories: "Were I to use information, this would be the form, the heaven-sent form. But . . . oh, well!" Evidently, packaging information attractively does not help when motivation to use it is lacking. The low priority that many people place on politics is likely to keep political learning spotty and thin, regardless of the manner in which journalists handle the news.

The reasons for interest in news vary, involving specific curiosity about happenings that are related to one's personal life or societal role or general curiosity to find out how the world is turning. Usually, interest spurred by a specific goal, such as the need to become informed about candidates just before an election, results in a greater impetus to learning than occurs when interest is unfocused.[35] Once people get into the habit of using the media because they are interested in the news, a spiral effect sets in. Exposure to fresh information produces new knowledge. In turn, this creates further interest that is satisfied by heightened attention to news. The spiral continues until a saturation level is reached.

When people say that they are very interested in politics in general, or in a specific aspect of politics, one should not jump to the conclusion that political concerns are paramount in their minds and that they will exert strong efforts to satisfy their curiosity. Nothing could be farther from the truth. In the hierarchy of interests and concerns in people's lives, politics yields to most other personally important matters. An invitation to dinner, a baby-sitting job, an ordinary shopping trip provided ready excuses for ignoring important, pre-announced political news events. Considering such behavior, inferences about the behavioral effects of expressions of high interest in political news must be made in light of competing interests of the individual.

For instance, most of our panelists had expressed great interest in the presidential election. A check of their diaries showed that, indeed, 11% of all of the diary stories were related to the election, a figure almost identical to the percentage of election news in the *Tribune* and on television. However, this meant that 89% of the diary stories dealt with topics other than the election. Moreover, 8 of the respondents never mentioned the elections when they were asked in successive interviews during the primary season to name "major problems and events facing the United States at the present time." Seven panelists named the election once, and four named it twice. None named it in all four interviews conducted in the spring and summer of 1976.

Most of the panelists had also expressed high interest in the presidential debates. Sixteen panelists thought that the event might aid them in making a more informed voting decision. Despite the high interest levels, 7 panelists were dropouts in each presidential debate. Of those who watched, only half managed to pay attention to the entire broadcast. Half of all respondents missed the vice-presidential debate. Two individuals missed all four debates and two others saw only one. Despite professions of high interest, the panelists were not generally motivated to catch up on learning about the debates through other sources. Only 6 reported that they tried to watch a rebroadcast of the events or to read about them in the print media.

The conclusion to be drawn from such behavior is that interest in ongoing events is, indeed, an incentive for learning. But its degree must be judged by the extent of relevant behavior and in comparison with other behaviors. Verbal affirmations of great or little interest, by themselves, defy accurate interpretation.

## Cynicism/Credibility

The final contextual factor to be considered also involves psychological responses to the environment. Studies of persuasion have shown that people are less likely to pay attention to messages, and less likely to believe them, if the credibility of the source of the message seems doubtful. Therefore, it stands to reason that people who have little trust in the media, or in the political leaders, will learn at lower rates than people whose trust is high.

We found it difficult to assess to what degree our panelists' learning was affected by credibility factors because they gave mixed signals about their trust in media credibility and in political leaders. They frequently referred to the unreliability and even deceitfulness of politicians in general. At the same time, answers to questions about trust in specific public officials did not reveal high levels of distrust. For instance, in expressing agreement or disagreement with a statement that Ford or Carter as president could be trusted, only two respondents distrusted Ford and only three distrusted Carter. On a 7-point scale, where 1 meant strong agreement and 7 meant strong disagreement that the candidates could be trusted, and with 4 as the neutral point, 18 of the 21 panelists rated Ford positively, while 10 did the same for Carter. Asked to react to a series of statements regarding trust in public officials, two-thirds of the panelists generally expressed some degree of trust.

However, a number of panelists voiced doubts about the credibility of what they termed "campaign rhetoric" or "political jargon." The implication generally was that politicians should not be blamed for the vacuous rhetoric since the nature of politics requires it. Audiences, for their part, should routinely discount what politicians say in the heat of the campaign. It appears, therefore, that even voters who trust political figures may discount their campaign pronouncements. Special political broadcasts, like debates, oratory at political rallies, and political advertisements appeared to be particularly suspect. Our panelists saw them as carefully rehearsed performances designed to manipulate their judgment of the comparative merits of the candidates—a "show" rather than an effort to depict reality. They watched such "shows" partly to keep in touch with the campaign and partly in hopes that something fresh and believable might indeed be said. But whatever was said was swallowed with the proverbial grain of salt.

Attitudes towards the media were similar to attitudes towards politicians. When our panelists appraised the media in general terms, they routinely complained about such distortions as sensational coverage, lack of perspective, and sometimes outright bias. They frequently told stories with cautionary adjectives like "supposedly this happened while the mayor was present." But when asked about believability for specific stories, specific media, or newspeople, our panelists rarely expressed disbelief except when a story ran directly counter to their personal experiences. Even then, they never talked about "lies," only about exaggeration and improper emphasis.

In general, then, lack of credibility of news sources and channels was not a major disincentive to learning, with the possible exception of learning from political speeches. When our panelists were skeptical about a story, usually on the basis of personal experiences, they would discount the questionable parts or supply their own interpretations. However, they rarely labelled a story as totally false or accused media and politicians of routine dishonesty and deception.

If one were to rank the credibility of various sources, personal experiences would rate at the top. They would be followed by credible interpersonal sources and media stories citing credible authorities. Run of the mill media stories would come last. As Walter Lippmann said long ago, once the "pictures in our heads" have been formed, they become vastly more important than actual conditions in "the world outside."[36] New learning slows down. How these pictures are formed is the subject of the next chapter.

## Notes

1. For a fuller discussion of the various models described in this chapter see, Sidney Kraus and Dennis Davis, *The Effects of Mass Communication on Political Behavior*,

University Park, Pa., Pennsylvania State University Press, 1976, pp. 115–148. The hypodermic model is discussed on pp. 115–117. Also see, Dennis K. Davis and Stanley J. Baran, *Mass Communication and Everyday Life: A Perspective on Theory and Effects*, Belmont, Calif., Wadsworth, 1981, pp. 25–26.

2. Ibid., pp. 117–131.

3. For similar findings, see Kraus and Dennis, cited in note 1, p. 126.

4. John Kessel, *Presidential Campaign Politics: Coalition Strategies and Citizen Response*, Homewood, Ill., Dorsey Press, 1980, p. 194.

5. Raymond A. Bauer, "The Obstinate Audience: The Influence Process from the Point of View of Social Communication," *American Psychologist*, 19, 1964, pp. 319–328.

6. Harold G. Zucker, "The Variable Nature of News Media Influence," in Brent D. Ruben (ed.), *Communication Yearbook 2*, New Brunswick, N.J., Transaction Books, 1978, p. 225. Also see, Lutz Erbring, Edie N. Goldenberg, and Arthur H. Miller, "Front-Page News and Real-World Cues: A New Look at Agenda-Setting by the Media," *American Journal of Political Science*, 24:1, February 1980, pp. 28–40.

7. For more details see, David H. Weaver, Doris A. Graber, Maxwell E. McCombs, and Chaim H. Eyal, *Media Agenda-Setting in a Presidential Election: Issues, Images, and Interest*, New York, Praeger, 1981.

8. For the New Hampshire panel, for example, in the summer of 1976, correlations of newspaper and personal agendas were .92 for unobtrusive issues and − .80 for obtrusive issues. For more detail, see, Weaver et al., cited in note 7, p. 131.

9. Using Spearman's rhos computed for four panels with 165 panelists, average correlations between media rankings of issue importance and panelists' rankings during the primaries were .75 for unobtrusive issues and .13 for obtrusive issues. By November, the original distinction between obtrusive and unobtrusive issues had all but faded away. Most issues had become obtrusive and the public therefore used its own priorities. See, Weaver et al., as cited in note 7, p. 101.

10. Jack M. McLeod and Lee B. Becker, "The Uses and Gratifications Approach," in Dan D. Nimmo and Keith R. Sanders (eds.), *Handbook of Political Communication*, Beverly Hills, Calif., Sage, 1981, p. 93.

11. See, for example, Charles K. Atkin, "Instrumental Utilities and Information Seeking," in Peter Clarke (ed.), *New Models of Mass Communication Research*, Beverly Hills, Sage, 1973, pp. 205–242; and Lee B. Becker, "Two Tests of Media Gratifications: Watergate and the 1974 Election," *Journalism Quarterly*, 53, Spring 1976, pp. 26–31.

12. Lee B. Becker, "Measurement of Gratifications," *Communication Research*, 6, 1979, pp. 54–73.

13. McLeod and Becker, as cited in note 10, contend that media behavior reflects prior interests and preferences.

14. Ibid., p. 74.

15. William Stephenson, *The Play Theory of Mass Communication*, Chicago, University of Chicago Press, 1967.

16. McLeod and Becker, as cited in note 10, p. 79.

17. Ibid., p. 81. Uses and gratifications studies have also shown that "the stability of individual gratification items appears sufficiently strong to rule out the possibility that audience members give frivolous responses to the gratifications sought items" (p. 82).

18. A brief exposition of these theories is contained in Lewis Donohew and Philip Palmgreen, "A Reappraisal of Dissonance and the Selective Exposure Hypothesis," *Journalism Quarterly*, 48, Autumn 1971, pp. 412–420.

19. Shanto Iyengar, Mark D. Peters and Donald Kinder, "Experimental Demonstrations of the 'Not-So-Minimal' Consequences of Television News Programs," *American Political Science Review*, 76, 4, December 1982, pp. 854–855.

20. Steven H. Chaffee (with Marilyn Jackson-Beeck, Jean Durall, and Donna Wilson), "Mass Communication in Political Socialization," in Stanley Renshon (ed.), *Handbook of Political Socialization*, New York, Free Press, 1977, pp. 227–228, 251–253.

21. Doris A. Graber, "Agenda-Setting: Are There Women's Perspectives?" in Laurily Keir Epstein (ed.), *Women and the News*, New York, Hastings House, 1978, p. 33.

22. Ibid., pp. 33–35.

23. Comparison of women's and men's approval of various policies showed Spearman's rhos ranging from .70 to .94.

24. David L. Swanson, "A Constructivist Approach," in Dan D. Nimmo and Keith R. Sanders (eds.), *Handbook of Political Communication*, Beverly Hills, Sage, 1981, pp. 173–175.

25. Prior knowledge scores are very useful as baselines for measuring new learning. However, they are seldom used. For a fuller discussion, see, Doris A. Graber, "Problems in Measuring Audience Effects of the 1976 Debates," in George F. Bishop, Robert G. Meadow, and Marilyn Jackson-Beeck (eds.), *The Presidential Debates: Media, Electoral, and Policy Perspectives*, New York, Praeger, 1978, pp. 109–111.

26. Gerald R. Miller, "On Being Persuaded," in Michael E. Roloff and Gerald R. Miller (eds.), *Persuasion: New Directions in Theory and Research*, Beverly Hills, Sage, 1980, p. 20. Miller notes that by the time adulthood is reached, "under conditions of voluntary exposure, the majority of individuals' persuasive transactions will involve messages that reinforce their existing response repertories."

27. Philip J. Tichenor, George A. Donohue, and Clarice A. Olien, "Mass Media Flow and Differential Growth in Knowledge," *Public Opinion Quarterly*, 34, Summer 1970, pp. 159–170.

28. Philip E. Converse, "Public Opinion and Voting Behavior," in Nathan Polsby and Fred Greenstein (eds.), *Handbook of Political Science*, vol. 4, Reading, Mass., Addison-Wesley, 1975, p. 97.

29. $r = .65, p < .001$.

30. The correlation coefficient between these two aspects of the debates was .75 ($p < .001$) when both variables were measured by learning of specific information.

31. $r = .75, p < .001$.

32. The relationships between labelling an issue as a matter of interest and concern and talking about it ranged from Spearman's rho 0.80 to 0.93.

33. Doris A. Graber and Young Yun Kim, "Why John Q Voter Did Not Learn Much from the 1976 Presidential Debates," in Brent Ruben (ed.), *Communication Yearbook 2*, New Brunswick, N.J., Transaction Books, 1978, p. 412.

34. The correlation between prior interest and learning about issues from the debate was $r = .21$ for learning about issues and $r = .37$ for learning about the candidates. This is significant at the .01 level.

35. See David H. Weaver, Doris A. Graber, Maxwell E. McCombs, and Chaim H. Eyal, *Media Agenda-Setting in A Presidential Election: Issues, Images, and Interest*, New York, Praeger, 1981, p. 154; and David H. Weaver, "Political Issues and Voter Need for Orientation," in Donald Shaw and Maxwell E. McCombs (eds.), *The Emergence of American Political Issues: The Agenda-Setting Function of the Press*, St. Paul, Minn., West, 1977, pp. 107–119.

36. Walter Lippmann, *Public Opinion*, New York, Harcourt Brace, 1922.

# 7

# Strategies for Processing Political Information

What are the various mental steps involved in processing news stories so that they become part of existing schemas? And what evidence do we have that these steps actually take place? These are the main questions to be answered in this chapter. We will examine the strategies people use for processing news, for limiting it to a manageable number of incidents and details, and for categorizing and transforming these details so that they fit into pre-established or newly-created patterns.

## STAGES IN INFORMATION PROCESSING

Figure 7.1 puts the entire process into perspective. As the legends at the bottom of the diagram indicate, the process begins with physical signals that reach the individual's sensory organs. (How these signals are initially screened has been described in chapter 5.) After perception, the new information is condensed and simplified for brief storage in short-term memory—the "sensory information store" of the diagram. It then becomes part of the "data pool" which is checked against the reservoir of "memory schemata" to determine whether it can be appropriately integrated. If integration is achieved, the information becomes part of the repertoire of schemas of the individual. Failing integration, either because no suitable schema is available or created or because an overload of information prevents preliminary processing, the information passes quickly from consciousness.[1]

Adults are likely to have appropriate schemas for integrating information prevalent in their culture or subculture. Childhood socialization has taught them what kind of information is of potential interest. They have also discovered that mental simplifications are essential for digesting information, and they have

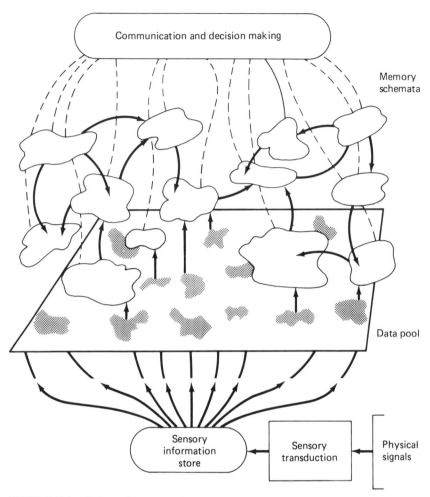

FIGURE 7.1.   Information-processing model. (From "On the Role of Active Memory Processes in Perception and Cognition" by Donald R. Norman and David G. Bobrow in *The Structure of Human Memory* edited by Charles Cofer, San Francisco, W. H. Freeman and Company, 1976, p. 118. Copyright 1976 W. H. Freeman and Company. Reprinted by permission.)

learned the types of simplifications that are appropriate and useful. Cues within the information help them to determine which schemas will be a suitable storage place for the information. For instance, a story about a fatal fire in a Hispanic neighborhood can be incorporated into general schemas about tragic unavoidable accidents, or it can become substantiation of schemas about disregard for safety in minority neighborhoods. The cues within the story are apt to cast the die. Cues within the information, as well as within the previously stored schema, also indicate how the new information should be processed to fit into established schemas or whether it requires the creation of new schemas.

The sequence of steps involved in information processing was described in greater detail by Robert Axelrod in his 1973 article on "Schema Theory: An Information Processing Model of Perception and Cognition."[2] His 11-stage model, outlined in figure 7.2, can be summarized as entailing the following steps. First comes reception of the message. Next, the integration process starts with a series of questions to determine whether and how the new information relates to stored concepts and whether it is worth processing. Does it cover a topic about which the receiver already has information? Is it a familiar or predictable consequence of familiar knowledge? Does it make sense in light of past experience? Does it convincingly contradict past experience? Is it worth considering? Is it unduly redundant? If answers to such questions indicate that the information is worthwhile and is reasonably well related to established thought schemas that can be readily brought to mind, it is integrated into them. If not, the new information or its source, maybe discredited and rejected or the new information may alter or replace the previous schema that has been called into question. The criteria which determine acceptance or rejection are discussed below.

In the process of integration, information becomes substantially transformed to make it a plausible complement to existing knowledge. Some aspects of the story are levelled and others are sharpened. Through this encoding process, elements of the story that seem essential to the perceiver are separated from non-essential details.[3] Cesar Ippolito described it this way. "I tend not to get most of the facts. I don't tend to remember them. I pick out just the things I can use in a general way. I try to integrate them into things. I tend to generalize." Expressing dissatisfaction with this approach, he continued: "I don't like that, I like to be as specific as possible." But he realized that shortcuts are essential when facing large amounts of information. "That's what has to come from reading lots of things fast and not concentrating. I can't take my time when I read the paper. I have to rush through."

Stories always lose detail and become more abstract during processing.[4] For instance, Deidre Sandelius, asked about the details of a story about marijuana use by the son of a prominent politician, replied "I don't really remember the details of the story as much as my own feelings about it." Darlene Rosswell's sole recollection of a presidential debate was that "Ford tried to cut down Carter." A series of unfavorable comments about a candidate may crystallize into the idea that "he is a loser." Information about international events may be translated into a confirmation or a denial that war is likely. A name may be forgotten but the fact that it was short or foreign or strange lingers.

Most panelists performed in this manner. They stored only a small portion of each news story. They were unable to recall even brief passages verbatim. They could not describe visual images with photographic detail. They rarely made mental notes of the specific source from which information originated. They routinely omitted recording contextual information provided along with

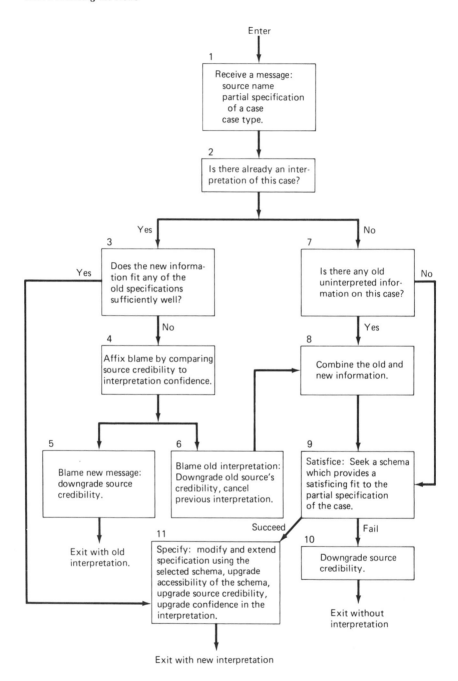

FIGURE 7.2. Process model for schema theory. (From "Schema Theory: An Information Processing Model of Perception and Cognition" by Robert Axelrod in the *American Political Science Review*, vol. 67, Spring 1973, p. 1251. Copyright 1973 the American Political Science Association. Reprinted by permission.)

the story.[5] Frequently they stored only the vaguest kind of judgments (e.g., "it sounded like a good idea," or "it made me feel uncomfortable").

During processing, information may acquire distinct slants that may make it more or less accurate. People are apt to distill information into true or false meanings and inferences and store only the distillation. Specific episodes usually become part of general concepts, with or without the loss of memory for the specific incident. This is especially true when many incidents resemble each other, as happens with routine political events.[6] For instance, a story about CIA misconduct may become part of a schema characterized as "the mess in Washington."

This type of processing is a parsimonious way of dealing with information overloads. People want to know the gist of a story; they do not want to memorize it. Since the ultimate purpose of most information gathering is the extraction of meaning, so that the significance of the story becomes apparent, it makes sense to process information for meaning right away. This saves the trouble of storing details and background information.[7] But the price that is paid is vagueness of memories, inability to recall details, and inability to separate various incidents. As Sandelius put it when she could not recall a story about a riot in the Middle East: "There's so much of that kind of thing. I can't separate one thing in my memory from the other."

The fact that people tend to store conclusions drawn from evidence, rather than the evidence itself, explains why they are frequently unable to give reasons for their opinions. They may, for example, say that they agree with the views of a particular politician without being able to give a single example of shared views. Consequently, social scientists have often erroneously concluded that the opinions were unfounded. In fact, these opinions may rest on careful earlier deliberations that have been long forgotten.[8]

The steps outlined by Axelrod entail three major types of processing strategies. They are *relatedness search, segmentation,* and *checking.* The latter two are subroutines that help in making successful relatedness searches. All of these strategies are evident in the interview protocols of each panelist, albeit in diffferent proportions. We cannot claim with complete certitude that these three types totally exhaust the repertoire of available strategies. But they were the only ones that surfaced in our research. We can say, on the basis of our extensive interview protocols, that these strategies are amply used and that they appeared to be adequate to cope with all the news processing tasks encountered in our study.

## MATCHING STRATEGIES

Relatedness search involves looking for similar situations in the individual's array of schemas. It helps people to store and to retrieve information via the "that reminds me of" route. Ordinarily, it involves three procedures: *straight matching, matching of spinoffs,* and *matching through analogies.* The process conforms to the theory of association that currently is the dominant theory of recall. "The fundamental principle of this theory is that each instance of recall is initiated by an event with which it was previously associated."[9] Schemas encompass distilled memories of such events. They are tapped when an information stimulus can be associated in some fashion with the memories encapsulated in the schema.

## Straight Matching

Straight matching involves a direct comparison of preprocessed incoming information with information already stored in memory. This will show to what extent the meanings inherent in the new information relate directly to meanings inherent in one or several existing schemas. Matching may show that the new information confirms the accuracy of existing schemas or that it raises questions about their accuracy or universality. Since schemas about current political happenings rarely encompass strong feelings and prized concerns, the panelists did not generally try to avoid dissonant information. Apparently, dissonance avoidance and active searches for supporting information come into play only when people care deeply about issues or when ego protection is involved. Perceptions and beliefs about current events rarely entail such consequences.

In fact, our interview protocols reveal that the panelists processed information just as often when it seemed to be a contrast and an exception to what they believed to be the general rule, as when it appeared to be something to be expected. Fascination with the odd, the surprising, the extraordinary is widespread. However, to be considered, information has to bear some relation to salient aspects of the schema. "Information that is undiagnostic, or irrelevant to the applicability of the schema" tends to be ignored.[10] Several panelists routinely rejected stories that seemed too familiar. Instead, they were on the look-out for deviations—the exceptions that prove the rule. Ippolito, for instance, stopped paying attention to routine campaign stories during the summer of 1976, but watched for exceptional news. "I kind of know where each of the candidates is. But if I see something that says they are going in a different direction, I'll flag it. If the man starts biting the dog, that's the kind of article I look for."

Straight matching is often acknowledged by some phrase that indicates that the new information matches expectations or past thinking and experiences. For example, Robert Creighton commented about a story about indictments for corruption in the city's sanitary district.

> It's pretty much business as usual. There's always a scandal at the sanitary district. I don't think it'll ever get cleaned up. They're people elected to public office and they are handling a tremendous amount of money and they don't get a lot of visibility. With that kind of situation, you're going to have somebody fooling around with the funds.

Similarly, stories about dirty campaigning evoked comments that these were commonly expected events. "I think it goes on in every election. Everybody always accuses everybody else of doing this, that and the other thing." Most reports about the activities of politicians were greeted with blasé acceptance. "This is typical of politicians—I expected something like that." Stories about rising rates, rising costs, rising taxes, were labelled as "old hat."

Telling companion stories was another common sign of a successful relatedness search. David Utley, for example, reacted to a story about a local tornado by telling several stories about tornadoes during his childhood. Martha Gaylord responded to a story about the Kennedy assassination with stories of other political assassinations. At times, companion stories would come from a related schema. Tugwell Quentin would follow a story about layoffs among teachers with a story about the folly of a widely-publicized school building program. A story about population growth stimulated him to recall stories about birth control and abortion. President Ford's veto of a daycare bill led Lettie Tisdale into a discussion about a columnist who had argued that mothers of young children should not work.

To make a match, people can use any one of their existing schemas or parts of schemas—"it's a bird; it's a plane; it's Superman!" The same information can be organized around specific persons, giving it a "person focus," or around situations, giving it a "situation focus."[11] Our interview protocols show very clearly that all of our panelists had favorite matching patterns, to the point where likely choices of patterns could be predicted from earlier interviews to later ones. In those instances, in which individuals had several suitable schemas available for filing particular information, schemas that had been used recently were more likely to be chosen again. Otherwise, the choice of a particular schema seemed to hinge on the interests and societal setting of the perceiver at the time the information was noted, on the cues inherent in the information, on the availability of closely matching schemas, and on their relative accessibility.[12]

Matches obviously need not be perfect. As Joseph Tanenhaus and Mary Ann Foley point out: "In recent years, psycholinguists and cognitive psychologists have come to share Wittgenstein's view that categories are 'fuzzy' rather than well bounded."[13] General shapes, rather than distinct outlines, are used for comparisons. Finding a match requires similarity along a number of dimensions. But it remains a matter for future inquiry which dimensions are used to assess similarities in particular cases and how these dimensions are chosen. Media emphases obviously play an important part. (Findings about the dimensions chosen for matching selected political concepts are reported in chapter 9.)

It is also uncertain how many dimensions need to be similar or dissimilar before a match or lack of match is perceived, but apparently a limited number of dimensions suffice. Nancy Cantor describes matching in the following manner:

> In typing an object (person, situation, self) the perceiver estimates the degree of similarity between the object and a *prototype* for each category into which the object might plausibly fit. Categorization is a probabilistic process based on *degree* of overlap in features between the new object and the prototype for each different category.[14]

Thus a person can be labelled "another Nixon" even if he is not a president and matches only a few salient characteristics and activities of his prototype.[15] Rosswell matched all stories concerning the inefficiencies of hospital staffs to just one aspect of inefficiency—unduly long waiting periods. She had developed her perceptions on that score as a result of being kept waiting for many hours in a hospital emergency room with her seriously-ill father. Whenever she encountered stories about poor hospital practices, she would sigh and say: "I know what it's like. You spend all this time, nobody says anything to you. You don't know what's going on. It's a mess." For Tisdale, every story concerning nurses immediately evoked memories of a gruesome murder case several years earlier which snuffed out the lives of eight victims.

Our study indicates that relatedness search is easier for people who have acquired a large store of information and who use it frequently than for people who lack a broad information base and practice in using it. This phenomenon has been repeatedly documented by social scientists who have observed that information rich individuals tend to acquire new information at far higher rates than is true generally of information-poor people.[16]

Relatedness search is also easier when cues to appropriate storage are supplied by the stimulus statement or have been generated by the individual. This explains why people generally find it easier to answer directed questions, rather than open-ended ones, or to recall matters once they have begun to generate their own cues through talking about a subject. Matching was easiest for our panelists when stories conformed closely to their expectations or to the ways in which they had originally committed the story to memory. Therefore, stories about economic failures in third world countries were processed more readily than stories about economic successes. Diary stories were retrieved more easily when questions about them dwelled on the same concepts that had been recorded in the diary.[17] Similarly, when information was recalled from memory, the form of the question affected not only which schemas were searched, but also the ease of recall. At times, our panelists would rephrase questions to match them more closely to their schemas, thereby making answers easier.

## Spinoffs from Episodes

Frequently, our panelists were interested primarily in spinoffs from a story, rather than the facts as such. What did it mean in terms of future events and consequences? What past or future behaviors did it suggest? What motives did it reveal? What would they have done under the circumstance? Relatedness searches then involved matching of these spinoffs. Matches were possible because schemas do not only record the status of persons and events, but also record sequences in human behavior and in the development of events, likely outcomes, as well as judgments about meanings, motivations, and merits. Incoming information may be matched against stored information for these features.[18] Such matching lends stability to judgments, but it also carries the danger of making improper generalizations. If the panelists could not evoke relevant information, they would often deduce spinoffs from news stories nonetheless and store only the spinoffs, rather than the details of the stories.

An example of ascribing previous consequences to new situations occurred when several panelists reacted to a story reporting a ceasefire in Lebanon. Rather than processing the story as part of a schema on problems in the Middle East, the panelists called on their knowledge of ceasefires in Northern Ireland. Since these had not worked well, the panelists reasoned that ceasefires never worked and that they would, therefore, fail in Lebanon, too. Similarly, from a story announcing increased subway fares, Betty Nystrom concluded that the subway system must be near bankruptcy because she recalled that rises in railroad fares had in the past signalled financial collapse of the railroads. In both instances, the conclusions drawn from spinoff matching were incorrect.

Inferences, too, may be generalized from one situation to the next. Stories about the Soviet Union's willingness to negotiate with the West were routinely interpreted as signals of economic difficulties in the Soviet Union, without re-evaluating the context of the particular incident. Fraud and corruption stories were automatically equated with lax adminstrative controls. All Southerners were presumed to be racists and their remarks were interpreted in that context. This type of reasoning avoids the necessity of fresh thinking about new situations. As happens frequently when broad generalizations are made about the outcomes of individual or collective behavior, the dangers of erroneous conclusions are substantial.

Individuals may also reason that the ways to cope with similar situations ought to be the same. Carol Fechbach, for instance, suggested that the United States should send troops to Angola to support its political friends because intervention on behalf of friendly powers had been a good policy for the United States and other powers in the past. Similarly, a number of news items involving serious political corruption by high-level officials, were characterized as "just another Watergate situation." This categorization then led to proposals that penalties should match those which the respondents deemed appropriate for the Watergate delinquents.

The panelists frequently reasoned on the basis of their schemas about human behavior that certain types of individuals or groups would act in predictable ways. For instance, our panelists expected politicians' actions to be motivated by desire to gain favorable publicity. Hence much of the information coming from politicians was processed as an example of publicity-hunting, rather than an instance of serious communication between government officials and their publics. Likewise, failures, to achieve desired results in a policy, particularly a domestic policy, were routinely, and often inappropriately, labelled by many panelists as examples of bureaucratic bungling.

If judgments have been made about the merits or ethics of a situation embedded in a schema, these may be transferred to novel situations without a re-examination of the original bases of judgment. An example of transferring judgments about the merits of the situation occurred when Karl Adams was asked to comment on a story regarding the legality of euthanasia. He said that he felt he should consider euthanasia legal since he already sanctioned abortion and capital punishment. Processing the story had involved checking his past position regarding legalized taking of human life. Again, probing existing schemas in this manner not only avoids the necessity of making new judgments, but it also increases the consistency of thinking employed in the creation and the development of schemas.

## Using Comparisons for Evaluations

At times, making comparisons becomes the chief objective of relatedness searches. When people must evaluate a policy or a public figure, they need standards for making evaluations. Comparable situations or behaviors provided such standards for our panelists. Ippolito, for example, described a story about Leicester, England, as follows: "Leicester is much like the Bronx and parts of St. Louis—parts of urban areas that are very economically depressed. It's just interesting to see that happen in England. Also they had the minority problems there—their equivalent to the black problem." Leo Evanski commented about a plan to racially integrate Chicago schools by busing children to the suburbs: "It's similar to that proposal they had in Detroit and I don't think it will ever work out. I don't think the kids will ever stand for anything like that in Chicago, or Detroit, or in Boston."

Panelists varied widely in their ability to make comparisons. If they had a few schemas available for making comparisons, they usually found it difficult to make value judgments. The most frequently encountered comparisons in our study involved presidential candidates. Many panelists judged presidential candidates by comparing them to selected predecessors. For one panelist, the ideal was Truman; for another, it was Franklin Roosevelt. In each case, the new information was matched in a rough-and-ready way against the stored information about the earlier president. When panelists were asked to evaluate the likely performance of current presidential candidates in coping with unemployment, inflation, foreign affairs, and similar problems, their judgments commonly were made on relative merit. Carter was judged in comparison to Ford. Since the point of departure of an evaluation is crucial to its outcome, it must be considered in interpreting the outcome. Unfortunately, most survey research questions fail to ask the "compared to what" question.

Several panelists were able to draw on analogies that were not readily obvious. Tugwell Quentin, when asked to evaluate big business, likened it to the military. "Business, I feel, is based on a war ethic." He then proceeded to describe business activities in terms appropriate to that metaphor. Similarly, several panelists evaluated the performance of the government by comparing it to private business. Adams, drawing on his experiences as an employee in both the private and public sector, compared the amount of work performed by private and public employees. Several panelists assessed the ethical problems presented by a physicians' strike by comparing it to strikes by lawyers and teachers.

## Apparent and Real Mismatches

Relatedness searches frequently lead to, or appear to lead to, mismatches. For instance, a story dealing with dishonesty by Medicaid providers led Betty Nystrom to comment about dishonesty by Medicaid receivers. She evidently had matched the story to the wrong schema or to the wrong part of the schema. But in that particular case, as in many others, alternative explanations were possible. Faulty memory, rather than faulty initial storing is one. A second one is that associative thinking may have been involved so that one type of fraud evoked memories of a different type of fraud (in this case, within the same program). In general, our panelists tended to connect fraud with the poor rather than the rich, especially in social service programs.[19] Hence it would be easy for Nystrom to connect fraud stories to care receivers, rather than providers.

Lane contends that three factors are apt to produce mismatches. They are *cognitive bluntness*, which occurs when people lack information; *emotional bluntness*, which results when strong emotions, such as anger or fear, block thinking; and *ideological bluntness*, which occurs when perceivers cannot interpret new information accurately because it is remote from their own beliefs.[20] This means that some types of information cannot be adequately processed by some members of the media audience.

We found numerous instances of faulty processing among our panelists when they professed that the situation in question was totally alien to their way of thinking.[21] Stories involving people and politics in third world countries were particularly susceptible to misinterpretation. The ability and even willingness to project oneself into a totally different cultural milieu appears to be quite limited, except when stereotypes are available. In the latter case, people will make projections in accordance with the stereotype. Mexicans are presumed to be lazy; Chinese are expected to be clever and industrious; African politics is imagined as primitive and corrupt. Thus, stereotyping often leads to obviously incorrect schemas and to naive theories about collective and individual human behaviors and courses of events.[22]

## News Stories as Stimuli

The kinds of straight matches that are possible when news stories are the information stimulus and the dimensions of these matches, very often hinge on the manner in which the news story presents the information. The exception is when individuals have developed strong preferences with respect to matches for specific types of news. In the case of most news stories, weak predispositions are the rule, except when the story can be matched to a personal experience. Accordingly, the mass media are one of the chief sources of cuing and their influence on matching strategies and subsequent schema development is very large. For instance, when a news story stressed the costs of nuclear weapons, our panelists were more likely to incorporate it into their schemas about defense spending, if these were available, than into their schemas about radiation dangers. They were also likely to remember those dimensions of the story that had been given greatest emphasis by the media story. This was especially true for our less well-educated and less interested panelists, who were most likely to acquiesce to cuing suggestions.[23]

People exposed to the same media sources tend to match information to the same kinds of schemas in response to the shared media cues. This explains why large numbers of stories carry similar meanings for the bulk of the media audience. A shared culture produces shared thinking without wiping out differences that spring from individual experiences and personality factors.[24] The impact of media cuing is heightened by the fact that schemas brought to the forefront of memory are more likely to be used for subsequent news stories than equally appropriate schemas that have not been recently rehearsed. Psychologists call this phenomenon "priming."[25]

Experimental evidence shows "that the criteria by which complex stimuli are judged can be profoundly altered by their prior (and seemingly incidental) activation" of one set of considerations as against another. For example, people who were asked to evaluate the president did so in terms of foreign affairs skills when recent media coverage had brought this aspect of presidential performance to the fore.[26] The topics stressed by the media, therefore, may serve as a rehearsal for relevant schemas that subsequently determine the criteria on which the public relies in evaluating politics and politicians. This can be dangerous when "the judgments people make are swayed inordinately by evidence that is incidentally salient. Conspicuous evidence is generally accorded importance exceeding its inferential value; logically consequential but perceptually innocuous evidence is accorded far less" importance than its inferential value may warrant.[27]

Similarly, during interviews and when opinion polls are taken, the cues inherent in the form of the question tend to influence which schemas are likely to be searched. Once a schema has been brought to the forefront of memory, it becomes part of the context that influences how subsequent questions are answered. This is the so-called "context effect," one that complicates the interpretation of interviews and polling results.[28] Prior questions and answers—which amount to evocation of prior schemas—influence subsequent answers, even if the questions are widely separated during an interview or within a questionnaire. These effects appear to be constant for all respondents, irrespective of their level of political information. Once a certain schema has been brought to the fore by earlier parts of an interview or questionnaire, the chances that it will be evoked again during later portions are great.

When news stories contained no obvious cues to the salience of various aspects of the story, when the story offered a variety of cues, or when panelists had their own strong predispositions, the panelists usually made their own choices. Depending on the nature of the information and the variations in their arrays of schemas, these choices were apt to differ, particularly with respect to the dimensions noted about a story. Stories about Patricia Hearst, a kidnapping victim accused of bank robbery, provided a good illustration of individual differences in selecting salient aspects of the same story.

Here is how Helga Holmquist, a law school graduate, recorded the essential elements of the story:

> Patty Hearst was kidnapped by the Symbionese Liberation Army. She subsequently seemingly adopted their viewpoint and took part in a bank robbery. Now, two years and eight months later, she is on trial for her part in that bank robbery. Her defense is that she was in fear of her life and that she was brainwashed by the SLA into adopting their viewpoint.

And here is the same story from the vantage point of Carol Fechbach, a very family-oriented young mother:

> The whole thing is so sad and I feel so sorry for the parents. It's just one of those terrible, sad things that happen that are out of your control. It's so unfair, yet there's not really anything one can do about it. I think it was horrible because it could have happened to anybody. Her whole life has been destroyed, and I don't think it was her fault.

Obviously, Holmquist stuck to legally significant details while Fechbach recorded the emotional impact of the story.

# SEGMENTATION

Segmentation is a major subroutine of ordinary matching strategies. Our panelists varied considerably in their ability and inclination to use it. *Segmentation* involves classifying stimuli in terms of similarity on separate dimensions of a stimulus, rather than on its totality. A story about changes in social security benefits for the aged, for instance, may be divided into three aspects. One may be the issue of personal versus public responsibility for the support of senior citizens. A second may be the quality of fiscal management in the public sector, and the third may be the adequacy of proposed financial support in a time of inflation. To a certain extent, segmentation occurs routinely because people rarely store all aspects of a story. Details that do not seem essential at the time and much of the context of a story are routinely separated out. This is the process called levelling and sharpening. It differs from the segmentation discussed here in that it involves a condensation of all features of a story, rather than a focusing on selected parts. Like ordinary matching strategies, segmentation involves three major approaches.

## Multiple Integration

When a complex story is broken into several components as a result of segmentation, this immediately increases the opportunities to integrate the story. This is true because one multi-faceted, complex stimulus has been transformed into several simpler, often single-faceted stimuli. For instance, a complex story about parents boycotting a school to prevent entry of students bused from a distant location does not have to be related to stories involving nearly identical situations. Instead, the story can be segmented and integrated as an example of political participation, an incident that disrupts public education, an example of radical or ethnic prejudice, or a case of sticking to accustomed practices at all costs. Each of these distinct perspectives, inherent in the story, provides an opportunity for integrating it into a different schema. Instead of having only one possibility for matching the story, there are four.

Several of these opportunities may be seized concurrently. Max Jackman's comments about a story on the defense budget are illustrative. He said that "there are two ways of looking at national defense. One is whether we need to keep up with Russia. More importantly, national defense is the biggest make-work program we have. And no one ever says that. I think one out of four people are involved in defense work or something like it." Rather than evaluating the defense budget as a matter of spending specific sums of money, he had chosen two other facets as bases for evaluation: (1) parity in defense capabilities and (2) the economic consequences of defense spending.

Multiple integrations make it easier to assimilate complex stories because a wider array of options becomes available when a variety of schemas can be tapped.[29] They also make it far easier to retrieve these stories in response to questions. As long as questions correspond to at least one of the schemas associated with the information, the story becomes available for retrieval.

At times, our panelists reconsidered their original processing decisions or expanded the number of schemas employed in a situation after mulling over their initial processing decisions. This happened either spontaneously or following later questions. Panelists repeatedly remarked that they had changed their mind about their original perspectives for processing information. For example, one panelist told us about viewing street crime as a matter of individual wrong doing until he became immersed in Marxism. Ample exposure to Marxist theories, coupled with receptiveness to change, encouraged him to revise earlier schemas and regard street crime as a consequence of capitalism. The process of checking, discussed below, is one way of systematically looking for different ways to store segmented information.

## Multiple Judgments

Segmentation may also be used to facilitate spinoff operations and comparisons. For instance, people frequently receive information about a situation or individual and want to store value judgments about the information. Many of our panelists found it difficult to make global judgments. Instead, if they were capable of making the intellectual effort involved in segmentation, they preferred to make a series of judgments.

For example, Adams, when trying to judge President Nixon's place in history, said that it was impossible to give an unsegmented assessment. It was his view that "Nixon is going to be one of our most famous presidents as well as one of our most infamous. I always thought he was not given enough credit for a lot of things he did, and too much credit for things he didn't do." Craig Kolarz, commenting on Governor Jerry Brown's refusal to live in the governor's mansion, noted "It could be a political scheme to make him look like he doesn't want to take the public's money, but maybe he really feels that way. I think it's 90% genuine and 10% to get votes and attention."

Panelists frequently segmented their judgments when assessing the merits of government intervention in various societal enterprises. Normally, there were many options. For example, government operation was judged as both good and bad, depending on whether it was viewed from the perspective of the poor or the middle-class. Alternatively, it might be judged both advisable and inadvisable by considering first the benefits of nationwide uniformity and then the high costs of national bureaucracies. Using a simpler approach, a single perspective might be selected as a basis for judgment.

## Restricted Perspectives

Segmentation may also be undertaken to limit, rather than to expand, opportunities for integrating information. There are three major reasons for limiting processing in this way. *Limited knowledge* is one. In many instances, our panelists were only familiar with one aspect of the information or one perspective on it. They segmented this particular element out of the situation because it was the only one for which they had an available schema.

More commonly, limited processing occurred because it saved labor. The individual needed only to file selected segments of a complex story. The rest of the segments could then be discarded. For instance, several panelists automatically filed news of street crime on the basis of racial categories of likely offenders and victims. This allowed them to fit the news neatly into their established racial stereotypes avoiding the effort of more complex and varied encodings.

Our panelists' appraisals of political candidates typically were segmented along a severely restricted number of dimensions. One dimension that was often used in isolation was the candidate's ability to win. Judgments about the candidates' merits also were frequently expressed as a single quality. Carter was characterized as bland, fuzzy, or honest; Ford was a "klutz"; Reagan was rich, inexperienced, or an actor. Several panelists looked only at party labels, ignoring all other aspects of categorization. Of course, expressing a one-dimensional characterization does not always mean that perception is one-dimensional. Other dimensions may be left unexpressed or the single expressed dimensions may be a condensation symbol. For instance, the party label, or the "actor" designation may encompass many dimensions which become apparent when further questions are asked.

The third reason for limiting perspectives relates to people's desire to *absorb* only *information* that is *of special interest* to them. There were many examples of such restricted perspectives. For example, several of our panelists reacted to

Mideast stories only in terms of their impact on the state of Israel. Panelists, who were particularly concerned about energy problems, often reacted to the same stories only in terms of their impact on the price and supply of oil to the United States. Panelists who had gone to law school shut out most of the Patty Hearst story except for the legal details. Panelists without legal training shut out all legal details, claiming that they were overly complex and boring. Several panel members expressed disinterest in the lurid aspects of a sex scandal involving a Congressman. Elaine Mullins commented: "What he does in his personal life, that he pays for himself, is up to him. I don't care to know about that. But when it comes down to me as a taxpayer paying for his mistress—no way! I wanna know where our money's going."

When only limited numbers of story segments are integrated, it may be difficult to retrieve them if the retrieval stimulus is couched into terms appropriate for a different segment. For instance, several of our panelists coded specific items of information about candidates only in terms of "effectiveness." If later questions about candidates were then asked in different terms, it often was difficult for panelists to retrieve the story. This problem accounted for the common practice of rephrasing a question in terms that linked it more readily to available schema. For instance, a series of questions about various traits of a candidate often was parried by the question: "Are you asking me if he is an effective candidate?" A "yes" answer than facilitated retrieving the effectiveness schema.

## CHECKING

Checking is the third major processing strategy. It involves going beyond the first schema that comes to mind for storing or retrieving and continuing to search for additional schemas needed to complete processing or to provide better alternatives. Evidence of checking comes to the fore when people "think out loud," examining several possibilities. Checking appears to be a "satisficing" rather than a "maximizing" endeavor.[30] This means that our panelists examined only a limited number of options, rather than running through the full gamut of possibilities. Their ability to locate appropriate schemas quickly varied with their general intellectual abilities and with the degree of familiarity with a particular situation. The result of the checking procedure, as well as the procedure itself, appears to be stored in memory. This conclusion is based on the fact that panelists tended to replicate checking procedures when confronted with similar information.

### Improving the Fit

The two main reasons for checking are to *acquire a better schema fit* for storage or retrieval of information and to *create a broader basis* for making judgments. Penny Liebman, for instance, in trying to make sense out of a story about the secretary of state's Latin American trip, wondered out loud if this was akin to his peacekeeping missions to the Middle East, a journey designed to assist American business or, perhaps, just a public relations venture. Betty Nystrom also checked several alternatives in trying to identify George Bush, then the head of the CIA: "He wasn't Ford's—no; was he—no; was he a judge from Illinois? From around here?"

Checking also helps in making judgments about individuals, institutions, and policies. For instance, when asked to appraise media performance, our panelists would frequently check through several areas of performance and then follow with either an overall or a segmented judgment. Newspapers were generally praised for the completeness of their stories, but condemned for sensationalism on the one hand and dullness on the other. Television earned praise for the quality of its pictorial coverage and condemnation for the sketchiness of news presentations and the lack of follow-up stories.

Several examples of checking to broaden the basis of judgment occurred when campaign stories raised questions about specific policies that the candidates might pursue in the future. Initially, most panelists assessed the personal characteristics of each candidate. Then, they speculated as to what a president with such a personality would be likely to do, given the circumstances in which his actions would take place. Finally, they checked the plausibility of their projections by comparing them to schemas about actions by previous presidents.[31]

Checking also aids in retrieving information from memory. For instance, in trying to remember what one has learned about the effects of budget cuts, one need not stop with the first policy area that comes to mind. Rather, one can check several policy areas (e.g., education, child welfare, or defense expenditures) to look for a variety of examples concerning the effects of budget cuts. One can then weigh these examples together or come up with the best example to make a particular point. Our panelists frequently gave one example and, when it proved defective, moved on to other ones that seemed better to them. If an extended search did not yield better examples, our panelists often returned to their initial choice, acknowledging that their first idea had been best after all.

## Rambling

For several of our panelists, checking appeared to be an inadvertent procedure that led to aimless rambling. For example, Rosswell drifted from a discussion of workers' performance in governmental offices, to tensions among racially-different groups, to problems of school racial integration, to teenage pregnancy. Nystrom responded to a story about United States' policy in the Middle East with the comment: "I am afraid that we are going to get into war over there. I feel sorry for those poor boys who lost their lives in Korea. And my nephew was wounded in Vietnam." Each switch could be readily traced to a key word that led to the recall of the next new schema. At the end of the mental journey, both panelists had forgotten the initial question and asked to hear it again. Obviously, this type of checking is a hindrance to clear thinking, rather than a help. It does, howewver, provide interesting clues to casual linkages among various schemas.

## THE CHOICE OF PROCESSING STRATEGIES

Which of the various cognitive procedures is undertaken, by itself or in combination, depends on the individual's cognitive style. This, in turn, is related to intellectual abilities and experience. Straightforward matching, without segmentation or checking, appeared to be the most commonly used and easiest strategy. It was employed by all panelists, regardless of their educational and intellectual achievements. It led to the highest incidence of inability to process information.

When our panelists could segment information, and chose to do so, it almost always seemed possible to incorporate information into established thinking processes. We reached this conclusion because panelists, whose answers exhibited ample segmentation skills, were rarely at a loss to comment in some way about the news to which they paid attention. By contrast, panelists whose statements showed little evidence of segmentation skills frequently were unable to answer questions about information to which they had been exposed. They also told us more often that they had ignored media information because they could not make sense out of it than did panelists more skilled in segmentation.

Checking appeared to be an even rarer tactic. Direct questions about whether or not checking had taken place generally yielded negative answers. Comparatively few panelists gave evidence of habitually running through a diversity of perspectives to arrive at the best schema for incorporating the information, or to provide the best responses to questions. However, this impression may be incorrect. It is possible that much checking, that was never articulated, occurred.

Checking seemed to be used most by two types of people: (1) those who were generally open-minded and (2) those who lacked confidence in their opinions. The open-minded people seemed to be looking for all possible alternatives since they were not prone to stereotypical information processing. The unsure ones seemed to lack confidence in the accuracy of their interpretation of a situation and hence continued to look for better answers.

## PROCESSING DIFFICULTIES

### Questionable and Difficult Information

Information that could not be processed readily through these three procedures often was rejected outright or resulted in unanswered questions and subsequent rejection of the information. The panelists occasionally suspected that the real meaning of stories had been deliberately concealed, making it unwise to process the information. For instance, a report that the governor had inexplicably endorsed a certain candidate elicited the comment: "I was surprised . . . and leery . . . what does he want?" Other phrases commonly used were "It doesn't make sense or "I can't figure it out." Adams, for example, did not know how to process a story about the building of huge bomb shelters in the Soviet Union. Accordingly, he commented:

> They could shelter 60 million citizens, industrial workers, moving all their industries to the suburbs, hardening missile sites, and things like that. When people start doing things like that, that worries me. I can't see why. I don't see that the U.S. has given them any reason in the last five years to think that we're going to bomb them back to the Stone Age or anything like that. And the only thing I can conclude from all these preparations is that they are preparing for something. But I can't figure what.

Panelists also told us that they frequently rejected stories if they expected to have difficulty with processing them. Tugwell Quentin, for instance, did not process a story about Senator Hubert Humphrey's quest for the job of Senate majority leader. "I really didn't see it in any context. I didn't have a frame of reference for it. I didn't know why it was important. It didn't strike a responsive chord. I didn't have any knee-jerk reaction to it." Similarly, Sandra Ornstein claimed that she got nothing out of watching the presidential nominating conventions on television. "There again, I don't even know what political people expect out of an acceptance speech. I don't know what format they are supposed to follow, or if there is a format they are supposed to follow, or what they are supposed to say."

Many stories were routinely ignored by most panelists because they seemed overly complex or totally unfamiliar. The bulk of news from abroad fell into that category. Most panelists admitted that they did not even try to make sense out of stories from far-off places. They automatically assumed that such stories would be complicated and dull. Doubts about the accuracy of stories also led to rejection. Holmquist said that she never paid attention to stories reporting unemployment statistics. She was "skeptical on two fronts. The figures don't reflect all the people out of work and they also include a lot of people who are the second member of a family, people looking for part-time work, and so on." Since she felt that she had no way to get corrective information, she chose to ignore stories of that type. Several panelists said that they always anticipated difficulties whenever they encountered news that appeared to be part of a continuing story to which initially they had not paid attention. Under those circumstances, they preferred to ignore the story. Others complained that story details were insufficient for processing. Martha Gaylord, for instance, said she could get only "bits and pieces" about the renegotiation of the Panama Canal treaty. This was insufficienct to "put it all together . . . I think the media never really get into the meat of the story. So I'm not familiar with the real guts of the story."

## Schema Alterations

Processing difficulties may also arise because new information questions the accuracy of existing schemas. In that case, rather than discarding the information, the existing schemas may be discarded or revised substantially. Whether the new information will be accepted, or existing conceptions retained, depends on a variety of factors. These include the complexity of the judgments that must be made in determining the merits of old and new conceptions, the amount and quality of old and new information, and the personal and social factors that buttress the old schema and support the newer one. The degree of receptivity to changes and the confidence respondents have in their own judgments also are important factors. In line with the predictions of most theories on attitude change, major schema revisions are resisted unless there are strong social or circumstantial pressures for revision.[32]

Sandra Ornstein's position is representative. Asked why she thinks that all politicians are crooked, she replied: "I just think that's inherent in me. I've known it for so long, and . . . most people say that politicians are crooks. And I do think that after all these years, being an old lady, I really think that it's just *in* me. I don't think that I could change anymore."

Though persistence is the rule, all our panelists regularly reported that they had revised their views about a limited number of political phenomena, particularly when a lapse of time or new events provided ready justification for the change. Donald Burton, for example, changed his mind about giving mail subsidies to charitable organizations after reading a story about a religious order that lost money in stock speculations. Tugwell Quentin reported that he had, in the past, approved of the death penality. But, after reading many stories about individuals who had been condemned to death, he had come to the conclusion that the penalty was barbaric. The phrases "I used to think so-and-so until" or "I suppose the world is changing," were quite common in our interview transcripts.

People frequently named a crucial event to which they ascribed their altered outlook. This event had become a new context for making judgments.[33] The assassination of John F. Kennedy, the Vietnam war, and Watergate were the most commonly named catalysts for schema changes involving political disillusionment. Many panelists also attributed major revisions of their political schemas to growing maturity. They reported that they used to think that political life conformed to the Ten Commandments, but that prolonged exposure to news about politics had altered these perceptions. Change appeared to be a gradual process for the most part, but could also be abrupt, linked to specific direct or vicarious experiences.

However, change of established schemas is troublesome, especially when schemas are based on personal experiences or on judgments accepted from highly trusted sources. Change involves the trouble of re-thinking the situation and revising the existing schema or tying the situation into a different schema in the person's cognitive structure. It may involve having to admit that one has been wrong in the past or laying oneself open to charges of inconsistency.[34] When concepts are interrelated, alteration in one schema may involve the need to alter others as well. New ideas may upset stereotyped response patterns. As Lane puts it, "Changing ideas is a strain not to be lightly incurred, particularly when these ideas are intimately related to one's self-esteem. The less education one has, the harder it is to change such ideas."[35]

For all these reasons, our panelists seemed reluctant, though never totally unwilling to change their schemas. Even Adams, one of the most erudite, refused to alter his judgment about President Kennedy despite compelling new evidence that indicated that Kennedy had failed in matters of great concern to him. Other panelists denied the validity of information or argued that it was an exception. This allowed the panelists to avoid changing their schemas while still maintaining consistency between the schema and the apparently discordant information. Sandelius, for example, who held highly favorable views of police, denied reports that police had violated somebody's civil rights: "That's a bunch of baloney." In response to a dissonant report that the police did not reach an accident scene quickly enough, she responded: "I'm sure there's got to be a lot going on in a situation like that. They're not all angels. But on the whole, I think the cops are doing a good job."

## Coping with Evaluation Difficulties

When our panelists had difficulties in finding appropriate schemas to make evaluations, they occasionally resorted to using generalized decision rules. Some of these were expressed in slogans or common sense logic. "It's darkest before the dawn"; "Once a loser, always a loser"; or "If it has not happened before, it is not likely to happen." For example, in trying to assess the safety of nuclear power plants, panelists commonly admitted that they were not competent to judge the merits of the situation. Nonetheless, several panelists pronounced the use of nuclear power as safe on the grounds that no major disasters had occurred in the past. Hence, none were likely in the future. Political candidates were routinely declared to be honest on the grounds that no information about corruption had been uncovered. Sven Peterson inferred that the United States Steel company was a major environmental polluter because the company was the subject of a suit by the federal government: "I would have to assume that they have a case or they wouldn't go through with all this nonsense."

When the accuracy of incoming information was in doubt, which happens often when political information is involved, our panelists used several ways to reassure themselves that the information was worth processing. A common approach for validating the information was to assess the credibility of the source. Information coming from credible sources, like a trusted politician or television commentator, was pronounced credible for that reason. Another approach involved testing the information for logical consistency with previously acquired information. If the information appeared to be reasonably consistent, it was labelled as likely to be accurate and processed accordingly. Checks of logical consistency of old and new information appeared to be reserved only for news that seemed doubtful initially.

Several panelists had routines for testing the logic of new information. Adams, for instance, played devil's advocate. As he put it: "It's my method to take the opposite view to see what holes can be put in that argument. By that method, it's easier to understand your own position and see where the faults in your own reasoning lie." He applied the devil's advocate technique not only to incoming information but also to the schemas that he had already stored. Most other panelists were content to leave their schemas untested except when undeniably conflicting information appeared to make a reappraisal imperative.

## Notes

1. W. Lance Bennett, "Perception and Cognition: An Information-Processing Framework for Politics," in Samuel L. Long (ed.), *The Handbook of Political Behavior*, 1, 1979, pp. 130–131; Roy Lachman, Janet L. Lachman, and Earl C. Butterfield, *Cognitive Psychology and Information Processing: An Introduction*, Hillsdale, N.J., Lawrence Erlbaum, 1979, pp. 415, 436.

2. Robert Axelrod, "Schema Theory: An Information Processing Model of Perception and Cognition," *American Political Science Review*, 67, 1973, pp. 1248–1266.

3. Bennett, as cited in note 1, p. 160; Lachman et al., as cited in note 1, p. 415. Also see, Percy H. Tannenbaum, "The Indexing Process in Communications," *Public Opinion Quarterly*, 19, 1955, pp. 292–302.

4. J. Richard Eiser. *Cognitive Social Psychology: A Guidebook to Theory and Research*, New York, McGraw-Hill, 1980, p. 94; Lachman et al., as cited in note 1, p. 415.

5. Robert E. Lane, *Political Ideology: Why the American Common Man Believes What He Does*, New York, Free Press, 1962, pp. 350–353. Lane has noted that people tend to morselize, rather than contextualize information.

6. Roger C. Schank and Robert P. Abelson, *Scripts, Plans, Goals, and Understanding: An Inquiry Into Human Knowledge Structures*, Hillsdale, N.J., Lawrence Erlbaum, 1977, p. 19.

7. Ibid., p. 163.

8. For a discussion of the inadequacies of measures for gauging the public's knowledge about candidates see, Thomas E. Mann and Raymond E. Wolfinger, "Candidates and Parties in Congressional Elections," *American Political Science Review*, 74, 1980, p. 631.

9. Solomon E. Asch, "The Process of Free Recall," in Constance Scheerer (ed.), *Cognition: Theory, Research, Promise*, New York, Harper & Row, 1964, p. 80.

10. Reid Hastie, "Schematic Principles in Human Memory," in E. Tory Higgins, C. Peter Herman, and Mark P. Zanna (eds.), *Social Cognition: The Ontario Symposium*, vol. 1, Hillsdale, N.J., Lawrence Erlbaum, 1981, p. 75. (Also see pp. 62–66.)

11. Nancy A. Cantor, "A Cognitive-Social Approach to Personality," in Nancy Cantor and John F. Kihlstrom (eds.), *Personality, Cognition, and Social Interaction*, Hillsdale, N.J., Lawrence Erlbaum, 1981, pp. 30–31.

12. E. Tory Higgins and Gillian King, "Accessibility of Social Constructs: Information Processing Consequences of Individual and Contextual Variability," in Nancy Cantor and John F. Kihlstrom (eds.), *Personality, Cognition, and Social Interaction*, Hillsdale, N.J., Lawrence Erlbaum, 1981, p. 70.

13. Joseph Tanenhaus and Mary Ann Foley, "Separating Objects of Specific and Diffuse Support: Experiments on Presidents and the Presidency," *Micropolitics*, 1, 1981, p. 351.

14. Cantor, as cited in note 11, p. 36.

15. Ibid., pp. 38–39; Higgins and King, as cited in note 12, p. 73.

16. Philip J. Tichenor, George A. Donohue, and Clarice A. Olien, "Mass Media Flow and Differential Growth in Knowledge," *Public Opinion Quarterly*, 34, Summer 1970, pp. 159–170.

17. See Lachman et al., as cited in note 1, pp. 280–282 for a discussion of the "encoding specificity" phenomenon.

18. Lachman et al., as cited in note 1, p. 415.

19. Lane, as cited in note 5, p. 330, reports similar findings.

20. Ibid.

21. Eiser, as cited in note 4, p. 8.

22. Walter Mischel, "Personality and Cognition: Something Borrowed, Something New?" in Nancy Cantor and John F. Kihlstrom (eds.), *Personality, Cognition, and Social Interaction*, Hillsdale, N.,J., Lawrence Erlbaum, 1981, p. 14.

23. George Bishop, Robert W. Oldendick, and Alfred J. Tuchfarber, "Effects of Presenting One versus Two Sides of an Issue in Survey Questions," *Public Opinion Quarterly*, 46, 1982, p. 78.

24. Experimental evidence shows that such cuing does indeed take place. See, Peter B. Warr and Christopher Knapper, *The Perception of People and Events*, New York, Wiley, 1968, pp. 258–264.

25. Shanto Iyengar, Mark D. Peters, and Donald Kinder, "Experimental Demonstrations of the 'Not-So-Minimal' Consequences of Television News Programs," *American Political Science Review*, 76, December 1982, pp. 852–853; also Higgins and King, as cited in note 12; and Allan M. Collins and Elizabeth F. Loftus, "A Spreading-Activation Theory of Semantic Processing," *Psychological Review*, 82, 1975, pp. 407–428.

26. Iyengar et al., as cited in note 25, p. 856; also Higgins and King, as cited in note 12. Also see, Donald R. Kinder, Shanto Iyengar, John A. Krosnick, and Mark D. Peters, "More than Meets the Eye: The Impact of Television News on Evaluation of Presidential Performance," *Midwest Political Science Association Paper*, 1983.

27. Iyengar et al., as cited in note 25, p. 855; also see, Shelley E. Taylor and Susan T. Fiske, "Salience, Attention and Attribution: Top of the Head Phenomena," in Leonard Berkowitz (ed.), *Advances in Experimental Social Psychology*, vol. 2, New York, Academic Press, 1978; Leslie Zebrowitz McArthur, "What Grabs You? The Role of Attention in Impression Formation and Causal Attribution," in E. Tory Higgins, C. Peter Herman, and Mark P. Zanna (ed.), *Social Cognition: The Ontario Symposium*, vol. 1, Hillsdale, N.J., Erlbaum, 1981.

28. Bishop et al., as cited in note 23; George Bishop, Robert W. Oldendick, and Alfred G. Tuchfarber, "Political Information Processing: Question Order and Context Effects," *Political Behavior*, 4, 1982, pp. 177–120. For a contrary finding, which argues that prior questions do not necessarily provide context, see, Lee Sigelman, "Question-Order Effects on Presidential Popularity," *Public Opinion Quarterly*, 45, Summer 1981, pp. 199–207.

29. See Herman A. Witkin, "Origins of Cognitive Style," in Constance Scheerer (ed.), *Cognition: Theory, Promise*, New York, Harper & Row, 1964, pp. 436–441.

30. The terms "satisficing" and "maximizing" have been borrowed from Herbert Simon, *Models of Man*, New York, Wiley, 1957.

31. Schank and Ableson, as cited in note 6, p. 70. They call such mental constructs "plans."

32. The extensive literature on attitude change is relevant here. See, for example, Chester A. Insko, *Theories of Attitude Change*, New York, Appleton-Century-Crofts, 1967; Richard E. Petty, Thomas M. Ostrom, and Timothy C. Brock, (eds.), *Cognitive Responses in Persuasion*, Hillsdale, N.J., Lawrence Erlbaum, 1981 (especially parts 2 and 3); and Richard Nisbett and Lee Ross, *Human Inference: Strategies and Shortcomings of Social Judgment*, Englewood Cliffs, N.J., Prentice-Hall, 1980, pp. 167–192. A simplified discussion is presented in Richard E. Petty and John T. Cacioppo, *Attitudes and Persuasion: Classic and Contemporary Approaches*, Dubuque, Iowa, Wm. C. Brown, 1981.

33. Bennett, as cited in note 1, p. 165.

34. J. B. Tedeschi, J. B. Schlenker, and T. Bonoma, "Cognitive Dissonance: Private Ratiocination or Public Spectacle," *American Psychologist*, 26, 1971, pp. 685–695.

35. Lane, as cited in note 5, p. 73.

# 8

## Thinking Categories: Their Origin and Substance

### HOW SCHEMAS ORIGINATE

Schemas represent social learning. Like other forms of learning, schemas are acquired from early childhood onward through overt teaching or operant conditioning and through imitating behavior observed in others. They may also result from independent discovery through actual personal experiences or through abstract reasoning processes.[1] Existing schemas may be expanded and refined in the same manner when direct and indirect experiences challenge their accuracy and completeness. Indirect experiences, that may lead to schema creation or modification, include mass media stories.

For example, Darlene Rosswell developed a schema about nursing homes on the basis of a media story about a disastrous nursing home fire. The fire was set by an attendant who had a past record of arson. Rosswell remembered the story ten months later because "I was not aware before of the problems nursing homes had." Independent reasoning expanded the schema beyond the facts included in the news story. Accordingly, Rosswell continued: "I'm sure that nursing homes don't pay very well, so they get any help they can without looking into the background of people. And I was not aware before that they probably just take anyone that applies to the job because they are short of help."

Schema creation and modification has been described by cognitive psychologists David Rumelhart and Donald Norman as follows:

> The typical course of such a learning process consists of an initial creation of a new schema by modeling it on an existing schema. The new schema, however, is not perfect. It may occasionally mispredict events and otherwise be inadequate. We then believe that the newly acquired schema undergoes a process of refinement that we have dubbed *tuning*.

Rumelhart and Norman point out that traces of the old schema, that are not overtly inconsistent with the new situation, are likely to be carried over to it. They note:

> It is through such carrying-over that the analogical process is both powerful and prone to error. Carrying over existing features of existing schemata allows us to make inferences about the new situation without explicit knowledge of the new situation. It allows us to learn a good deal very quickly. It also can lead to error.[2]

Most people have the capacity to "take in and interpret perceptual experiences, to draw inferences and implications and to make predictions from them, to attribute causality and to reshuffle old ideas into novel combinations without benefit of new perceptual input."[3] People can, in this way, develop their schemas either through restructuring information they already have, by using hindsight and reflection, or through incorporating new information into existing schemas.[4] Like other behaviors, schema creation and development needs to be practiced. Levels of proficiency are related to the extent of practice, to environmental conditions, and to intellectual abilities.

The fact that schemas that are developed in childhood are likely to shape future intellectual development throughout life drives home the importance of preadult socialization as a source of good or evil. As Charles Lindblom has warned, socialization is not always benign. It possibly "is intellectually confining, is sometimes crippling, may reduce understanding, and may obstruct the development of skill in evaluation." Worse, it may be "an instrument through which the advantaged, with their advantages in the control of communications, teach the disadvantaged to accept their disadvantages."[5]

Schema acquisition bears the imprint of the particular culture in which learning takes place.[6] Hence, children raised in the same culture learn the schemas common to their culture and the processing strategies that lead to them. The cultural imprint is further deepened throughout life because information sources reflect general cultural or subcultural values. Ultimately, the schema system is, in Lane's words, an "enormous brain-filling, painfully learned store of principles, doctrine, dogma, premises, values, theories, prejudices, habits, codes, defenses, and the like" developed and passed on by people who share common experiences and processing rules.[7]

Schemas that are culture-bound include ideas about the appropriate times and places for events to take place and ideas about minutiae of behavior expected from people who participate in these events. They encompass ideas about the causes of good and evil and the ways to cope with the everyday vagaries of life. They also include ideas about the purpose of life and broad norms of behavior to be followed by human beings, singly and in groups, in a variety of social roles.[8] The culture, as Lane points out, may give didactic answers to many social problems. Thus, the young may learn that poverty comes from ignorance and lack of education, that unemployment is the consequence of laziness, social malfunctions, or fate. They may learn which dimensions of a given situation are worth noting and which can be safely ignored.[9] "There is a culturally given metaphysics, an ethics, an epistemology, and a value scheme."[10]

The fact that the bulk of schemas are apparently learned early through socialization in the culture may explain why, generally speaking, people express little surprise about happenings. They have learned what to expect and view situations from perspectives that make situations conform to expectations. Ongoing events, whether experienced directly or vicariously through media stories, "are easily interpreted and explained by" reference to a culturally-shared philosophy that is "in accord with an ethical scheme," that has been internalized since childhood.[11]

Once established, schemas resist disconfirmation. According to Shelley Taylor and Jennifer Crocker, "Disconfirming instances of a schema rarely lead to revision of the basic schema itself, but rather provide a basis for differentiation of the schema." As an example, Taylor and Crocker describe a man who believes that women are docile, quiet, and unintelligent. If such a man meets a woman who contradicts the stereotype, he rarely changes his schema. "Rather, he may simply develop a new stereotype such as "castrating female" or "career woman," keeping his original stereotype for most women and considering his new stereotype to be a kind of exception to the rule. Eventually, as his experience increases, the number of stereotypes he has available also increases—mother, princess, bitch, castrating female, showgirl—and any behavior a female performs can fit within at least one of these stereotypic conceptions without disconfirming the overarching stereotype."[12]

Since schemas become guides to information selection, the dimensions that they exclude are apt to be ignored in subsequent information processing. Hence, the odds favor schema maintenance over schema growth or creation of new schemas.[13] When one asks whether we "use the data our senses bring to us to construct hypotheses about how the world works," or whether we use our hypotheses about how the world works to determine what data to process, the answer, of course, is that people do both. But, as Taylor and Crocker point out, "at least in the adult social perceiver, hypothesis-driven processing is very much the rule, being both common and maximally efficient."[14] In the simpler words of Lippmann,

> For the most part, we do not first see, and then define, we define first and then see. In the great blooming, buzzing confusion of the outer world, we pick out what our culture has already defined for us, and we tend to perceive that which we have picked out in the form stereotyped for us by our culture.[15]

Early acquisition and hardening of schemas may explain why people carry social consciousness norms throughout life, rather than thinking predominantly in terms of self-interest. Children learn to think in terms of social rather than personal benefits, and the mass media reinforce this inclination. "In adulthood, then, they (children) respond in a highly affective way to symbols which resemble the attitude objects to which similar emotional responses were conditioned or associated in earlier life. Whether or not the issue has some tangible consequence for the adult voter's personal life is irrelevant."[16] Accordingly, economic policies and racial policies, among others, are evaluated in sociotropic terms, contrary to the predictions of rational choice theorists.[17]

Most people rely primarily on culturally provided explanations because they lack the interest, and often the capacity, to break out of the cultural norms and think independently. On the whole, most people tend to be conventional and conforming. Such "perceptual habitation in politics . . . may well account for the stereotypical perception of social problems."[18] Society, therefore, may depend for timely major changes on people who take idiosyncratic views of reality and who are willing to form and propound schemas that diverge widely from cultural norms. Unique experiences and a bent for non-conformist thoughts and actions characterize such individuals. However, as discussed in the previous chapter, willingness to make occasional changes is not limited to a few unique individuals. Most of our panelists were willing at times to make major changes in their schemas, particularly when they thought that social conditions were changing in significant ways. A few people routinely reevaluated their schemas. Sven Peterson, for instance, told us "I tend to look back on things in retrospect and see what happened. I'm not very good at evaluating things right at the moment."

## THE SUBSTANCE OF SCHEMAS—A BRIEF REVIEW

Before describing typical features of the schemas encountered in the interview protocols, several basic features of all types of schemas need to be recalled. At the simplest level as described in chapter 2, schemas are commonsense models of the life situations that an individual has experienced directly or vicariously. They contain information about the substantive elements usually encountered in the situation and the likely interaction of these elements. Since they are sharply stripped-down versions of reality, the average schema has only a limited number of basic components.[19]

For instance, among our panelists, schemas about various public policies generally revolved around five dimensions. There were (1) statements about who or what caused particular problems; (2) statements about the nature of institutions involved in the policy; (3) statements concerning the role played by human actors; (4) statements about the policy in terms of cultural values; and (5) statements about the policy's relation to humanistic concerns.

To give an example, when the panelists discussed stories about defense policies of the Ford administration, collectively their reports exhibited the following aspects: (1) statements about the causes that prompted high defense expenditures; (2) statements about rivalries between the United States and the Soviet Union that had produced severe tensions; (3) statements about the role of the President in coping with the problems; (4) statements about the need to preserve the American way of life from communism; and (5) statements about the need to protect helpless people from communist tyranny. (Chapter 9 presents additional, more detailed examples.)

Extensive probing failed to disclose other aspects. The schemas articulated by individual panelists usually had fewer than five dimensions. In the case of defense policy, the most commonly used aspect was evaluation of the policy in terms of its effects of the danger of war and the consequences for the nation and the panelists' future. Discussion of the interrelation of defense spending and social welfare spending also was common. Schemas were rarely organized in terms of its effects of the danger on war and the consequences for the nation and Marxism and capitalism. The reason is that average Americans do not usually learn to think in these ways.[20] (Later in this chapter, the discussion will point to several other dimensions that might have been chosen for processing but that were avoided.)

It should not be surprising that schemas dealing with current affairs are simple when compared to many other types of schemas.[21] The average person lacks direct experience with the complexities of politics. The information from which schemas are largely built is indirect, coming primarily from the mass media. Although it is available in massive amounts, it lacks the richness and diversity of natural situations. It frequently stresses dimensions that have little interest for most members of the media audience and it is deficient in contextual information that would make political situations more understandable. In addition, or perhaps because of these shortcomings, the development and enrichment of political schemas is not a very high priority for most people most of the time. Rather, it is a chore performed with little enthusiam and limited expenditure of effort.

Accepting the fact that political schemas tend to be simple, and often simplistic, they nevertheless vary in richness depending on the nature of the subject matter, the main sources of relevant information, and the intellectual capabilities of individuals. For situations that are familiar, yet laced with excitement, and that are frequently in the news, such as street crime, schemas tend to be richer and more complex than when situations are unfamiliar and bland and receive little publicity (e.g., trade policy). In many instances, of course, schemas contain information that is absent from routine news stories. We have already mentioned that our panelists were able to talk about causes of reported crimes even when news stories did not.[22] This added information came from accumulated past information and from independent reasoning based on stored data.

Schemas based largely on information gleaned from television tend to be less diverse than schemas based on print information. Schemas distilled from direct experiences, rather than indirect presentations, were likely to be richest of all. When experiences are direct, an intelligent, sensitive perceiver has a chance to observe the complexity of various aspects of the situation and to select those features and perspectives which hold greatest personal interest. People who are able to segment information and engage in checking also tend to have more complex and richer schemas than their less intellectually sophisticated fellows.[23]

## THE INTERRELATION OF SCHEMAS

In general, the interview protocols provide little evidence of schema organization into major, logically coherent patterns. To use a set of terms developed by Lane, our panelists did not have overarching interrelated beliefs but, instead, were either "morselizing" or contextualizing" information.[24] This means that most, though by no means all, such schemas about various current events appeared to be either totally isolated or embedded in limited contexts. They were not viewed as part of a large social tapestry in which all pieces were meaningfully interrelated. For example, the image of government as inefficient was free-standing for some panelists and linked to the notion of inefficiency of all large institutions by others. But it was rarely part of an overall conception of how human beings interact in a capitalist or socialist society.

Bem ascribes the prevalence of morselized thinking to the fact that much political information is acquired primarily for social interactions, rather than from a desire to know.

> Opinion molecules . . . are conversational units. They give us something coherent to say when a particular topic comes up in conversation. Accordingly, they do not need to have logical interconnections between them. . . . I suspect that the majority of our knowledge comes packed in little opinion molecules like these, just waiting for the topic to come up.[25]

Most of our respondents also seemed unaware or unconcerned about real or seemingly logical inconsistencies within individual schemas or among several of their schemas. They were not greatly troubled when specific schemas contradicted general schemas. Karl Adams, for instance, argued that the notion of professionalism precluded the right to strike. Yet he excused a physicians' strike for higher wages on the grounds that they were underpaid. At the same time, he condemned a lawyers' strike. Sandra Ornstein argued that a woman should not need anyone's consent for having an abortion. But then she continued: "But I do think it would be a very good idea if a minor would get parents' permission. And I think it would be a good idea for the wife to get the husband's permission. I think those things should be discussed in the family." Recognizing the apparent inconsistency of her views, she added: "I'm on both sides of the fence." Similarly, the fact that many panelists had schemas about proper personal and political behavior, including their own, did not keep them from violating what they perceived to be the appropriate norms. "I ought to, but I don't" was a frequent comment.

Despite their apparent lack of concern about inconsistencies among some of their schemas, all panelists stated that consistency in thoughts and consistency between words and deeds were desirable qualities.[26] At times, panelists did make attempts to rationalize or even correct inconsistencies. Such inconsistencies in inconsistencies should be neither surprising nor disturbing if we remember Milton Rokeach's observations about belief systems. "When we say that a person has a belief system it brings forth the idea that it is a logical system, and that if it isn't logical, it isn't a system. We propose that logical systems, considered as human products, are but a subclass, a special kind of psychological system." For the most part, in psychological systems, "the parts may be interrelated without necessarily being logically interrelated.[27]

Although there was little evidence that our panelists had elaborately organized, hierarchically-structured belief systems, it was not true, as many social scientists have argued, that knowledge of the beliefs of such average people had little predictive value.[28] As indicated earlier, and discussed more fully in the next chapter, general schemas were routinely used to structure specific schemas, many schemas were interlinked, and morselized schemas usually appeared with regularity. By knowing the panelists' schemas and schema structures, we could therefore predict with a high degree of accuracy how they would process additional information.

The fact that we detected more structure and regularity in our panelists' belief systems than most survey researchers have been able to do in the past is due to the differences in methodology. To accommodate the more constrained questions required by survey research, survey researchers have established fixed criteria for judging belief consistency. These criteria are based on belief structures held by political elites and appropriate evidence is sought accordingly. This approach has led investigators "to measure attitude constraint in the mass public in such a way that other modes of attitude and belief organization would not be detected even if they existed."[29] The conclusion was then reached that average people lack belief systems. As Lane points out:

> The mistake underlying reliance on the constraints implied by statistical clustering, scalar ordering, or acceptance of an idea cluster by an authoritative elite is based on the fallacious view that if some people see idea elements properly clustering in a certain way, others should too. Such "constraints" or clusterings refer to neither logic nor rationality.[30]

Our study, unlike survey research, permitted us to collect a much larger amount of information about individuals than is possible in a mass survey and to record it exactly as the panelists articulated their conceptualizations. This makes it much easier to detect connections between beliefs and to discover regularities in thinking patterns. However, there appears to be no single blueprint for what goes with what. Which concepts are linked depends on the organizing principle that is used.

For instance, several panelists opposed health care financed by the government. But some did it because they believed in minimal government; others did it because they considered these services too expensive. Knowing the substance of beliefs—opposition to government-financed health care—does not tell us the nature of the underlying structure. To discover that structure, one must have answers to the "why" questions about beliefs as well.

Other investigators have obtained similar findings. Pamela Johnston Conover and Stanley Feldman, for example, have demonstrated experimentally how specific beliefs can be interrelated in different patterns. They discovered that economic beliefs tended to be unrelated to racial beliefs for individuals who valued concepts of free enterprise. By contrast, for individuals who took a social responsibility approach to economic problems, racial and economic beliefs were linked. Thus, there was more than one way to make logical ties between these two domains of politics. The choice hinged on individual value structures. Conover and Feldman concluded that "overall our respondents appear to have well-developed, interrelated sets of schemas that they use to structure various types of political information at different levels of abstractions."[31] We can say the same about our panelists, if we think in terms of clusters of related schemas, rather than overall belief systems.

Constraints among beliefs about politics may be based on ordinary logic as well as political logic. The two are not necessarily the same. It may be logical for a reform-minded administrator to fire an inefficient employee; but this action may defy political logic if the employee is well-connected to powerful political personalities on whose goodwill the administrator depends. Cognitive abilities and social learning permit people to make general logical connections, but it takes interest and exposure to American politics to know the constraints of American political logic. "Obviously, constraint can be a function of either cognitive ability or political exposure but which condition is the more important depends on the issue and its centrality to prevailing political conflicts."[32]

Consistency among beliefs may even be learned by rote. In an age of ample election news, many people learn issue constraint by taking their cues from the candidates or from media stories. "The net effect to be expected from the candidate issue-bundling process is the enhancement of mass issue consistency on the salient issues of particular presidential campaigns."[33] Once people have learned to make associations among issues by modeling their belief systems on those to which they are exposed, their systems may have de facto consistency. Accordingly, there seems to be more constraint in people's beliefs when national issues are involved than when local issues are at stake. This happens because people have more exposure to thinking about national than about state issues.[34]

## SCHEMA DIMENSIONS

We are now ready to examine the types of schema dimensions that emerged when our panelists described and analyzed news events in 1976. Since interview coding was open-ended, there was no limit on the numbers of schemas and schema dimensions that might have been discovered. As we shall see, actual discoveries were limited. For each of them, we shall present a number of examples that appeared frequently in the inverview protocols. Thus far, the emphasis in the political science literature has been on the study of whole belief systems, ignoring research on the mental schemas that constitute the building blocks in any belief system. Our study, therefore, builds on only a slender base of prior work.

Our panelists used six types of dimensions in their schemas to process current news in 1976. We have coined descriptive labels to identify them as (1) simple situation sequences, (2) cause-and-effect sequences, (3) person judgments, (4) institution judgments, (5) cultural norm applications, and (6) human empathy perspectives. There were variations in the frequency with which each type was used, reflecting personal idiosyncracies, educational differences, and differences in political outlook and interest. Nonetheless, it is significant that the same limited array of basic schema dimensions appeared without fail in each of the interview protocols of the 21 panelists. The fact that other scholars who have investigated political culture and political belief systems have observed similarly organized schemas provides additional support for the accuracy and general applicability of our findings.[35] Of course, the array of political schemas tapped via news story stimuli may not exhaust the political schemas available to individuals. In different contexts, when political questions unrelated to current news are asked, schemas and schema dimensions may emerge that our research did not tap.

## Simple Situation Sequences

When people are asked about a news story, one would expect that they would generally retell merely the facts of the story. Surprisingly, this was not the case with our panelists. For most of the stories that they recalled, they had processed meanings beyond a recapitulation of the mere facts. Occasionally, we tried to encourage them to repeat facts by asking them to tell the story to an imaginary friend who had not heard about it. The resulting stories were generally poor in detail, with omission of many salient points. Often they contained serious factual errors. This evidence suggests that news stories are not generally processed to recapture a precise facsimile for retelling. Rather, the thrust of processing goes toward condensing the story to the bare essentials of factual occurrences and toward extracting what these occurences mean in particular contexts.

The major exceptions to this pattern are stories of striking events, such as the assassination of President John F. Kennedy and Reverend Martin Luther King, Jr. or the first landing of American astronauts on the moon. These types of events are routinely remembered and retold sequentially with a fair amount of detail. Additionally, people have stock scenarios about what usually happens in familiar events, such as labor union strikes, school integration efforts, or primary elections. But while these scenarios are apparently used in judging whether or not a particular story is usual or unusual, they are not generally articulated during story telling, unless one asks for them specifically. Then, people will report the image they have of the prototypical situation which always differs in some respects from the story at hand.

## Cause-and-Effect Sequences

The most common way to process news stories is to view them from the perspective of likely causes of observed effects.[36] When an event is reported, the question becomes "Was this predictable under current social conditions?" News stories are readily incorporated into existing schemas if the facts they report constitute a predictable outcome of familiar current situations. For instance, most panelists believed that unemployment produced crime. Therefore, stories about rising crime were not surprising when published during times of high unemployment. The fact that the outcome should have been expected even seemed to take some of the sting out of undesirable events. New information that conformed to familiar causal sequences either was incorporated, in greater or lesser detail, into established schemas or more frequently, it was discarded as "nothing new"; therefore, it was not needed to flesh out existing schemas.

## Simple Causal Linkages

We encountered three varieties of cause-and-effect linkages in schemas: *simple ones, complex ones,* and *future projections.* In simple cause-and-effect approaches, the linkage between cause and effect was direct. The panelists believed that situation A would cause situation B. There were no multiple steps or circular reasoning. However, a particular outcome often was linked directly to multiple causes.

The following examples represent simple causal sequences. Stories about tax increases were frequently processed as the predictable direct results of excessive spending by government. Pollution stories were integrated as the inevitable outcome of high industrialization and heavy automatic traffic. Poor schools were linked to inadequate spending for public education and poor student discipline. Rampant crime was the inevitable consequence of insufficient punishment. In Lettie Tisdale's words, criminals rob and steal because they know

> they'll get away with it. That's why there's so many crimes 'cause they let the police go and lock 'em up and then they pay a little to get out and that's it. I think there should be something did about it. They should be punished.

Stories about predictable events were regarded as neither novel nor surprising, and they were often labelled as boring. Hence most panelists would read headlines only, or headlines and opening paragraphs. Since much of current news is nothing more than the repetition of such familiar occurrences, it was treated with disdain. In fact, we asked at the start of each interview whether anything of lasting significance had been reported during the past month and found that the answer was more often "no" than "yes" for the majority of the panelists.

Most panelists expected the same causes to continue to produce the same political effects with only slight changes within the realm of possibility. Given this attitude, stories that reported substantial improvements in long-standing political problems received attention from most of our panelists because they were perceived as major deviations from the expected. Occasionally, such stories were used to modify existing schemas—as mentioned, all of our panelists were quite willing, at times, to change their minds. More commonly, such stories were labelled as exceptions that did not alter the rule, or the stories were rejected as unbelievable and the established schema was reaffirmed. Reasons for calling a story unbelievable ranged from reservations about the source of the story, to doubts about the accuracy of the media, to assertions that past experience indicated that the story must be incorrect or merely a temporary deviation that would be eventually corrected. The reasons for adopting one or the other of these processing alternatives remain to be ascertained.

At times, our panelists made obviously faulty causal connections. As Taylor and Crocker point out, "schemas provide an illusory data base, because they provide default options for missing data; and when they are salient, they are applied relatively indiscriminately to data sets for which the match to the schema is less than perfect."[37] Political laymen and professionals alike may fall into this trap as Ernest R. May illustrates in a fascinating book about *"Lessons" of the Past*.[38] The "Munich Conference" schema, for instance, was applied by several American presidents to justify defense policies in situations that were only superficially comparable to the schematized event.

On many occasions, our panelists' search for causal explanations failed. When the causes were elusive, they expressed disappointment. "I wish I knew— it baffles me—I can't make heads or tails out of this" were common expressions that indicated that the respondent could not readily find an appropriate schema that provided a meaningful cause-and-effect sequence. If no appropriate schemas could ultimately be found, such stories were more readily forgotten than more familiar tales, as judged by tests checking recall 2 to 9 months after exposure.

## Projections to the Future

People are very curious about future happenings. The mass media capitalize on this curiosity by using news stories as indicators of future events. But even when they fail to do this, many people attempt their own predictions.[39] Our panelists often tried to project the unknown outcome of current events covered by news stories to their ultimate consequences. For instance, in reading about a march by women eager to gain favorable attention for the Equal Rights Amendment, panelists would search for clues to its prospective success or failure. When passage of a new law was announced, the question became "Will it work?" or "What will it do for me?" By comparing the event to past cause-and-effect sequences, one can predict the likely path of events and, at times, evaluate the outcome. This is different from ordinary effect-to-cause linkage whereby one accounts for an effect that has already happened by linking it to a cause.

Examples of predictions include Robert Creighton's declaration that stories about Carter's strong primary election winning streak indicated that Carter would be able to unify the party even before the convention "because that's generally what happens." Another example was Paul Diedrich's assertion that Senator Jackson's affinity for Jewish causes meant that he would be prone to favor these causes unduly. Spurred by stories about racial integration plans for schools, several panelists projected that these plans would be costly in money and convenience and that they would not improve the quality of education received by black children.

Projection may also be used as a technique to bring discrepant information into alignment with existing schemas. For example, stories contradicting the schema that social conditions make continuous rises in the crime rate inevitable were brought into line by pointing out that the deviant trends would be reversed in the near future. The current trends were construed as temporary aberrations.

## Complex Causal Linkages

While simple cause-and-effect linkages were quite common in story processing, complex cause-and-effect linkages were rare, averaging 1 in 10. An example of a complex cause-and-effect linkage was Karl Adams's remark that stories about rising crime rates should be interpreted as evidence of the bankruptcy of liberal philosophies. The complex reasoning leading to this particular linkage was that anti-business policies generated by liberals produced unemployment. In turn, unemployment produced crime because it left people idle and vulnerable to temptations to increase their wealth through crime or to take out their frustrations on society. Thus, the causal chain went from liberalism to anti-business philosophy to unemployment to rising crime. It was triggered, in reverse, by crime stories.

Several politically sophisticated panelists distinguished between instrumental and symbolic aspects of stories. Adams remarked that he paid attention to news about Illinois Senator Stevenson's endorsement of a local Chicago Congressman because it was Stevenson's "Declaration of Independence." Rather than interpreting the story as merely proclaiming support for a fellow politician, Adams thought that Stevenson was signaling Mayor Daley that he was willing to defy the mayor, who had endorsed a different candidate. Another example was Sven Peterson's comment that senators who strongly attacked the CIA during congressional hearings were not really concerned with the merits of the agency's conduct. Rather, their major concern was the improvement of their own image as fighters for just causes.

Another type of complex reasoning is acknowledgment of the obvious cause-and-effect linkage that explains a particular story and indicates how it should be stored, followed by an indication that there are ancillary reasons beyond the apparent ones. A story about reassigning teachers in Chicago in order to racially integrate faculties illustrates searching beyond apparent reasons. Several panelists alleged that Chicago school authorities, who were reassigning the teachers, actually were opposed to teacher integration. These panelists perceived the story as involving the status of teachers' unions in Chicago, rather than integration policy. In their view, the reassignment was intended to destroy the power of unions by destroying their control over teacher assignments.

Reference to ulterior motives was common in three types of situations. The panelists looked for hidden reasons when they distrusted the veracity of particular message senders or when they suspected that message senders were trying to be manipulative. It also happened when panelists were generally distrustful of people and believed that the world was full of conspiracies. Finally, it occurred when the reported events ran counter to the schemas the panelists had developed about how society functions.

## Person Judgments

News stories frequently involve the activities of various types of individuals, many of them easily recognizable as members of distinct demographic groups. These groups could be as narrow as specific types of college students or as broad as ethnic, religious, or occupational groups.[40] Stories about such groups could be readily processed because our panelists had general schemas about human nature, goals, and behaviors as they are and as they ought to be. Stories about student rowdyism, ethnic or religious lobbying, or business corruption fit neatly into these schemas.

Adams's schema about actors is a good example. Commenting on Ronald Reagan's candidacy, he said:

> I wouldn't trust a movie actor as President. I've known actors and theater people during my college days, and my opinion of the way they live isn't great. I mean, it's just different and I wouldn't trust them with governing the country. Now I realize you can't generalize about individuals, but its a gut feeling I have.

In the process of incorporating stories into their person schemas, the panelists often articulated their theories about the meanings to be attributed to particular human characteristics, behaviors, and roles. Such theories constitute examples of general schemas about personality.[41] They could either be part of schemas dealing with situations and public policies, when panelists chose to concentrate on human behavior dimensions, or they could be part of schemas focusing on specific persons or people in general.

### General Human Behavior Schemas

When confronted with stories focusing on various individuals, our panelists seemed to ask themselves first of all whether or not they were familiar with the person in question or knew someone similar to her or him. Stories about unfamiliar individuals and types of people normally were ignored or quickly forgotten unless the fresh faces in news stories reflected situations of great interest or prominence. For instance, new schemas were formed for important characters in sensational discoveries, in brutal crimes, or when new stars were rising in the galaxy of presidential hopefuls.

Whenever the story subjects were familiar persons or types of persons, the panelists tried to square the newly reported action with their previous impressions of these people. If current action conformed to past activities or likely behaviors, it was treated as confirmation of existing schemas. In such cases, the story was often described as "nothing new" and was given slight attention. Expected human behaviors include behaving selfishly at the risk of hurting others, doing favors for relatives and personal and political friends, and denying and covering up one's mistakes. Lawyers were expected to be contentious, spokesmen for groups were presumed to be biased, and first ladies were supposed to be concerned with social problems. Young radicals were expected to mellow with age and to join "the establishment." Adams articulated typical human behavior schemas in connection with a story about union leader Cesar Chavez. Adams observed:

> When people are younger, when the issues are upfront, then everybody's an activist. But when things sort of settle down, and the nitty-gritty of the whole situation comes about, and you have become a level-headed thinker, and you have to deal with things intelligently—you can't act emotionally. You have to become an administrator, you have to wheel and deal, you have to reason with people, compromise with people. It's a mellowing, I think, type of experience.

Human behavior schemas, or prototypes, also included ideas about the impact of various contexts on people's behavior. For instance, many panelists shared the view that young people with time on their hands were apt to cause trouble for society, ranging from social activism for unorthodox causes to serious crime. Such ideas made the panelists expect that social protest activities would be carried on largely by young, single, and usually unemployed people, and that most perpetrators of violent crimes also belonged to this segment of the population.

Stories indicating that familiar individuals' current actions contradicted established schemas elicited expressions of surprise, followed by 1 of 3 strategies. There were attempts to interpret the story in ways that would make it conform after all. For instance, "good" behavior by "bad" politicians, such as President Nixon, was explained as a ploy to deceive the public. If rationalizations proved impossible, the story was rejected or the established schemas were altered. The first of these strategies was the most common, followed, in order, by the other two. If the persons involved in prominent stories were unfamiliar, attempts were made to find similarities between the newcomers and familiar characters. These similarities were then used to develop new schemas that harmonized with existing ones.

Stereotypes about human behavior are extremely useful for processing information. They permit drawing broad conclusions from tiny story fragments. The simple sentence that John Doe is a candidate for Congress can activate the candidate stereotype so that John Doe immediately becomes all the things ascribed to typical candidates. In the process, John Doe may, of course, be saddled with attributes of various kinds that are not mentioned in the story and that he may not possess at all. Stereotyping simplifies, but it also distorts, often in major ways.[42]

Our panelists did not hesitate to ascribe schema characteristics to all members of the same group. As Deidre Sandelius put it, when explaining why she views all politicians as dishonest:

> And then this person who you voted for is convicted of some serious offense . . .

to me it goes off onto all other politicians. After the events of the past few years, I have a real distrust of politicians. I really don't believe what they are saying.

Similarly, stories about the use of bribes by Lockheed officials in their conduct of business evoked this comment: "It's the kind of thing I think goes on a lot. Business is a lot of wheeling-dealing, under-the-table sort of politics . . . it will keep on going. It's just a human way of doing things." Obviously, these schemas go beyond characterizing behavior by a specific institution or individual. Rather, they indicate schemas about habitual behaviors by big business and by politicians.

However, stereotypical thinking was rarely absolute. Our respondents frequently acknowledged that there were exceptions to the rule. This provided them with an easy explanation when members of stereotyped subgroups behaved in atypical ways. Our findings, therefore, match those of sociologists Mary Jackman and Mary Senter whose analysis of national survey data showed that "qualified images of groups generally prevail over categorical descriptions."[43] Person schemas like other schemas, appear to focus on only a limited array of themes. They appear to be cued by an observable feature, such as national origin, past and current occupations, body position, or voice characteristics. The choice of specific themes depends on routine preferences of individual panelists or on specific current information needs.[44]

Although most panelists had a variety of processing approaches to person schemas, they tended to cling to a favorite approach most of the time. This may represent a conscious attempt to assimilate information in a form that has proven useful in the past, or it may be the result of schema accessibility. As noted earlier, schemas that have been most recently and most frequently used tend to be most readily accessible. The better-educated panelists often processed news about persons in more sophisticated ways than their less well-educated counterparts.[45] They were able to give more examples of particular traits and could draw more inferences from available data. They also could fill in missing data more amply.

For example, when Lettie Tisdale, the panelist with the least amount of formal education, was asked what she had learned about Jimmy Carter throughout the campaign, she responded: "I learned that he was a good man. And him and his family was good. Seems like he would make a nice candidate. I hope that he will, you know, do good after he had won." By contrast, college graduate Tugwell Quentin, like Tisdale a member of the low-interest, difficult-access group, mentioned more specific traits and more diverse themes. He replied:

> Jimmy Carter is southern and he has a strong religious background; and he has a naval background; and he is apparently a rather progressive businessman. Domestically he seems to have a rather strong interest and ability. In foreign affairs, I don't think he has any background at all.

Some panelists dwelled on people's physical characteristics while others assessed personality features or evaluated the person's merits against the backdrop of a specific situation. Judgments about people's honesty were especially common.

In part, this was true because honesty was deemed to be a crucial element in determining whether to take messages conveyed by individuals seriously. However, it was also true because honesty is an important positive dimension by which people judge their own worth. They tend to apply familiar self-judgment criteria to the judgment of other persons.[46] While honesty is no assurance of other good qualities, lack of honesty presumably depreciates sharply the value of other good qualities.

Our panelists' schema contained a number of criteria for assessing honesty. If physical appearance could be judged, people were described as having or lacking an "honest look." For instance, Cesar Ippolito, a staunch Democrat, gave honest looks as the reason for voting for a Republican governor. "I voted for Ogilvie instead of Walker because I felt Oglivie looked like an honest man. I thought Walker was a crook. With Walker there is something that you instinctively know is crooked, the way the guy looks, that's what turned me off on him." Avoidance of eye contact in televised encounters was universally interpreted as a sign of dishonesty, whereas a straight look into the eye and firm, unhesitating responses were interpreted as evidence of honesty.

Aside from these signs, our panelists found it difficult to articulate the specific criteria by which they gauged an honest look. They obviously had distinct images available for relatedness searches, but had not analyzed them or put them into verbal form. Facial expressions, body stances and movements, as well as dress and grooming, all seemed to play a part. Judgments about who looked honest and who did not were surprisingly uniform, despite the difficulty of articulating criteria. It was the case of the man asked to describe a mountain who replied "you'll know it when you see it."

Honesty was also inferred from stereotypical cues or from the absence of contrary proof. Several panelists judged Ford to be honest "because he is a family man" and because no stories about dishonesty had been published. Betty Nystrom remarked that if Ford had been dishonest, the media "would have it out of him and you would hear it." If panelists' schemas or comments reported in the media pointed to questionable claims, such as Jimmy Carter's pledge that he would never tell a lie to the public, this was usually construed as dishonesty. The same was true when inconsistencies between a person's pronouncements or between words and actions became apparent. Most judgment schemas about persons evidently did not include the idea that inconsistencies might involve rational readjustments to changing conditions.

Many of the characteristics included in person schemas were quite trivial. For instance, Helga Holmquist reported watching a telecast to capture "the announcers' comments and the little tidbits . . . stupid little things like Jimmy Carter's the first presidential nominee to wear his hair covering the tops of his ears . . . you know, junky things, little human interest things." Watching the television screen for bodily characteristics often distracted panelists from listening to the person. Deidre Sandelius, for instance, told us about watching Carter during the presidential debates and missing much of what he said: "I spent a lot of time watching Carter that night . . . his right index finger is slightly deformed."

Others came away from watching political figures with general comments like "he has a clean, good guy look."

Instead of attempting to make their own judgments for incorporation into a schema, some panelists routinely accepted personality judgments made by third parties and conveyed through the media or through interpersonal discussions. People with low esteem for their capacity to make sound judgments were most likely to adopt this strategy in processing news about people. A majority of the women fell into this group. Some panelists were also willing to accept third-party judgments by persons whom they considered to be experts in judging particular types of people. For instance, Darlene Rosswell always deferred to the judgment of her father when it came to appraising politicians because she felt that he was paying attention to political information while she was ignoring it.

## Politicians

One population subgroup for which our panelists had distinct schemas consists of politicians. Contrary to the notion that politicians reflect the characteristics of their constituents, panelists saw them as a breed apart—power hungry, double dealing, unscrupulous. In the words of Elaine Mullins: "To me a public official is a different kind of person from what, like I am . . . It's involved with a need for power." The comment that "in politics, dirty tricks don't really upset me" was typical.[47] Politicians also were expected to be inordinately concerned with making headlines and with putting the desire for re-election above moral behavior. A stock phrase, repeated in almost identical wording whenever politicians misbehaved, was "this is typical of politicians . . . I expect something like that . . . I just take it sort of matter of fact that that's what politicians do." Panelists frequently said that they would not want to serve in politics because it required reprehensible behavior.

How can these kinds of feelings be reconciled with scholarly reports that politicians are favorably evaluated? An analysis of Gallup polls over a 40-year period, for instance, showed that "despite wars, depressions, and public scandals, despite the growing distrust of and cynicism towards government leaders . . . . Fully 76 percent of all public figures were evaluated positively by respondents to Gallup polls between 1935 and 1975."[48] The answer is that our respondents were not critical of individual politicians. Reprehensible conduct elicited no indignation. Just as one would not be surprised when a boxer or a wrestler inflicts bodily injury on his opponent, one also expects that many politicians will double-deal, betray, and engage in various forms of corruption. Unscrupulous behavior was blamed on circumstances beyond the individual politician's control. The world had become too complex for even the best and the brightest to cope with its ills successfully and to resist temptation. This type of fatalism creates feelings that nothing can be done to remedy political faults. It becomes a disincentive for paying close attention to tales about the perennial failures of the political system. Stories about ineptitude and corruption are met with expressions of boredom and resignation like the rhetorical query "what else is new?"[49]

The ability to win elections was commonly used as an indicator that candidates for public office were capable. In our panelists' schemas, victory meant that the candidate had the general public's approval, and the public's judgments deserved respect. Hence, it was sound politics to jump on the bandwagon. Stories about election victories, accordingly, were processed as evidence that the winners were qualified. Winners then were usually credited with other desirable qualities that were part of the schema about the nature of capable political candidates. Penny Liebman, for instance, changed her negative views about Carter following a string of victories in presidential primaries. Her explanation was that "there must be something to the man that he's getting so much response. I was a little leery of him at first, but I'm beginning to think maybe he's got something." Other frequently used traits for categorizing politicians were intelligence, savvy, articulateness, and general philosophy. Occasionally candidates were categorized as liberal or conservative or middle of the road. But most panelists found it difficult to explain what these terms meant to them and to give examples.

A nationwide panel study, reported by a team of researchers from the University of Michigan, provides comparable data about the limited dimensions evident in schemas about politicians. The researchers used factor analysis to identify five themes which routinely appeared in the images which their respondents had formed of presidential candidates in elections from 1952 to 1980. They labelled these themes competence, integrity, reliability, charisma, and personal characteristics.

- *Competence* involved past political experience, ability as statesman, comprehension of political issues, realism and intelligence.
- *Integrity* entailed honesty, sincerity, trustworthiness, and corruptibility, or their equivalents.
- *Reliability* referred to characterizations concerning the candidate's dependability, strength, hard-working attitude, decisiveness, aggressiveness, or their opposites.
- *Charisma* involved references to leadership, dignity, humbleness, patriotism, the ability to get along with people and to inspire them.
- *Personal characteristics* entailed appearance, health, manner, background, family, and the like.[50]

Throughout the study, the respondents used the competence category most often, with integrity and reliability following. Comparisons between the 1956 and 1960 panels and between the 1972 and 1976 panels showed that competence, integrity, and reliability rankings were used routinely. Rankings of charisma and personal characteristics were less routine and depended on the nature of particular campaigns.[51]

Several of our panelists, obviously socialized to the belief that rationality and democratic theory require that political choices be made on the basis of issues, expressed unease about judging candidates on the basis of their election successes or even on the basis of personality. But they indicated that they lacked criteria in their schemas to judge what kinds of policy proposals should be part and parcel of their conceptions of the good candidate. Such criteria may be difficult to construct when issues are constantly changing. Moreover (as discussed in Chapter 4), media stories emphasize personalities and campaign events more than issues and candidates tend to be very fuzzy about the issues because they do not want to alienate potential supporters. Therefore, the raw material for including issue themes in candidate schemas is more difficult to gather.

The impression that issues are frequently omitted from schemas about political candidates may be deceptive, however. Issues may be the basis for concluding that a candidate is capable or compassionate, or smart, or likeable. After the conclusions are drawn, the facts may be forgotten. Carol Fechbach's remarks were typical when she was asked to elaborate on her comment that she did not like Sargent Shriver's stands on issues. "Nothing specific. The things that I know about these people were formulated a long time ago and I've just forgotten. I'm sure they're things at one time I knew the specifics on, and I just forgot."[52] Evidence for the kind of "alchemy" that transforms issues into personality assessments also comes from our panelists' reactions to news stories that stressed issues. Comments about the presidential debates, for example, referred mostly to conclusions about the candidates' performance and capabilities, rather than the issues that were discussed.

Several panelists did have key issues, such as tax policy, defense policy, or social security policy which they used in judging incumbents. Linking incumbents to issues appeared to be much easier than doing it for candidates who had not held office before. In fact, nearly all panelists linked incumbents to at least a few issues. The fact that news stories provide more issue information about incumbents helps to explain the difference.

Aside from general notions about the nature and behavior of politicians in and out of office, people have, of course, schemas for particular politicians. Most of these schemas appeared to be quite sparse. Some were readily condensed into one-line or even one-word commentaries. Cesar Ippolito, for instance, summed up his views by calling Carter "a smooth-talking, wily modern Southerner." He labelled Humphrey as "the 'Happy Warrior,' the Al Smith of the 70s." Wallace was characterized as "a great campaigner with no real program for the country— a real populist." Ford was "a good businessman from Grand Rapids who should be running the Chamber of Commerce there." Brown, as Ippolito saw him, was "a phoney, a politician playing games with words." Many of the brief characterizations used by our panelists bear close resemblance to the stereotypes that television commentators so frequently develop for political figures.

After exposure to a lot of news about political candidates, most panelists showed signs of being satiated. They skipped large numbers of political stories, saying that they presented nothing new, nothing worthy of close attention. As Darlene Rosswell put it, "It's always the same old stuff, I just listen lightly, not full attention, and usually nothing perks my ears up. Nothing says 'oh this is new,' you know, or they're really doing something about it." For several panelists, the saturation boredom reaction seemed to set in more quickly for stories about politicians than for other familiar, repeated themes. This meant that it was exceptionally difficult to change their schemas about politicians through the flow of news stories.

## Institution Judgments

### *Institutional Activities*

Just as the panelists had a variety of schemas about the behavior of persons, so they had schemas about the behavior of institutions. When discussing institutional dimensions, the panelists usually focused on the quality that may be expected of governmental and private sector performance. They rarely dwelled on the proper scope for governmental or private sector activities, the necessity for action, or the level of government that ought to be involved.[53] However, our panelists did have schemas about the scope of activities that governments ought to pursue. These surfaced during discussions of various public policies unrelated to particular news stories. These schemas reveal the characteristic split between ideological and operational outlooks described by Lloyd Free and Hadley Cantril in their study of *The Political Beliefs of Americans*. Ideologically, most panelists did not want government to do or spend a great deal. But when asked about specific activities, they advocated a broad scope for government action. Operationally, government was expected to do anything that private institutions cannot do well or have failed to do.[54] When stories disclosed serious social problems in matters such as economic welfare, environmental protection or health, the panelists routinely mentioned the need for government intervention. At such times, their usual fears that government action meant inefficiency, wastefulness, and high expenditures seemed to be forgotten.

The national government was assumed to be the political actor unless it was quite explicit that the activities to be carried out belonged at the state or local level. There was, in 1976, no hint that our panelists' schemas contained warnings about the evils of excessive concentration of power at the federal level at the expense of state and local authorities. Nor was there any hint that the federal government was perceived as an unknowing and uncaring outsider, compared to their own state and local government. Quite the contrary! The concepts of the new federalism that became prominent during the Reagan years did not surface in their comments.

When it came to insights into the actual modus operandi of government, most of our panelists seemed to have vague ideas about the subject. A few appeared to have general schemas about institutional behavior, commenting that all institutions basically operated the same way. Most panelists thought of the president as the most influential political actor who shaped policy and carried it out. Public policies were his personal successes or failures. Congress was viewed as an occasional brake on presidential action, and individual Congressman were regarded as the citizen's link to government. Bureaucrats were perceived as generally lazy, entangled in red tape, carrying out the letter of the law rather than its spirit. Occasionally, some panelists would indicate that they associated specific mental outlooks with certain agencies. Thus a CIA operative's expressed distrust of the Soviet Union was "a viewpoint which you'd expect him to have and which a lot of people in Defense and the CIA have." But, on the whole, most of our panelists did not seem to have multifaceted schemas about the ways in which governmental bodies were set up to perform their duties and about the ways in which their activities were shaped by internal and external political pressures. Therefore, stories about governmental activities generally could not be analyzed in terms of their correspondence to normal behavior by such bodies.[55]

Few panelists were able to detect missing information in stories about governmental action. To spot missing information, people must have ample schemas from which they can draw information normally associated with such stories or perceive information logically following from the facts supplied in the story. Most panelists lacked such well-rounded schemas about governmental operations. It was an exception, for instane, when Robert Creighton, a politically astute individual, noted that a story about limitations on campaign spending mentioned only the comparatively small number of groups whose contributions were to be kept in check. It omitted to mention that the bulk of individuals and social groups remained unshackled.

## Behavioral Norms

Our panelists had distinct ideas within their schemas about the norms by which the behavior of political institutions should be judged. When processing relevant stories, they checked for compliance with these norms.[56] Prominent among institutional behavior norms is fairness. For example, Martha Gaylord used the fairness angle in processing a story about a United States veto against United Nation membership for the Palestine Liberation Organization. "I disagree with the decision," she said. "It's unfair. I think the Arabs have been getting screwed for a long time. I think that's a mistake we made and we should rectify it." Consistency is another common norm. Our panelists believed that governmental action should be consistent. Stories that recorded inconsistencies often were noted and interpreted as evidence of undesirable governmental behavior.

The degree of public approval is another criterion that was frequently employed to assess the merits or strengths of public institutions and programs. Stories reporting wide public support of institutions and policies tended to receive attention and produced favorable evaluations of the institutions in question. The widespread interest in knowing what is publicly approved or condemned is also reflected in avid attention to stories reporting public opinion-poll results. The panelists generally equated failure to win substantial public endorsement with weakness and lack of merit. Thus a story that an anti-abortion candidate had received few votes in the Massachusetts primary was interpreted by several panelists, falsely, as it turned out, as reflective of the general weakness and undesirability of the anti-abortion movement.

The most constant element in processing stories about governmental activities was the assumption that government is inefficient. Our panelists, especially those who had had direct experience with governmental activities, expected government bureaucracies—all bureaucracies for that matter, at home and abroad—to be slow, bogged down in senseless red tape, and wasteful of human and material resources. Adams's judgment was typical when he declared that "I don't like anything the federal government is going to manage because they screw everything up." Sven Peterson complained that: "A hell of a lot of dollars are being spent and the people meant to benefit aren't. I guess people are beginning to realize that the government is terribly ineffective." The post office was mentioned frequently as the prototype of inefficient behavior. When stories raised questions about the expediency of a government takeover of ailing industries, such as oil or steel, the inefficiency of the post office was likely to be cited as a yardstick for appraising such plans.

Inefficiencies generally were viewed as the inescapable results of the complexity of the problems with which governments are forced to deal. They were not ascribed to the incapacity of government personnel.[57] In third world countries, they were blamed on inexperience, lack of adequate technology, and abject poverty. Penny Liebman made a typical excuse for the failure of governmental institutions to deal with problems by commenting: "It must be very hard to come to some solution and get the job done and all that without causing other problems; otherwise somebody would have come up with something." Sandra Ornstein had this to say about inadequate performance by the court system: "They're probably functioning as best they can, given the situation, given that they just don't have enough manpower. There's so much red tape, there's so much plea bargaining that goes on. I think they do their best and it's not their fault if they are not functioning too well." The belief that solutions are hard to discover may spring from the fact that our panelists found it difficult to think of solutions themselves. They usually conceded that government officials were more likely to have answers than average citizens, but added that many governmental problems defied solution even by experts.

As part of the notion of inefficiency, bureaucracies were deemed incapable of appropriate foresight and planning. Various disasters were interpreted as evidence of this tragic inability. Peterson's comment following a story about the collapse of a major dam is illustrative: "As usual, after a disaster happens, the government went out and started making regulations . . . I remember thinking at that time that it's always some human mistake that screws things up."

While domestic policies were occasionally perceived as successful, despite bureaucratic bungling, governmental action was routinely expected to be ineffectual in foreign policy. Hence, when stories about retreats or inaction in the face of adverse developments were published, our panelists characterized them as expected behavior. For instance, stories about failure to object to Cuba's sending of troops into Angola were interpreted as evidence of characteristically weak foreign policy stands.

Stories about governmental performance were also commonly evaluated by casting them into historical or circumstantial perspectives. For instance, 1976 election events and candidates were compared to their historical counterparts or evaluated in light of the political circumstances in 1976. Stories about the level of national expenditures were assessed in light of the gross national product. From that perspective, as one panelist put it, "we're not going overboard with defense spending like all these critics and people are saying." A story about the ouster of a civilian government in Argentina, placed into historical perspective, showed that this was a routine event. As Paul Diedrich commented,

> In light of Argntine history and the history of many other South American republics, it's, I suppose, almost inevitable when things go badly—inflation and economic troubles that Argentina has been through—that the military or at least the right wing groups would step in.

Other, less frequently used, criteria for judgment were the impact that certain policies were likely to have on selected groups of people at home or abroad; the economic and political costs of particular behaviors; technical feasibility, including environmental impacts; and conformity of the policy to cultural and subcultural norms and traditions.

Stories about governmental corruption and attempts to conceal it were also taken in stride. As Tugwell Quentin phrased it: "I have a feeling that whenever the government is spending huge sums of money, there's a lot of graft and inefficiency going on. It is just something I expect. It doesn't shock me or anything." Our panelists regarded corruption as a widespread, inevitable partner of power vested in public and private institutions. They shared Lord Acton's view that power inevitably corrupts. But corruption was regarded as a natural by-product of big government which can and must be tolerated.[58]

A belief that many political institutions and many politicians are corrupt is not the same as a belief that the entire political system is corrupt.[59] Our panelists were supportive of the American political system in general and viewed it as working for the public's welfare. Even those with leftward leanings argued that it should be retained and only changed incrementally, not radically. Therefore, stories about political movements designed to overturn "the American way" and stories about attempts to bring about political change outside normal political channels generally received attention and negative comment. Reports about government action to stop protesters who had used violent means, elicited approval.

## Cultural Norms

Besides schemas about actual behaviors of people and institutions, and the manner in which these behaviors ought to be carried out and judged, our panelists also had schemas reflecting generalized norms of the political culture. These norms were often labeled as "the American way" and appeared to be shared by all our panelists. As Stanley Feldman puts it: "The liberal political culture of the United States establishes basic parameters within which politics and private affairs are perceived and interpreted."[60] Our panelists voiced such norms repeatedly in appraising the conduct of individuals and institutions.

The most basic schema involving cultural norms about politics is that democracy is the best form of government and that governments and people ought to behave democratically. Stories raising issues about democratic behavior were processed accordingly. In fact, when news stories characterized behavior as democratic or undemocratic, our panelists usually accepted the classification and judged the story accordingly. Code words sufficed, even when the story provided little support for the judgment.

While support for democratic government was universal, our panelists varied substantially in the criteria they applied for judging what is or is not democratic. Obviously, schemas about the parameters of democracy are not identical.[61] Freedom of expression was widely accepted as an essential element of democracy, but there was little consensus about whether this applies to expressions of radically different political philosophies or even severe criticism of governmental policies. Similarly, our panelists agreed that democratic governments and people should act fairly towards all population groups, consider all sides of controversial issues, and respect the right of individuals to be different. But the panelists applied these concepts in quite different ways when they processed news stories. While Tugwell Quentin, for instance, said that it was fair and democratic for the state public utility commission to allow raises in electric rates when costs had skyrocketed, Darlene Rosswell called it totally unfair and undemocratic. She argued that public utility commissions should protect low-income consumers from high prices for essential services.

Our panelists' schemas about what constitutes appropriate behavior for the good citizen, unlike their schemas about democracy, were surprisingly similar in content. Moreover, they smacked of stereotypes propounded in grade and high school civics classes. These schemas were rarely used for story processing because stories raising issues about good citizenship were scarce, but they frequently were expressed when people appraised their own information-seeking behavior. Schemas about good citizens invariably show them voting in elections, based on their own well-informed decisions. As Lane describes it for his respondents: "In Eastport, the common man asserts his independence, asserts that he would not, even to relieve his ignorance, consult anyone in particular about the issues and candidates in an election—but would rather make up his own mind."[62] To make well-informed decisions requires devoting time to election news at some point during the electoral contest. All of our panelists reported paying attention to election news stories, spurred by this sense of civic duty to reach their own decisions.

Good citizens also keep abreast of other important national and local political issues. The fact that these issues may be beyond their capacity to understand is not considered a valid excuse for ignoring them.[63] Helga Holmquist, for instance, berated herself for ignoring news stories about Angola: "I don't pay as much attention to things as I should. Sometimes I'm embarrassed. Like on Angola. I'm not interested in Angola and I don't understand what's going on there. But I should force myself to become informed on this issue. It's a duty, I feel." Paying attention to news includes paying attention to public messages from political leaders, even if these messages, in Ippolito's words, are "typical Ford bullshit." It does not, however, include acquiring "school knowledge," such as remembering the length of a senatorial or judicial term. Good citizens perform their civic duties out of a sense of genuine concern, rather than forced duty.

Our panelists expressed guilt whenever they realized that they had missed important political stories, thereby running afoul of their own conceptions of good citizenship.[64] But this feeling did not lead to major improvements in subsequent attention to news. Ornstein, who had commented that keeping abreast of election news "shouldn't really be a duty, you should *want* to do it," explained the gap between ideal behavior norms and actual behavior. She continued: "But I don't think a person can force theirselves; you can't *force* a person to take a deep interest in something that they're not interested in."

Another basic schema that commonly comes to the fore in judging stories about political activities is that the needs of the poor, the weak, and the disadvantaged must be given the highest priority. Whenever a situation involves real suffering which government can alleviate, it must step in, irrespective of the costs. Underlying these beliefs is a basic schema that the United States is a boundlessly rich country that can afford to be generous to its citizens. Standards of generosity for the poor of other countries are a different matter; their claims are definitely subordinate to those of the domestic poor. Belief in the right of the unfortunate to be aided by government is supplemented by the notion that able-bodied people must be willing to take responsibility for their own lives. Belief in the work ethic and in human equality implies that anybody who is willing to work hard can achieve economic success.[65]

A major prerequisite for success is a good education. Therefore, every citizen must have the opportunity to be well-educated. The notion that education is the key to a better life is, as Lane has pointed out, "the humanistic 'religion' of the West."[66] Since education leads to better jobs, better citizenship, and reduced asocial behavior, most of our panelists believed that society ought to supply all members of the public with an ample array of educational opportunities. Stories related to public education readily captured attention, even for people who had no school-age children. These stories were always evaluated from the perspective that the best type of education ought to be provided for all who can benefit from it.

## Human Interest and Empathy

One of the more potent incentives that encourages people to attend to news stories is the desire to learn about the personal life, joys, tragedies, and varied activities of other people, particularly those in high places or in familiar settings. Several schemas appear to be involved in this dimension. One relates to self-perception. Our panelists seemed to ask themselves: "Is the situation depicted in the news story similar to what I have experienced directly or vicariously, or similar to what I would do, under the circumstances?" Schemas involving personal experiences would then be tapped. Besides personal experiences, people also appear to have schemas about miscellaneous events that happened to other people and that wrench the observer's emotions. Finally, our panelists tended to be alert to stories of all kinds which had human-interest appeal because they personally knew the people involved in the story or because they were familiar with the site of the story.

For instance, in response to a tornado news story, Leo Evanski remembered only the scars left in familiar areas. He explained: "When I see things on TV of places I've been to, it means more to me." A story about former First Lady Pat Nixon's stroke received attention because it involved a familiar person and evoked sympathy. By contrast, Holmquist said that she did not remember much about a Guatemalan earthquake. "I don't really feel touched emotionally by it. It certainly is a terrible tragedy, but I think that it's been too distant so that it hasn't really been brought home to me on a personal level." More general schemas of concern were involved in processing a story about a mother and her children killed in Ireland (with the political aspects of the story forgotten), an earthquake in China ("I feel very sorry for those homeless people"), and expressions of sympathy for victims and their families in air crashes and major fires.

Stories processed for their direct personal relevance involved human-interest information germane to the panelists' jobs, to their daily personal life and leisure activities, or stories that they perceived as worth telling to interested family members, friends, or associates. For instance, Donald Burton personalized a story about a cable car accident in Italy by processing it as a cue for future behavior. He commented that the story "confirmed that I should stay out of cable cars."

Similarly, panelists often indicated that they were interested in certain stories only if there was a personal angle. As Quentin put it: "People aren't really concerned about something unless it directly affects their well-being. If there isn't that direct threat, it's somebody else's problem." Adding a cultural dimension, he noted: "We have been brought up as a society to operate for our own personal needs, and there isn't a great deal of consideration given to those who follow us." This appraisal, of course, runs counter to the previously noted pattern of sociotropic thinking among our panelists.

Several panelists expressed disinterest in a scandal at a local hospital because "the names of the people involved did not ring a bell." Others said that they did not intend to form impressions and opinions about public housing policies because such policies did not affect them personally.[67] When respondents did not know anybody involved in a scandal at a local hospital or when they were not personally affected by public housing policies, they disregarded stories on these topics. In the same vein, many panelists expressed disinterest in stories occurring abroad when they did not know where the places involved in the stories were located.

## OVERALL EVALUATION

Our examination of the schemas revealed in response to news stories leads to three major conclusions. First of all, most people have a *broad array of schemas* that cover events that are likely to crop up in news stories. Therefore, they can perform effective relatedness searches for large numbers of stories. Secondly, these schemas, for the most part, exhibit a *limited number of dimensions*. In news story processing, as observed in this study, six types of schema dimensions were employed. Among these, cause-and-effect dimensions and human interest and empathy dimensions were used most often. Thus, the vast number of individual schemas display a fairly simple internal structure. Finally, the individual schemas reported here as illustrations reveal a *good deal of shared stereotypical thinking* by all of our panelists. This should not be surprising since the news in general, and political events in particular, are comparatively removed from the individual's life. When shared stereotypes suffice, why should the panelists go to the trouble of thinking independently? The central elements in our panelists' political belief systems "may be strong affective commitments to certain symbols, which remain constant for many years due to long histories of reinforcement." Belief in these symbols and stereotypes "may constrain the individual's political responses to numerous other stimuli, such as policy issues, political events, media presentations, or electoral candidacies . . . the individual's private life may be quite peripheral to his or her political belief system, and both may be mutually quite unconstraining."[68]

This chapter has focused on common characteristics of schemas and schema dimensions drawn from the interview protocols and diaries of all the panelists. The next chapter will indicate the scope of individual variations in the use of schema dimensions and themes. It will also analyze the reasons for variations in the complexity and sophistication of individual schemas.

### Notes

1. W. Lance Bennett, "Perception and Cognition: An Information-Processing Framework for Politics," in Samuel L. Long (ed.), *The Handbook of Political Behavior*, vol. 1, New York, Plenum Press, 1981, p. 101. The importance of pre-adult political learning for subsequent poltical orientations is discussed in Paul Allen Beck and M. Kent Jennings, "Pathways to Participation," *American Political Science Review*, 76, 1982, pp. 103–110.

2. David E. Rumelhart and Donald A. Norman, "Analogic Processes in Learning," in John R. Anderson (ed.), *Cognitive Skills and Their Acquisition*, Hillsdale, N.J., Lawrence Erlbaum, 1980, pp. 357–358.

3. Roy Lachman, Janet L. Lachman, and Earl C. Butterfield, *Cognitive Psychology and Information Processing: An Introduction*, Hillsdale, N.J., Lawrence Erlbaum, 1979, p. 302.

4. See also, Bennett, as cited in note 1, pp. 91, 101; and Jonathan Baron, "Intelligence and General Strategies," in Constance Scheerer (ed.), *Cognition: Theory, Research, Promise*, New York, Harper & Row, 1964, p. 416.

5. Charles E. Lindblom, "Another State of Mind," *American Political Science Review*, 76, 1982, pp. 17–18.

6. Bennett, as cited in note 1, p. 87.

7. Robert E. Lane, *Political Ideology: Why the American Common Man Believes What He Does*, New York, Free Press, 1962, p. 425. The impact of different subcultural experiences is discussed on p. 311. See also, Bennett, as cited in note 1, p. 123.

8. Lane, as cited in note 7, p. 418. Bennett, as cited in note 1, p. 123. Susan T. Fiske and Donald R. Kinder, "Involvement, Expertise, and Schema Use: Evidence from Political Cognition," in Nancy Cantor and John F. Kihlstrom (eds.), *Personality, Cognition, and Social Interaction*, Hillsdale, N.J., Lawrence Erlbaum, 1981, p. 174.

9. Lane, as cited in note 7, pp. 310, 417. Also see, Roger C. Schank and Robert P. Abelson, *Scripts, Plans, Goals and Understanding: An Inquiry Into Human Knowledge Structures*. Hillsdale, N.J., Lawrence Erlbaum, 1977, p. 70.

10. Lane, as cited in note 7, p. 418. Many specific examples of schema content can be found in Richard E. Nisbett and Lee Ross, *Human Inference: Strategies and Shortcomings of Social Judgment*, Englewood Cliffs, N.J., Prentice-Hall, 1980.

11. Ibid. p. 419.

12. Shelley E. Taylor and Jennifer Crocker, "Schematic Bases of Social Information Processing," in E. Tory Higgins, C. Peter Herman, and Mark P. Zanna (eds.), *Social Cognition: The Ontario Symposium*, vol. 1, Hillsdale, N.J., Lawrence Erlbaum, 1981, pp. 119–120; Nisbett and Ross, as cited in note 10, pp. 167–192.

13. Reid Hastie, "Schematic Principles in Human Memory," in E. Tory Higgins, C. Peter Herman, and Mark P. Zanna (eds.), *Social Cognition: The Ontario Symposium*, vol. 1, Hillsdale, N.J., Lawrence Erlbaum, 1981, pp. 53–55.

14. Taylor and Crocker, as cited in note 12, p. 87.

15. Walter Lippmann, *Public Opinion*, New York, Harcourt Brace, 1922, p. 31.

16. David O. Sears, Carl B. Hensler, and Leslie K. Speers, "Whites' Opposition to 'Busing': Self-Interest or Symbolic Politics?," *American Political Science Review*, 73, 1979, p. 371.

17. Ibid. Also see, Donald R. Kinder and D. Roderick Kiewiet, "Economic Grievances and Political Behavior: The Role of Personal Discontents and Collective Judgments in Congressional Voting," *American Journal of Political Science*, 23, 1979, pp. 495–527; Donald R. Kinder, "Sociotropic Politics: The American Case," *British Journal of Political Science*, 11, 1981, pp. 129–162; and Donald R. Kinder, "Presidents, Prosperity and Public Opinion," *Public Opinion Quarterly*, 45, 1981, pp. 1–21.

18. Bennett, as cited in note 1, p. 116. Also see Lane, as cited in note 7, p. 376.

19. Richard R. Lau, "Common Sense Representations of Common Illnesses," *Health Psychology*, 2, 1983, 167–185. Also see David O. Sears and Jack Citrin, *Tax Revolt: Something for Nothing in California*, Cambridge, Mass., Harvard University Press, 1982, 79–95.

20. For similar findings see Lane, as cited in note 7, p. 349.

21. Other types of schemas are discussed by David L. Swanson, "A Constructivist Approach," in Dan D. Nimmo and Keith R. Sanders (eds.), *Handbook of Political*

*Communication*, Beverly Hills, Sage, 1981, p. 179; Fiske and Kinder, as cited in note 8, p. 179; Hastie, as cited in note 13, pp. 43–77.

22. Hastie, as cited in note 13, pp. 42–44.

23. For a discussion of ways to measure the ability to make multiple judgments, see, Bennett, as cited in note 1, p. 82.

24. Lane, as cited in note 7, p. 319.

25. Daryl J. Bem, *Beliefs, Attitudes, and Human Affairs*. Belmont, Calif., Brooks Cole, 1970, p. 39.

26. For similar findings, see, Karl A. Lamb, *As Orange Goes: Twelve California Families and the Future of American Politics*, New York, Norton, 1974, p. 110.

27. Milton Rokeach, *The Open and Closed Mind: Investigations into the Nature of Belief Systems and Personality Systems*, New York, Basic Books, 1960, p. 33. Sears and Citrin, as cited in note 19, p. 92. They found consistency in affect, rather than rationales, in tax revolt schemas held by California voters. These voters objected to a series of unrelated aspects of the tax situation, with the negative attitude tying the schemas together.

28. Robert Axelrod, *Structure of Decision: The Cognitive Maps of Political Elites*, Princeton, Princeton University Press, 1976, p. 277.

29. W. Lance Bennett, *The Political Mind and the Political Environment*, Lexington, Mass., Lexington Books, 1975, p. 9.

30. Robert E. Lane, "Patterns of Political Belief," in Jeane Knutson (ed.), *Handbook of Political Psychology*, San Francisco, Jossey-Bass, 1974, p. 103. Shawn Rosenberg, "The Study of Political Reasoning: An Alternative to the Belief Systems Approach," *American Political Science Association Paper*, 1982. He points out that quantitative studies of belief systems have failed to account for much of the available data. Only 2 1/2 to 30% of the population show ideological thinking by various criteria. Inter-item correlations have ranged from 4–25%, leaving the remainder unexplained. Even factor analysis, which generates factors from available data, rather than a priori, can only explain half the variance.

31. Pamela Johnston Conover and Stanley Feldman, "Schema Theory and the Use of Q-Methodology in the Study of Mass Belief Systems," *American Political Science Association Paper*, 1982, p. 15. For similar findings see, Jennifer L. Hochschild, *What's Fair? American Beliefs about Distributive Justice*, Cambridge, Harvard University Press, 1981, pp. 232–237.

32. Paul Allen Beck, "The Structure of Policy Thinking: State Versus National Issues," *American Poltical Science Association Paper*, 1982, p. 20.

33. Edward G. Carmines and James A. Stimson, "Racial Issues and the Structure of Mass Belief Systems," *Journal of Politics*, 44, 1982, p. 19.

34. Beck, as cited in note 32.

35. See, for example, Lane, as cited in note 7; Lamb, as cited in note 26; and Robert S. Lynd and Helen Merrell Lynd, *Middletown in Transition: A Study in Cultural Conflicts*, New York, Harcourt, Brace, 1937.

36. Taylor and Crocker, as cited in note 12, p. 96. For a description of common causal sequences, see Nisbett and Ross, as cited in note 10, pp. 113–138.

37. Taylor and Crocker, as cited in note 12, p. 124.

38. Ernest R. May, *Lessons of the Past*, New York, Oxford University Press, 1973.

39. The nature of typical predictions is discussed in Nisbett and Ross, as cited in note 10, pp. 139–166.

40. The most widely known experiment demonstrating schemas about population subgroups involves interpretation of a drawing. In this drawing, a white man carries a

razor in a subway car, presumably to attack fellow passengers. In memory tests about the drawing, most white subjects reported that a black man carried the razor because their schemas pictured blacks as more likely assailants. Gordon W. Allport and Leo J. Postman, "The Basic Psychology of Rumor," *Transactions of the New York Academy of Sciences*, series 2, 8, 1945, pp. 61–81.

41. For similar findings, see, Claudia E. Cohen, "Goals and Schemata in Person Perception: Making Sense from the Stream of Behavior," in Nancy Cantor and John F. Kihlstrom (eds.), *Personality, Cognition, and Social Interaction*, Hillsdale, N.J., Lawrence Erlbaum, 1981, pp. 47–55. Person schemas are discussed in Thomas M. Ostrom, John B. Pryor, and David D. Simpson, "The Organization of Social Information," in E. Tory Higgins, C. Peter Herman, and Mark P. Zanna (eds.), *Social Cognition: The Ontario Symposium*, vol. 1, Hillsdale, N.J., Lawrence Erlbaum, 1981, pp. 15–30.

42. E. Tory Higgins and Gillian King, "Accessibility of Social Constructs: Information Processing Consequences of Individual and Contextual Variability," in Nancy Cantor and John F. Kihlstrom (eds.), *Personality, Cognition, and Social Interaction*, Hillsdale, N.J., Lawrence Erlbaum, 1981, pp. 91–93; and Eugene Borgida, Anne Locksley, and Nancy Brekke, "Social Stereotypes and Social Judgment," in Nancy Cantor and John F. Kihlstrom (eds.), *Personality, Cognition, and Social Interaction*, Hillsdale, N.J., Lawrence Erlbaum, 1981, 154–155.

43. Mary R. Jackman and Mary Scheuer Senter, "Images of Social Groups: Categorical or Qualified?," *Public Opinion Quarterly*, 44, 1980, p. 357.

44. For similar findings, see, Arthur H. Miller, Martin P. Wattenberg, and Oksana Malanchuk, "Cognitive Representations of Candidate Assessments," *American Political Science Association Paper*, 1982, p. 8.

45. Miller et al., as cited in note 44, found the same.

46. Hazel Markus and Jeanne Smith, "The Influence of Self-Schema on the Perception of Others," in Nancy Cantor and John F. Kihlstrom (eds.), *Personality, Cognition, and Social Interaction*, Hillsdale, N.J., Lawrence Erlbaum, 1981, p. 257.

47. Michael M. Gant and Dwight Davis, "Negative Voter Support in Presidential Elections," *Midwestern Political Science Association Paper*, 1982, p. 11. They note that there has been a consistent increase in the proportion of citizens who evaluate their preferred candidates negatively. This reached 44% in 1980, compared to 13% in 1952. They ascribe this to the fact that television campaigns make negative information pervasive and loyalty to candidates and parties is decreasing.

48. Richard R. Lau, David O. Sears, and Richard Centers, "The 'Positivity Bias' in Evaluation of Public Figures: Evidence against Instrument Artifacts," *Public Opinion Quarterly*, 43, 1979, p. 347. Also see, Barbara Hinckley, "The American Voter in Congressional Elections," *American Political Science Review*, 74, 1980, pp. 644–645.

49. Donald R. Kinder, "Presidents, Prosperity, and Public Opinion," as cited in note 17, p. 17. He points out that "when the economy falters, support for the president erodes . . . because citizens hold the president accountable for the deterioration of national economic conditions." This conflicts with our findings. However, Kinder also notes that people do not blame the president for matters presumed to be beyond his control, such as their personal economic status. This agrees with our findings, as well as those of Kay Lehman Schlozman and Sidney Verba in *Injury to Insult: Unemployment, Class, and Political Response*, Cambridge, Harvard University Press, 1979.

50. Miller, as cited in note 44, pp. 16–28. Note that these definitions of "personal characteristics" differ from the definitions used elsewhere in this book. See chapter 4, pp. 66–67.

51. Ibid. p. 22.

52. For similar observations, see Miller, as cited in note 44 and sources cited there; Thomas E. Mann and Raymond E. Wolfinger, "Candidates and Parties in Congressional Elections," *American Political Science Review*, 74, 1980, p. 629; and Shanto Iyengar, Mark D. Peters, and Donald R. Kinder, "Experimental Demonstrations of the 'Not-So-Minimal' Consequences of Television News Programs," *American Political Science Review*, 76, 1982, 852–853.

53. See Lane, as cited in note 7, p. 192, for similar observations.

54. Lloyd A. Free and Hadley Cantril, *The Political Beliefs of Americans*, New York, Simon and Schuster, 1968. Lane, as cited in note 7, p. 190, reports that for his respondents "by all odds, the most important instrument for reform was government."

55. See Lane, as cited in note 7, p. 146, for similar observations.

56. For a discussion of socially-shared reference scales, see Bennett, as cited in note 1, p. 71.

57. See Lane, as cited in note 7, p. 420, for similar observations.

58. See Lane, as cited in note 7, p. 170, for similar observations.

59. See, for example, Lee Sigelman, "The Presidency: What Crisis of Confidence?" in Doris A. Graber (ed.), *The President and the Public*, Philadelphia: Institute for the Study of Human Issues, 1982.

60. Stanley Feldman, "Economic Self-Interest and Political Behavior," *American Journal of Political Science*, 26, 1982, p. 464. For examples of socially-shared reference scales for gauging societal events, see Bennett, as cited in note 1, p. 71.

61. For similar observations, see Robert D. Putnam, *The Beliefs of Politicians: Ideology, Conflict, and Democracy in Britain and Italy*, New Haven, Yale University Press, 1973, p. 166.

62. Lane, as cited in note 7, p. 19.

63. Ibid. p. 35, for similar observations.

64. Ibid. pp. 33–34, for similar observations.

65. Feldman, as cited in note 60, pp. 456–457, also found that people blame poverty mostly on individual faults.

66. Lane, as cited in note 7, p. 325.

67. Timothy B. Rogers, "A Model of the Self as an Aspect of the Human Information Processing System," in Nancy Cantor and John F. Kihlstrom (eds.), *Personality, Cognition, and Social Interaction*, Hillsdale, N.J., Lawrence Erlbaum, 1981, pp. 194–199. Rogers presents evidence that stories involving the self are remembered better than stories without self-involvement.

68. David O. Sears, Richard R. Lau, Tom R. Tyler, and Harris M. Allen, Jr., "Self-Interest vs. Symbolic Politics in Policy Attitudes and Presidential Voting," *American Political Science Review*, 74, 1980, p. 682. Schlozman and Verba, as cited in note 49, report that unemployed people rarely question the ideological foundations of American politics that are part of their schema heritage.

# 9

## Patterns in Information Processing: Similarities and Variations

No two people think exactly alike about all matters that have come to their attention. Each person has a unique configuration of concepts about her or his world that provides guidance for thinking and action. This configuration of concepts can be visualized as a cognitive map.[1] One can think of it as a total map, just as one might think of a map of the world which reveals all parts simultaneously, or one can think of it as a partial map. Just as a map may show only one country, only physical features, or only major highways, so cognitive maps may show limited aspects of the total configuration of thinking patterns. The essential aspect of a cognitive map is the fact that it depicts the interrelation of a variety of the features that occupy a person's cognitive space.[2] In this chapter, besides discussing some general aspects of all panelists' cognitive maps, we shall focus on cognitive maps for each person that depict a small sector of their thinking, namely the conceptualization of a number of public policy issues.

### EXPECTATIONS FROM SCHEMA THEORY

The discussion of individual cognitive maps provides a good opportunity for examining once more the fit between our data and schema theory. If schema theory does, indeed, give a good account of the way people conceptualize current affairs, what kinds of mental configurations would one expect to find? How well have these expectations been met? Assuming that schema theory is valid, why would one expect schemas, and the connection among various schemas, to differ from individual to individual? After all, this is contrary to the belief system literature which assumes that there are, or ought to be, shared ideological guidelines by which beliefs are interrelated.

To answer the first question: Since schemas are created for efficiency in coping with vast amounts of information, much of it repetitive, one would expect that they would be limited in the dimensions that they encompass. One would also expect that the dimensions that would be included would be those that people find easiest to judge in most situations and that answer the most basic questions people tend to ask. Just as a child explores the world by asking "why," so average American adults are likely to be more concerned with "why things happen" than with "how they happen" when matters of observation, rather than participation are concerned.

Finally, and most importantly, one would expect that our panelists would be quite consistent in using their readily available schemas. Related news stories, despite differences among them, would nonetheless evoke the same dimensions in the same schemas. These stories would also lead to the same inferences, interpretations, and judgments, and to descriptions of the same expected developments and behaviors. Major changes in images, following dissonant information, would be rare. Instead, one would expect the panelists to interpret dissonant information so that it fits into their prevailing schemas or to neutralize it by calling it an exception or denying its validity.

One would expect a great deal of uniformity among the panelists' schemas whenever these schemas were based largely on stock images distilled from media stories in subject areas where individuals lack countervailing information and find parts of the media images easy to absorb. Media stories tend to repeat stock images, albeit with new details, when the same types of situations recur. These repetitions rehearse and deepen the initial schema.

One would also expect uniformity among panel members in schemas and parts of schemas that involve basic cultural orientations because these are part of a common heritage taught to children by their parents, their teachers, and their religious and social contacts. One would expect differences among panelists in schemas that included matters based on direct and on vicarious individual experiences.

Average Americans are not generally socialized to organize their thinking about politics in line with an overarching ideology. American democracy is a conglomerate of basic beliefs and values, many of them irreconcilable in reality. This melange does not readily lend itself to a comprehensive, hierarchical organization of ideas about individual and public behavior, private or public institutions, and private and public policies. Consequently, linkages made by political leaders and by the media among the various aspects of political life are unsystematic, made in different ways at different times, depending on the needs to be served and the principles chosen as best serving these needs. The guiding concept is pragmatism, rather than a single logic. Accordingly, one would expect that average Americans, lacking models, would not organize their schemas in overarching ways. One would even question that an overarching structure is possible, given the nature of the ingredients of American democracy.

Our panelists, and other Americans, are, therefore, limited to being contextualizers in some areas and morselizers in others. This should not disturb them greatly since the chief objective in schematic thinking is ease and efficiency in handling vast amounts of information so that the essence of the information can be used quickly for ordinary human interactions and judgments. Contrary to cognitive consistency theories, schema theory rests on the assumption that people are not highly motivated to make their thinking consistent with general principles and to apply the same general principles to related matters. It follows that people do not go to great lengths to avoid information that contradicts principles that they hold. That is, they do not routinely check their beliefs for consistency. Of course, this does not preclude high levels of consistency in thinking, as long as information available from the environment is presented from consistent perspectives.

Contextualizing should follow shared patterns in those areas where linkages have been well publicized by political leaders and the media or where it forms part of ordinary political socialization. Accepting readily available schemas is a way to economize on intellectual effort. The linkages of elections to democratic rule, fallibility to human behavior, increased taxes to excessive government spending, and crime to poverty are examples of standardized schema linkages readily adopted from mainstream thinking. However, American culture provides an array of complementary and clashing general value schemas into which more concrete schemas can be embedded. The clashing concepts of individualism and equality are examples. An individual's schemas can be embedded in either one or both. Educational policies, for instance, can be linked either to concepts of fostering individual achievement or to concepts of equalizing opportunities for all. Depending on which linkage is made as a result of individual proclivities, or as a consequence of cues contained in the information, the context for linking schemas and for evaluating policies will differ. In areas where cultural cues are weak or lacking, linkages often are idiosyncratic.

Since schemas involve the organizing of cognitions, it stands to reason that mental acuity and practice in the use of mental maneuvers, as well as familiarity with a subject area, would have an impact on the sophistication of schematic thinking. Hence, one would expect that people with less mental acuity and less experience in handling information, as well as people lacking expertise in certain areas, would have political schemas exhibiting a more limited number of dimensions. These dimensions would be more apt to fall into the person schema and human interest and empathy categories because people have more facility in handling such schemas, since they know from experience with themselves and others how people feel and interact. In areas where information is highly complex and unfamiliar, a total absence of schemas would not be surprising.

Do our data match these expectations or do they exhibit different patterns? And what might be the shape of these different patterns? To answer the latter question first: The data would disconfirm schema theory if fluctuations in panelists' reports about stories mirrored fluctuations in story content. For instance, panelists' reports about stories featuring the same theme might parallel variations in story presentation. This would suggest that there is no underlying schema for processing information. Variations might occur in the nature of story dimensions, in the complexity of dimensions, and in inferences and interpretations drawn from the stories. One might expect, for example, that stories which included a broad array of dimensions would produce reports containing broader dimensions than would stories with a narrower array. Likewise, when stories contain more complex dimensions, such as a discussion of issue positions of candidates, one might expect that these would be reported. One might expect that inferences drawn from a story might be closely linked to story content, rather than reflecting generalized conclusions with no close tie to the particular story.

Similarly, in the absence of schemas, one would not expect story reports to include elements that were *not* part of the story. One would not expect people to routinely use the same limited array of patterns for organizing stories when these patterns were not part of the story content. If items of information were stored discretely, rather than being incorporated into culturally shared images of behavior sequences, one would not expect to find shared perceptions about behavior sequences in instances when media stories did not describe such sequences. In instances when consequences of events cannot be logically deduced, one would not, in the absence of schemas, expect panelists to provide repeated, detailed scenarios based on the same underlying conceptions. For example, in the absence of a schema, one would not expect Lettie Tisdale to recount identical, often inappropriate, scenarios for every major disaster story or Darlene Rosswell to cast every story dealing with President Ford into the "Ford is a Nixon puppet" frame, irrespective of the substance of the story.

# INDIVIDUAL AND GROUP COGNITIVE MAPS

## The Research Design

During our interviews, certain public policy issues cropped up repeatedly. To examine how well or poorly our data conform to schema theory expectations, we will examine the conceptualizations of nine public policy issues by each panelist. This will make it possible to detect interissue as well as interpanelist differences in areas of political thinking that are likely to involve various types of schemas and schema dimensions. Did our panelists use the types of schemas discussed in chapter 8 in processing news about these issues? Were there instances in which schematic thinking was not apparent? If schematic thinking was apparent, were schemas limited in dimensions and were these dimensions fairly simple, often shared, and often stereotypical? Were they used consistently with little change, regardless of story detail? Looking at the entire array of issues, were there signs of overarching ideologies?

Of the 9 issues, 4 dealt with matters of the economy that were of major concern to the panelists. They were inflation, taxes, unemployment, and welfare. In addition to these, we looked at 1 very active foreign policy area—policy towards the Middle East and 4 social policy areas. The latter entail human resource problems, represented by public education and by the problems of unethical behavior in the conduct of government, and physical resource problems resulting from waning energy resources and pollution of the environment. All of these issues had been discussed in newspapers and on television more than 50 times throughout the year. A few, like education and the Middle East, had been the subject of several hundred newspaper and television stories.

In addition to the nine issues described in this chapter, we examined the conceptualization of affirmative action in the field of employment, national health insurance, adequate national defense at reasonable costs, United States policy with respect to the Soviet Union, United States relations with Latin American countries, the problems of large cities, and problems of economic recession and recovery. We also looked at conceptualizations of political leaders at various levels of government. The findings for the additional issues parallel those reported here. Quite naturally, as reported in earlier chapters, the conceptualization of political leaders showed a much heavier emphasis on person schemas than is true of the conceptualization of public policy issues. Public policy issues are also unique in their neglect of schemas involving simple situation sequences.

Discussion of the nine issues examined below cropped up in a variety of contexts in nearly every interview. The panelists frequently mentioned these issues as topics of concern to them or to people in the community in general or as topics of conversation. They were then asked for reasons why they considered the problems presented by these issues to be important. The issues also cropped up in connection with specific news stories discussed in the interviews or diaries. In the interviews, panelists were asked what they remembered about these stories and about their reactions to the matters reported in the story. In the diaries, they chose their own ways of reporting the stories.

During the second half of the interview cycle, we asked a series of open-ended questions about each of these issues. The panelists were requested to define the nature of problems presented by the issue and to indicate whether they considered them serious. In this way, we hoped to discover the major dimensions in the panelists' thinking regarding well-publicized issues about which they were genuinely concerned. We also asked the panelists to explain why these problems existed and to suggest what might be done to cope with them. These questions tested the panelists' ability to put problems into an appropriate current and future context. Finally, we asked the panelists for the sources of information on which their answers were based.

In each case, most panelists considered the problems presented by these issues to be serious. The only exception was United States-Middle Eastern policy, which did not look like a serious problem to six of the panelists, despite the fact that Arab-Israeli problems had received the most ample publicity in 1976 among foreign policy issues. We included this item, nonetheless, because we wanted to assess conceptualizations of a foreign policy issue. Moreover, demonstrating a major opinion cleavage in the panel, 15 panelists had characterized conditions in the Middle East as the most serious foreign policy issue facing the United States.

In most instances, panelists had few ideas or none at all about issues that, in their opinion, presented no serious problems. The reasons for lack of concern were diverse. They were expressed in terms of institutional behavior and human interest and empathy schemas. Problems of the Middle East were slighted by those panelists who felt that a case of controlled institutional violence was involved. They viewed the area as perennially turbulent and felt that the United States had always managed to cope with this turbulence.

Donald Burton was unconcerned about taxes and ethics, and Lettie Tisdale shared this view about welfare issues, because they perceived existing problems as normal difficulties of public institutions trying to carry out their missions. Carol Fechbach felt the same about taxes, inflation, and energy problems, adding that the media, as usual, tended to exaggerate the problem by making it news when it really was routine. Darlene Rosswell, too, thought that the seriousness of pollution was a reality only in media stories. Martha Gaylord felt that the energy problem was no cause for worry because she perceived American research institutions as highly capable; true to form, they would be able to solve the problem. Helga Holmquist explained her lack of concern on a more personal basis. Using a human interest and empathy schema, she concluded that inflation, unemployment, and unrest in the Middle East had not had any major adverse effects on her own life. Hence they were not serious to her. Craig Kolarz, Sandra Ornstein, and Sven Peterson felt the same way about taxes. Finally, David Utley put the problem of inflation and taxes into a worldwide comparative perspective. He concluded that, by comparison with the economic suffering of foreign people, his personal economic discomfort was quite minor.

When it came to sources, nearly all of the panelists named a combination that included print and electronic media as well as personal experience and conversation. Obviously, they were quite aware that their thinking about political issues was based on more than media sources, a fact that was borne out by comparisons of news story content with panelists' accounts. More than half of the panelists cited personal experience, in addition to media, as an information source for problems of inflation and taxes and for public school problems. Half of the panelists also cited conversation as a source for information on inflation and school problems. Conversation, of course, frequently transmits media information so that it becomes a secondary form of media exposure. When no personal sources of information were mentioned, panelists often indicated that their views were based directly on media stories or even ascribed their views to specific news commentators. In those instances, of which there were many, their schemas were, indeed, stripped-down versions of the images provided by media stories on the particular topic. Otherwise, the versions of the problems, as presented by the panelists, deviated from media content in a number of respects, especially, as noted in previous chapters, in linking problems to specific causes.

## The Findings: Explaining a Complex Table

The findings in table 9.1 present a complex picture. The table is arranged according to issue groups, starting with economic issues, followed by foreign policy and social policy areas. Ampersands indicate that a panelist did not regard a particular issue as serious. The panelists are arranged by interest/availability groups to facilitate comparisons with earlier tables. As before, within each group, panelists are arranged by ascending age. The letters in the table identify major and minor schema dimensions used by each panelist for each issue, with minor dimensions placed in parentheses.

The letters are followed by numerals. These show how many themes formed part of the set of dimensions. A theme is a particular subject area within a schema dimension. For example, a respondent who discusses inflation in terms of causes and effects, may have two themes within that schema dimension. Examples would be attributing high inflation to both excessive business profits and excessive consumption of goods and services.

## Intraschema Themes

We will begin our discussion of the findings with a look at the themes that our panelists related to the nine policy issues. Table 9.1 shows that parsimony once more prevails, in accordance with the underlying principle of schematic thinking. By and large, as recalled in the diaries and during interviews, the themes included in the panelists' schemas were sparse, compared to themes included in media stories, even after repeated encouragements to provide further information, and even after combining the records from all interviews and diaries. Just as most people in national election studies can generally supply no more than one or two diverse reasons for liking specific candidates and parties, so our panelists described most problems along only one or two dimensions, each containing a very limited number of themes.

Only half the panelists mentioned 3 themes for more than 1 of the 9 issues and Deidre Sandelius and David Utley never mentioned a third theme. For the 9 issues considered here, there were only 4 instances when panelists mentioned 4 themes: Robert Creighton on unemployment; Elaine Mullins and Martha Gaylord on pollution; and Max Jackman on the Middle East situation. It is possible, though unlikely because of the multiple interview design, that additional themes remained unmentioned by all panelists. If prevalent themes escaped mention by all, it seems reasonable to assume that they were of little importance to the panelists. Given the nature of the issues under discussion, the chances are small that deliberate suppression of certain themes by all panelists was involved. Many respondents did give several examples of individual themes. For instance, a respondent who considered poor academic programs a major school problem might mention poor mathematics programs during one interview, poor reading programs during another, and poor programs for teaching social skills in a third. We would code these under the single heading of "defective programs."

Table 9.2 shows that the number of themes that the panelists as a group utilized varied from issue to issue. On the high end, 12 panelists thought in terms of 3 themes about problems of the public schools, and 7 used 3 themes

TABLE 9.1. Conceptualization of Public Policy Issues*

| Name | Inflation | Taxes | Jobs | Welfare | Mideast | Ethics | Schools | Pollution | Energy |
|---|---|---|---|---|---|---|---|---|---|
| | | | | *1. High Interest, Easy Access Group*** | | | | | |
| Adams | E 2 | P(E) 2 | E 3 | P 3 | & | P 2 | P 3 | P(I) 2 | P 2 |
| Burton | I(E) 2 | &(P) 2 | E 2 | P 1 | & | &-- | P,I 3 | E 2 | E(I) 2 |
| Creighton | E 1 | I 1 | E 4 | I 2 | & | P(C) 2 | P 1, | E(I) 3 | P,I 2 |
| Diedrich | I 1 | I 2 | H(E) 2 | P 1 | I 2 | P 1 | P(I) 2 | P,I,E 3 | P(I) 2 |
| Evanski | — | I 2 | H(I) 2 | P,E 2 | E,I 2 | P 1 | P 3 | P,I 2 | E(I) 2 |
| | | | | *2. High Interest, Difficult Access Group* | | | | | |
| Fechbach | &I 1 | &E 1 | E 2 | P 1 | E1 | P 1 | I 2 | E 3 | &I 1 |
| Gaylord | E 2 | I(H) 2 | P,I 2 | P,I 2 | — | C 1 | I,P 3 | E,I 4 | &I(E) 3 |
| Holmquist | & | I 2 | &P 2 | P,I(H) 3 | &I 1 | P 1 | E 1 | E 2 | E,P,C 3 |
| Ippolito | I 1 | I 1 | E,I,P 3 | I 2 | I 1 | P,I 2 | I 3 | I 3 | E,I 3 |
| Jackman | P 1 | I,P 2 | P,I 2 | P,I 3 | I,E 4 | E,I 2 | I 3 | I,E 2 | E,I,C 3 |
| | | | | *3. Low Interest, Easy Access Group* | | | | | |
| Kolarz | E 1 | & | H,P 2 | P,I 3 | E1 | P 1 | P,E 3 | I,E 3 | I 1 |
| Liebman | E 2 | I 2 | E,I 2 | I,E 3 | I,E 3 | P 1 | I 2 | E 3 | E,I 2 |
| Mullins | E 3 | I,E 3 | E 3 | E,I,P 3 | E,I 3 | P 2 | I(E) 3 | I,P 4 | E,P 3 |
| Nystrom | I 1 | I,P 2 | P(E,I) 3 | P 2 | I 2 | I,P 2 | I,E 3 | P(I,E) 3 | E,I 2 |
| Ornstein | I 1 | & | H,P 2 | P,C(I) 3 | — | P 1 | I 2 | P,I 2 | — |
| | | | | *4. Low Interest, Difficult Access Group* | | | | | |
| Peterson | — | &I 2 | E 2 | P,I 2 | & | P 2 | I,E,P 3 | E 1 | E(I) 2 |
| Quentin | I(E) 3 | I 2 | E(I) 3 | I(H) 2 | E,I 2 | C,P,I 3 | E,I,P 3 | C 1 | C 2 |
| Rosswell | I 1 | E,P,I 3 | H,P 2 | P 1 | &I 1 | P 1 | I 3 | & | E,P,C 3 |
| Sandelius | — | I 1 | H,E 2 | P 1 | E 1 | P 1 | P,I 2 | I,P 2 | E 2 |
| Tisdale | — | — | H,P,I 3 | & | H,I 2 | — | P 1 | I 1 | I 1 |
| Utley | &E 1 | &I,E 2 | H,I 2 | P 1 | I 1 | I,P 2 | I,E 2 | E,P 2 | I,P 2 |

* Based on 27 or more mentions of each of these issues in every panelist's interview protocols. Within each group, conceptualizations are arranged in order of frequency of occurrence. Parentheses indicate that the panelist treated this approach as subordinate. Key: E = Cause and Effect Schemas; P = Person Schemas; I = Institution Schemas; C = Cultural Norm Schemas; H = Human Interest and Empathy Schemas. The numbers refer to major themes within each schema type.

** Within each group, the panelists are arranged by age in ascending order. The ampersand indicates that the panelist did *not* consider the issue to be serious.

TABLE 9.2. Use of Multiple Themes for Policy Issues

| *Issue* | *Numbers of Themes**| | | |
|---|---|---|---|---|
| | *1* | *2* | *3* | *4* |
| Inflation | 10 | 4 | 1 | — |
| Taxes | 6 | 11 | 2 | — |
| Jobs | 2 | 12 | 6 | 1 |
| Welfare | 6 | 7 | 7 | — |
| Mideast | 7 | 5 | 2 | 1 |
| Ethics | 11 | 7 | 1 | — |
| Schools | 3 | 6 | 12 | — |
| Pollution | 3 | 8 | 7 | 2 |
| Energy | 4 | 10 | 6 | — |
| | 52 | 70 | 44 | 4 |

* Based on 27 or more mentions of each issue in every panelist's interview protocol.

in discussing welfare and pollution problems. By contrast, only 1 panelist used triple themes for inflation, which turned out to be the most baffling issue in the array under consideration. Areas where the number of themes were generally low were inflation, ethical conduct in government, and Middle Eastern problems.

Considering the panelists as a group, if one calls a 50:50 ratio between single-theme and multi-theme "medium" diversity, then pollution, welfare, and school issues earn that rating. Unemployment and energy rate a "high" because two-thirds of the panelists used multi-theme schemas. By contrast, inflation, taxes, Mideast issues and ethical conduct in government receive a "low" rating because single-theme schemas are the prevailing mode.

The interview protocols make it clear that our panelists were reluctant to think about inflation, taxes, and Mideast issues, claiming that their complexity baffled them. This explains a dearth of multi-theme schemas. The issue of ethics in government, in accordance with media stereotypes, was considered by most panelists as a case of personal failings that did not lend itself to multiple conceptualizations. The issue of jobs was pushed into the "high" category because nearly every panelist who had lived through the Great Depression employed a human interest and empathy schema, in addition to other schemas. If the themes in this schema are ignored, unemployment joins other economic issues in the "low" theme category. Finally, the "high" rating of energy issues may be explained by the fact that news about the activities of OPEC in controlling the world flow of oil had been plentiful throughout 1976. This meant that relevant schemas had been rehearsed often and ample material was available for expanding the dimensions and themes of these schemas. In general, panelists had richer schemas for those issues that were particularly interesting or salient for them and that had been recently rehearsed.

The themes encountered within various schema types varied in nature from panelist to panelist.[3] But, as the complete listing of themes below reveals, the total array was nonetheless quite limited in numbers as well as in conceptual breadth. Such narrowness, if it is indeed pervasive throughout American society, means that issues are not considered in their full complexity. Constricted perceptions then impair the scope of public opinion formation and diminish the role that public opinion can play. On the other hand, consensus about policies becomes easier when the foci of the public's attention are limited and widely shared.

The particular themes included in specific schemas often were related to each panelist's special needs. Where Paul Diedrich, for instance, might store legal aspects of a story about a lawsuit against a local utility, Cesar Ippolito might store administrative details about the role of regulatory agencies that interested him as a bureaucrat. In turn, Tugwell Quentin, an avid environmentalist, might concentrate his thinking on themes related to environmental pollution. Such divergencies in theme selection were encouraged by the fact that news stories contain a wide array of diverse, often ambiguous, cues that encourage selectiveness and lend themselves to varied processing approaches.

Like other scholars, we found that the themes various people use in information processing rarely lead to directly opposite conclusions. For instance, the panelists did not divide themselves into distinct groups—one group seeing government as the solution to the unemployment problem, the other seeing it only as the cause. Instead, themes involved mixtures of these conceptions. "People simply do not view the political world from opposite sides of the same field."[4] As Conover and Feldman point out:

> This lack of bipolarity is critical because it casts serious doubts on traditional conceptualizations of political belief systems which tend to assume that people structure their beliefs in terms of one or two bipolar structures—typically labeled liberal-conservative dimensions.[5]

In table 9.3, the themes that were used most frequently are marked with an asterisk. Under the heading of each issue, the lists are arranged by schema dimension. Assignment of themes to schema dimensions was done on the basis of the conceptual coding procedures described in chapter 2. For instance, observations about causes of the problem that stressed *who* was responsible for it and *who* could correct it were coded as falling into person or institution dimensions depending on whether individuals or identifiable groups were involved. We called this the culprit/savior approach. On the other hand, if the observations stressed *what* was happening and *what* caused and could cure it, naming events or policies involved, it was coded as part of the cause-and-effect dimensions. We called this the events/policy approach to processing. The cultural dimensions category was used for observations which were explicitly related to cultural norms, and the human interest and empathy category was used to record emotional reactions to issues. (The reader may wish to review table 9.3 only selectively before turning to the discussion of schema dimensions.)

## Schema Dimensions

Table 9.1 shows how each panelist used various schema dimensions in discussing the nine issues. In each case, the patterns displayed in the table, which reflect

TABLE 9.3. List of Themes

---

### *Themes in Inflation Schemas*

---

In *Cause-and-Effect Dimensions:* High wage demands by unions*; high business profits*; high energy costs*; shortage of goods; excessive consumption; low productivity; strikes; valuation of the dollar.

In *Person Dimensions:* Greedy rich people profit from inflation.

In *Institution Dimensions:* Governments spend wildly*; governments waste money because of inefficiency*; greedy corporations raise prices*; greedy special interest groups extract too much money from the public.

---

### *Themes in Taxes Schemas*

---

In *Cause-and-Effect Dimensions:* Expensive social programs*; generally high cost of government.

In *Person Dimensions:* People request too many services from government*; ineligibles collect welfare payments*; taxpayers cheat.

In *Institution Dimensions:* Government spends wildly*; government wastes money because of inefficiency*; government coddles rich taxpayers*; government overpays its workers; government sends too much money abroad.

---

### *Themes in Unemployment (Jobs) Schemas*

---

In *Cause-and-Effect Dimensions:* Technological advances*; recession*; weakening of nation's economy; inflation; crime-unemployment link; unemployment-high tax link; excess population; undue automation.

In *Person Dimensions:* People lack skills*; people take advantage of high unemployment benefits*; people are lazy; people have excessive expectations; parents do not instill the work ethic.

In *Institution Dimensions:* Greedy labor unions demand excessive wages*; schools provide insufficient job training; employers practice racial discrimination; government coddles lazy people; government economies produce job losses; government neglects aid to private business; economists make misleading predictions.

In *Human Interest and Empathy Dimensions:* Empathy with Depression type trauma*; fear that unemployed will suffer hunger.

---

### *Themes in Welfare Schemas*

---

In *Cause-and-Effect Dimensions:* Unemployment*; lack of daycare facilities; excessive strain on the economy.

In *Person Dimensions:* Recipients cheat*; recipients and providers are greedy*.

In *Institution Dimensions:* Agencies do not control fraud adequately*; agencies have generally poor management practices*; agencies yield to demands for high benefits*; agencies provide no incentives for leaving welfare rolls; agencies do not aid clients in finding work.

In *Cultural Dimensions:* American culture condones cheating.

In *Human Interest and Empathy Dimensions:* Pity for economic difficulties of welfare clients.

---

### *Themes in Mideast Policy Schemas*

---

In *Cause-and-Effect Dimensions:* Concentration of world oil supplies in Middle East*; danger of war; unrepresentative Middle Eastern governments.

In *Institution Dimensions:* Soviets are expansionist*; U.S. is interventionist*: U.S. State Department performs poorly; Arabs misbehave; Israelis misbehave; U.S. lobbies pressure for advantages.

In *Human Interest and Empathy Dimensions:* Pity for people caught up in hostilities.

TABLE 9.3. *Continued*

## *Themes in Ethical Conduct Schemas*

In *Cause-and-Effect Dimensions:* Insufficient pay.
In *Person Dimensions:* People are greedy*; people lust for power*; people are corruptible in the face of temptation*; people lack high moral standards.
In *Institution Dimensions:* Agencies do not control corruption sufficiently*; agencies recruit greedy people; agencies have generally poor management practices.
In *Cultural Dimensions:* Americans disregard own cultural values*; social pressures force people to seek instant success; the American spirit of competition breeds corruption.

## *Themes in Schools Schemas*

In *Cause-and-Effect Dimensions:* Lack of money*; racial integration policies*; overcrowding; inadequate technological equipment; poor discipline; ban on physical punishment.
In *Person Dimensions:* Students are undisciplined*; teachers are incapable*; parents are uninterested*; students are unmotivated.
In *Institution Dimensions:* Schools offer poor quality programs*; Schools offer outdated curricula*; schools are poorly managed; school bureaucracies are unresponsive to parents; school administrators lack an educational philosophy.

## *Themes in Pollution Schemas*

In *Cause-and-Effect Dimensions:* Heavy road traffic*; heavy air traffic*; industrialization*; high cost of anti-pollution devices*; coal burning; pollution controls injurious to the economy; relaxation of controls due to bad economic conditions; nuclear testing; aerosol sprays.
In *Person Dimensions:* People drive cars needlessly*; people dump wastes carelessly*; people buy unduly large cars; environmentalists are overzealous; people smoke too much.
In *Institution Dimensions:* Heavy industry dumps industrial waste*; Big Business greed prevents adequate controls*; government does not enforce laws adequately*; enforcement agencies are inefficient.
In *Cultural Dimensions:* Americans are unconcerned about welfare of future generations.

## *Themes in Energy Policy Schemas*

In *Cause-and-Effect Dimensions:* Exhaustible resources*; insufficient production*; excess population.
In *Person Dimensions:* People waste energy*; environmentalists prevent development of resources.
In *Institution Dimensions:* Government does not do enough research*; industry does not do enough research*; foreign governments manipulate supply*; government does not provide enough public transportation; Big Business greed prevents alternative fuels; greedy Arabs restrict supply.
In *Cultural Dimensions:* U.S. society is unduly oriented towards consumption; U.S. society is unduly wasteful.

* Themes used most frequently.

information compiled from all the interviews, are constant ones. They did not vary from interview to interview, as one might expect in the absence of schemas.[6] As indicated by dashes in the table, some panelists lacked schemas in one or more domains. This meant that they did not process stories about that particular issue at all, making them "aschematics" for that particular issue. It does not mean that they processed stories in a non-schematic way.

We discovered no areas where schematic processing was absent and no schema types beyond those noted in table 9.1 except for simple situation sequences. As indicated, these were rare. We surmised that simple situation sequences might be used as a form of preliminary processing. But, except for extraordinary historical events, they were quickly forgotten because they were more a matter of memorization than of information transformation. In the absence of more extensive processing, most simple situation sequences might fit less well into an individual's thinking structure. This may make them more transient than other types of schemas. These suppositions receive support from experimental research that has shown that recall of situational details from television stories is difficult for most people, even if they are tested about the content of a 30-second segment of news within 60 seconds of exposure.[7] At the end of a 30-minute newscast, the average viewer is able to provide simple situation sequences for no more than 1 or 2 of the 15 to 18 stories that form part of an ordinary newscast.

Table 9.4 provides an overview of the frequency with which different schema dimensions were used in the conceptualization of problems. As is true of the use of various themes, the use of different dimensions focuses attention on different aspects of the same problem. It, therefore, determines ultimate concerns, evaluations, and policy preferences. If pollution is thought of as primarily involving the problem of teaching people personal tidiness, the implications for government are quite different than when it is viewed as the consequence of nuclear testing. Table 9.4 shows varied use of the three dimensions that are dominant in these issue areas. For the tax issue, institutional dimensions were dominant. For issues concerning ethics in government and welfare, person dimensions prevailed. In dealing with news about the nine issues, the culprit/savior approach, which involves looking for the role played by political actors, was far more common than the events/policy approach, which assesses happenings and corrective policies.

TABLE 9.4. Frequency of Schema Dimensions

| *Issue* | Schema Dimensions* | | | | |
|---|---|---|---|---|---|
| | *E* | *P* | *I* | *C* | *H* |
| Inflation | 7 | 1 | 8 | — | — |
| Taxes | 4 | 4 | 16 | — | — |
| Jobs | 10 | 9 | 6 | — | 8 |
| Welfare | 3 | 16 | 10 | 1 | — |
| Mideast | 8 | — | 12 | — | 1 |
| Ethics | 1 | 17 | 4 | 2 | — |
| Schools | 6 | 11 | 14 | — | — |
| Pollution | 11 | 8 | 9 | 1 | — |
| Energy | 11 | 7 | 10 | 4 | — |
| | 61 | 73 | 89 | 8 | 9 |

* Based on 27 or more mentions of each issue in every panelist's interview protocol. Subordinate issues have been excluded. Key: E = Cause-and-Effect Schemas; P = Person Schemas; I = Institution Schemas; C = Cultural Norm Schemas; H = Human Interest and Empathy Schemas.

The culprits and saviors were far more likely to be institutions than individuals. In fact, when only the culprit/savior approach involving individuals is compared to the events/policy approach, the two approaches are used with nearly equal frequency. (In the next chapter, we will touch on some consequences flowing from differential uses of various schema dimensions.)

Do the four tables presented thus far show any demographic patterns? The answer is "no." With one small exception, to be noted later, there were no discernible patterns in the use of schema dimensions and schema themes linked to demographic characteristics.[8] The closest thing to a pattern is a basic similarity among all panelists in the use of different schema dimensions for particular issues. It is most apparent for taxation, ethics in government, and welfare. The information contained in the tables also contradicts our assumption that less intelligent and less experienced individuals would be more likely to use person and human interest and empathy schemas. Neither were differences in intellectual abilities reflected in the richness of dimensions and themes or, with minor exceptions, in the availability of schemas in various policy domains.

## The Cultural Norm Cocoon

As described in chapters 2 and 8, schemas are hierarchically organized. Besides specific conceptualizations, such as those just outlined, they also contain more normative ideas. (The nature of these culturally-shared norms was outlined in chapter 3 when we talked about the panelists' belief infrastructure.) Specific schemas are usually discernibly embedded in these normative ideas. The schemas held by our panelists about the nine issues provide examples. For instance, the Horatio Alger concept of achievement by virtue of individual effort comes through clearly in the panelists' thoughts about welfare, unemployment, and public education, even when it is not specifically articulated. The notion of government as the problem-solver of last resort is equally clear, despite the universal disdain for the capabilities and ethics of bureaucracies. Notions of fairness, particularly for the disadvantaged, obviously structured schemas concerning taxation, unemployment, and Mideast problems.

Most panelists reflected a varied array of cultural norms in their schemas. At times, these included clashing norms, such as viewing welfare alternately, or even in the same comment, from the "Horatio Alger" and "give unto the poor" concepts. Karl Adams was the exception when it came to variety in cultural norms. He conceptualized all nine issues largely in terms of the "man, the sinner" concept. Whether this was a transitory stage of mind, brought about by interpersonal problems in his work situation or whether this is a permanent characteristic of his cognitive mapping is difficult to tell. But whatever the pattern, all panelists applied it consistently throughout the interviews. Once more, this is in line with the predictions from schema theory.[9]

As mentioned before, our panelists generally took a public-regarding approach to public policy issues, viewing them from the standpoint of the public good, rather than personal advantage. However, this perspective changes when people perceive issues as touching them very directly. In the array of issues considered here, four panelists always took an explicitly public-regarding stance. They were Creighton, Mullins, Utley, and Quentin. All of them often used phrases such as "it seems best for the country" or "we, as Americans." In each case, early strong socialization stressing the need for this public benefit orientation seemed to be a factor. Adams, Jackman, and Ippolito also thought largely in public-regarding ways, but were less explicit about this orientation.

The remainder of the panelists periodically evaluated problems exclusively in personal terms, citing specific personal experiences. Judging inflation in terms of personal budget problems, schools in terms of childhood experiences, or pollution in terms of one's garbage-filled alley, were examples. Martha Gaylord explained one common reason for discussing public policy issues in personal terms, saying that: "It is just very hard for me to conceptualize when you're talking about a whole country." Sandelius gave another typical reason: "Unless it happens to you. . . . it really doesn't make much of an impression on you, and none of this *has* on me. . . . some of these big social issues really throw me."

## Conceptualization Levels

The ability to think in broad terms about the general public good may well be linked to the ability to generalize.[10] While the panelists varied in the level of generality at which they preferred to express themselves and while they differed in their ability to make generalizations, all of them were capable of generalizing. They did so frequently, often on the basis of a single experience. While this is risky, most of them felt that they could afford such cognitive shortcuts because mistakes in schematic thinking about news stories generally entailed few costs. Adams, for instance, felt that his success in life rested on combining formal education with practical training. Hence, he generalized from this single experience that unemployment and welfare problems could be solved by exposing most people to combinations of theoretical and practical training. Since he had no responsibilities for unemployment programs, it mattered little whether he was right or wrong. Similarly, Betty Nystrom judged all political events in Evanston on the basis of her work for one local government agency in the East. The results of her musings, one way or another, were unimportant to her and to the community at large.

How well the panelists were able to generalize seemed to hinge on their intellectual abilities, on the nature of the information and the manner in which it was presented, and on their eagerness to generalize. However the ability to excel in abstraction did not always coincide with the desire to abstract. Several very capable generalizers preferred to think in fairly narrow and specific terms in many instances. When news stories included clear generalizations, even the less intellectually gifted were likely to process the information in abstract terms.

At the very least, they were usually able to articulate the proffered generalizations even when they did not fully grasp their meanings.

People evidently learn many generalizations about political issues from the media or other sources. Subsequently, they may fit specific experiences into these learned general schemas. When assessing levels of generalization in various subject areas, one needs to examine the origin of these generalizations before drawing conclusions about people's differential desires and abilities for making generalizations in specific knowledge areas. As the authors of *The Changing American Voter* point out in a related context: "In general, the data on levels of conceptualization do support the hypothesis that the way in which citizens conceptualize the political realm is dependent on the political content to which they are exposed. . . ."[11]

Most panelists were able to view problems from the vantage point of the present, as well as projecting them into the future. Again, there was one exception: Carol Fechbach's inability, or unwillingness, to project issues into future contexts. The only plausible explanation for her behavior was her crowded time schedule which limited her thinking at length about news and made her rely heavily on her husband to do her thinking about current issues. In discussions with him, future perspectives might have been ignored.

All panelists were able to view problems from the vantage point of others, but few used this approach unless the interviewer asked them to do so. Even then, several panelists balked at using particular vantage points. For instance, when asked how business people might feel about various social policies, some panelists demurred on the ground that they had never been in business. Occasionally, the very existence of diverse viewpoints was denied. Deidre Sandelius, for example, when questioned about how a black person might feel about integration, responded: "I can't see why you make a differentiation of how a black would feel and how a white would feel. A black's gonna feel the same—they're a *person.*"

## Schema Linkages

As noted earlier, we failed in our attempts to detect an overall structure in the data in Table 9.1 which might indicate belief systems characteristic of particular types of respondents. Except for some similarity in conceptualization patterns among the over-50 age group—the Depression generation—none of the demographic categories or the interest/access categories produced any meaningful patterns.[12] It also proved impossible to predict the conceptualization of specific issues across issue groups. Neither the economic issues, nor the human resource issues, nor the physical resource issues were related in any statistically significant ways.

Some panelists linked several issues explicitly, of course, either through general concepts, such as a belief in free enterprise or through making causal connections. For the nine issues considered here, unemployment, in particular, was often linked causally to inflation, taxes, welfare, crime, and domestic and world-wide recession. Likewise, taxes were frequently linked with inflation, welfare, and corruption. Pollution and energy problems were also seen as causally related, and the causal tie between pollution control and unemployment was repeatedly mentioned. Of the 4 panelists, 3 repeatedly made such causal connections, with Robert Creighton and Elaine Mullins the high scorers, and Lettie Tisdale, Deidre Sandelius, Craig Kolarz, Max Jackman and Helga Holmquist at the low end.

But such connections and even linkages based on broader principles, are a far cry from the well-organized belief structure that is the "Holy Grail" so long sought by political scientists. Even when one is satisfied with extremely loose ideological orientations, such as "liberal" and "conservative" in the American context, the outlines of belief structures are blurred, blending into each other and overlapping on many points. Our panelists might call themselves liberals or conservatives, but even by their own definitions of these terms, so many of their schemas did not fit with the professed orientations that the term "system" would be misapplied.[13]

Since information processing evidently follows schematic rules, political scientists need to look to individual cognitive maps, rather than to generalized belief systems, displaying a universally-shared logic, in their search for belief structures. Once we had identified how particular panelists conceptualized specific issues in their schema structure, how they linked them, and how they encased them in normative beliefs, we could predict the persistence of these conceptualizations and linkages. While we could not forecast in each case which specific features of the conceptualization were going to be expressed, we knew the range of features available for inclusion. We could, therefore, anticipate that the specifics would be consistent with the general schema, without knowing what precise form the specifics would take. When incorrect predictions occurred, they were usually explained by the fact that the panelist under consideration had several available schemas to process the particular information, and we had chosen the wrong one.

Since the schema dimensions employed for processing ordinary political news are quite limited (even the themes within these dimensions are not numerous) and since the belief infrastructure in which specific schemas are embedded is well-known, the task of individual cognitive mapping is a feasible one. It has been done repeatedly by political scientists studying political elites.[14] It is also done routinely by professional campaign consultants who probe the beliefs of voting groups on specific issues, and it is done by advertising professionals who engage in psychographic analysis.[15]

## MENTAL ABILITIES AND MIND-SET

Before concluding our scrutiny of cognitive maps, we must briefly review the impact of mental abilities and mind-set on schematic thinking. Throughout this book, we have often referred to intelligence, learning, education, socialization, and similar matters as important factors in information processing. In light of the fact that intellectual abilities did not seem to affect the uses made of schema dimensions and the richness of themes, can one still maintain that intellect is a major factor in information processing? The answer is "yes," although the scope of influence of intelligence is more limited than we anticipated.

## The Role of Intelligence

*Intelligence*, as Webster defines, is the ability to learn, understand, and retain knowledge, the ability to respond quickly and successfully to new situations, and the use of the faculty of reasoning in solving problems.[16] On the basis of our interviews, we had rated our panelists on all of these qualities and found predictable, substantial differences. When we checked the interview data in light of these ratings, we found that panelists at lower intelligence levels omitted more stories from processing and had more difficulty in retrieving complex information than was true of people at higher levels.

The ability to comprehend the meaning of complex stories was most closely related to intelligence. Comments ("I don't understand what they are trying to say" or "this is beyond me") appear regularly in the protocols of panelists of normal, yet limited intellectual resources. They are rare in the protocols of the intellectually gifted. When televised or radio news was the source of information, speed of comprehension was an added factor. Although most panelists complained that newscasts were too fast-paced, panelists who were slow in comprehension found it exceptionally difficult to keep up the pace. They were most likely to process the last items prior to a pause in news because the pause provided them with the time needed for slower processing.

Intelligence was also a factor in story retrieval. Panelists rated as more intelligent were apt to process information more systematically and made use of their system in retrieval. Specifically (as discussed in chapter 7), the ability to segment information facilitates retrieval. While all panelists knew how to segment, the more intelligent used the technique more often and more adeptly. This made it easier for them to retrieve information. In many instances, the more intelligent also showed greater sophistication in telling what they deemed to be the gist of the story. Primarily, this involved greater language facility and better ability to articulate ideas. It did not involve increased use of dimensions and themes.

Finally, the capacity to retain information in memory is linked to intelligence, directly or indirectly. The indirect route involves schema rehearsal that enhances memory. Since the more intelligent panelists had better retrieval capacities, they rehearsed information more readily than the less intelligent. However, this advantage was counterbalanced for some panelists by problems of memory overload. Among the highly intelligent, several complained often that they had exposed themselves to more information than their memories could handle. Burton and Ippolito, for example, diagnosed memory overload as the source of their frequent failures of memory. According to Fiske and Kinder, the problem appears to spring from deficiencies in processing techniques because "the escalation of information need not interfere with rapid retrieval, if the information is organized."[17] The fact that information overload interferes with processing and memory was also evident since several panelists' memories worked far better when their information intake was limited and when there were no distractions during processing.

## The Role of Experience and Education

Experience has often been called "the best teacher." Do people who have experience in political matters and whose thinking abilities have been honed through higher education have more sophisticated schemas? The answer is a qualified "yes." Fiske and Kinder claim that "the involved and the expert in a particular domain will more easily bring to mind applicable schemata; they will also employ such schemata in more sensitive ways." Moreover, "through practice, experts acquire more—and more complexly organized—knowledge, which include strategies for dealing with particular domains."[18]

This observation held true only to a limited extent for our panelists. Those who had worked in government bureaucracies, had personal experiences with the health care system, or were professionally active in legal matters, generally had more complex and sophisticated schemas in these areas. But there were several exceptions. Helga Holmquist, for instance, despite the fact that her intellectual abilities had been sufficient to graduate from a top-level law school and despite the fact that both she and her husband were working in government, exhibited surprisingly simplistic schemas about governmental institutions. The explanation in her case, and others, seems to be that learning from experience is not automatic. Just as availability of news does not mean that it will be used, in the absence of interest and motivation, so experience does not automatically produce greater learning and sophistication if interest and motivation are lacking.

For the same reason, it is also doubtful that higher education automatically produces greater sophistication in thinking patterns, even though it strengthens cognitive skills, supplies concepts for organizing political information, and often spurs political interest.[19] In the absence of interest in a particular area of knowledge, and motivation to process the relevant information, our college-educated panelists had less sophisticated schemas than their less-educated, but more interested counterparts. Overall, intelligence and experience seemed to be stronger predictors of sophistication than higher education by itself. Fiske and Kinder, in like fashion, concluded from a series of experiments on political cognition that interest and motivation are key factors. The politically involved, because of their interest in and attentiveness to political information, excel "in the nature of schemata available to them, in the ease by which such schemata are invoked, and in the facility with which such schemata are employed in information processing."[20]

## The Role of Reference Groups

Feelings of shared interest are powerful forces in aligning people's thoughts with those professed by their reference groups. In the realm of political thinking, the influence of political parties and economic reference groups is deemed especially significant. Therefore, we need to look at the role that these reference groups played in our panelists' processing of political information. Unfortunately, our panel does not lend itself well to exploring the impact of partisanship. Of the panelists, 14 leaned toward the Democratic party and 7 leaned towards the Republicans. But in every case, partisanship was lukewarm. No panelist had strong enough feelings for her or his party to refuse to vote for a member of the opposition party or to refuse to consider the reasonableness of the positions taken by members of the opposition. Therefore, we cannot assess the impact of strong partisanship.

For weak partisans such as our panelists, everything else being equal, schemas tend to reflect positions taken by prominent party leaders and publicized in the media. But when things were not equal, when panelists had pre-existing countervailing schemas, partisanship lost its potency. It must also be remembered that the media only rarely emphasize partisan positions strongly and clearly, usually when election news and major congressional activities are involved.

Nonetheless, partisan influence is significant. Party affiliation is often a matter of childhood socialization. For this reason, even weak partisans might acquire many of the cognitive and normative orientations underlying their party's issue positions during childhood and adolescence. They will, therefore, be predisposed, to some extent, toward adopting party positions on specific current issues. In this way, party identification may be a significant influence on information-processing throughout an individual's life, even when the individual does not feel strong ties to a particular party.[21]

Using similar reasoning, Teresa Levitin and Warren Miller argue that the concepts of liberalism and conservatism become important political organizing principles, even when people do not understand or misinterpret the content associated by political scientists with these labels.[22] For many people, these concepts become code words with positive or negative connotations, which they usually learn early in life. Whenever these code words are subsequently attached to political information, as happens frequently, the sensitized individual is apt to react to the information in accordance with the sentiments attached to the cue.

Our interview protocols do not contain sufficient data to assess the validity of this supposition. With the exception of Lettie Tisdale, all of the panelists had rated themselves on a 7-point, conservatism-liberalism scale. They had also explained their understanding of the meanings of these concepts. However, most of their definitions strayed far from those underlying the use of these terms in the news. Accordingly, our panelists frequently questioned the accuracy of these labels as used by the media. When the panelists failed to take their cues from the labels, one could not tell whether doubts about the appropriateness of the label or impotence of the label was the reason.

Since economic self-interest is generally considered a powerful force in shaping opinions, did the schemas used by various panelists differ along economic lines? The answer, for most issues, is "no." Among the panelists, 5 could be called rich, 6 were poor, and the remaining 10 earned moderate incomes. But both rich and poor, as well as the middle-incomed, blamed big business and talked about inequitable tax structures; all three groups, attributed a great deal of unemployment to laziness and believed that welfare recipients often cheated to get undeserved benefits. However, the poor approached problems somewhat more often from the vantage point of economic group interests. They also processed information more often in terms of the need for government intervention. But these distinctions were neither marked nor pervasive.

To a limited extent, schemas also reflect what has been called "status incongruity." This phenomenon occurs when an individual is raised at one social status level and then rises above or falls below it after his or her thinking patterns have been formed.

Sven Peterson was an example. He had been raised in a well-to-do professional family, but worked in a menial, low-paying job and lived in a poor neighborhood. In his case, the result was a mixture of viewpoints. He retained many of the orientations learned in childhood, but coupled them with some new orientations more appropriate for his current economic status.

## THE VERDICT

What conclusions can we draw? The final verdict after matching findings from individual cognitive maps against the predictions derived from schema theory is that the fit is good. Cognitive processing does follow patterns that are best explained in terms of schema theory. In the realm of political news, our panelists coped with the floodtide of information through a manageable, limited array of schemas that were simple and sparse in basic dimensions, as well as in the number of themes included in the dimensions.

The simplicity of this basic structure was no bar to varied, occasionally sophisticated, information processing when one looks at the schemas exhibited by the group as a whole. What Putnam pointed out for political elites, held true for our panelists as well, albeit generally at lower levels of sophistication:

> Some concentrate on broad social and moral principles, while others emphasize specific situations and details. Some argue deductively from general political or social or economic theories, while others rely on induction from their own experience. Some refer to benefits or losses to particular groups in society, while others refer to technical or financial practicality or administrative efficiency. Some refer to past or future utopias . . . Some consider political feasibility . . . Some place an issue into a historical context. Some attribute blame for a problem while others phrase their analysis in "neutral" terms.[23]

Despite substantial uniformity in the general shape of schema systems, much of it abetted by uniformity in media presentations, diversity among the schemas created by each panelist thus remained a striking reality.

### Notes

1. Robert Axelrod, *The Structure of Decision: The Cognitive Maps of Political Elites*, Princeton, Princeton University Press, 1976, p. 55. Axelrod defines a cognitive

map as follows: "A cognitive map is a specific way of representing a person's assertions about some limited domain, such as a policy problem. It is designed to capture the structure of the person's causal assertions and to generate the consequences that follow from this structure."

2. For a fuller description of cognitive maps, see Axelrod, as cited in note 1, pp. 3–17, 221–248.

3. For an analysis of internal variations in schemas, see, Dana Ward, "Genetic Epistemology and the Structure of Belief Systems: An Introduction to Piaget for Political Scientists," *American Political Science Association Paper*, 1982, p. 28.

4. Pamela Johnston Conover and Stanley Feldman, "Schema Theory and the Use of Q-Methodology in the Study of Mass Belief Systems," *American Political Science Association Paper*, 1982, p. 10. The authors discovered only one instance in which the several perspectives used as a backdrop for analyzing a given policy were direct opposites. This involved a non-militaristic and isolationist schema that was the mirror image of a militaristic, internationalist schema. Also see, David Lowery and Lee Sigelman, "Understanding the Tax Revolt: Eight Explanations," *American Political Science Review*, 75, 1981, pp. 970–972.

5. Conover and Feldman, as cited in note 4, pp. 11–12.

6. Ibid. Kenneth P. Langton and Octavian Petrescu in "Cognitive and Situational Antecedents to Worker Participation," *American Political Science Association Paper*, 1982. The authors found that workers, confronted with scenarios about possible strike situations, "view a single situation from multiple perspectives." They also note that "situational perceptions do reflect the patterning of past learning, but the fit is by no means perfect."

7. Jacob Jacoby and Wayne D. Hoyer, "Viewer Miscomprehension of Televised Communication: Selected Findings," *Journal of Marketing*, 46, Fall 1982, pp. 12–26.

8. Lowery and Sigelman, as cited in note 4, p. 972. They point out that demographic lines blur when issues are viewed from a symbolic perspective. Also see, M. Stephen Weatherford, "Economic Voting and the 'Symbolic Politics' Argument: A Reinterpretation and Synthesis," *American Political Science Review*, 77, 1983, pp. 158–174.

9. For similar findings, see Axelrod, as cited in note 1, p. 153.

10. Riley W. Gardner, "The Development of Cognitive Structures," in Constance Scheerer (ed.), *Cognition: Theory, Research, Promise*, New York, Harper & Row, 1964, p. 151.

11. Norman H. Nie, Sidney Verba, and John R. Petrocik, *The Changing American Voter*, Cambridge, Mass., Harvard University Press, 1976, pp. 121–122. Eric R.A.N. Smith, "The Levels of Conceptualization: False Measures of Ideological Sophistication," *American Political Science Review*, 74, 1980, p. 685. Smith makes the same point with respect to ideological thinking. "When rhetoric is more ideological, people's discourse will reflect this. But that does not mean that their thinking has become more systematic." Also see, John C. Pierce, "Party Identification and the Changing Role of Ideology in American Politics," *Midwest Journal of Political Science*, 14, 1970, p. 34.

12. Susan T. Fiske and Donald R. Kinder, "Involvement, Expertise, and Schema Use: Evidence from Political Cognition," in Nancy Cantor and John F. Kihlstrom (eds.), *Personality, Cognition, and Social Interaction*, Hillsdale, N.J., Lawrence Erlbaum, 1981, p. 171. The authors begin their chapter by stating categorically that "our central message is that people differ enormously both in schema availability and in schema use."

13. See also, Pamela Johnston Conover and Stanley Feldman, "The Origins and Meaning of Liberal/Conservative Self-Identification," *American Journal of Political Science*,

25, 1981, p. 640. Also see, Donald R. Kinder, "Enough Already About Ideology: The Many Bases of American Public Opinion," *American Political Science Association Paper*, 1982.

14. See, for instance, Axelrod, as cited in note 1; Robert D. Putnam, *The Beliefs of Politicans: Ideology, Conflict, and Democracy in Britain and Italy*, New Haven, Yale University Press, 1973; Robert D. Putnam, *The Comparative Study of Political Elites*, Englewood Cliffs, N.J., Prentice Hall, 1976; and Hans D. Klingemann, "Measuring Ideological Conceptualizations," in Samuel H. Barnes et al., (eds.), *Political Action: Mass Participation in Five Western Democracies*, Beverly Hills, Calif., Sage, 1979.

15. See, for example, William D. Wells, (ed.), *Lifestyle and Psychographics*, Chicago, American Marketing Association, 1974; Barbara Everitt Bryant, "Marketing Newspapers with Lifestyle Research," *American Demographics*, 3, January 1981, pp. 21–25.

16. Jonathan Baron, "Intelligence and General Strategies," in Constance Scheerer, (ed.), *Cognition: Theory, Research, Promise*, New York, Harper & Row, 1964, pp. 403–405, 427. He argues that the mark of "intelligence" is that people have great facility in processing information. Highly intelligent people develop insights into strategies for learning which they can apply consciously to information processing. The less intelligent acquire such strategies through imitation and repetition but they do not learn how to use them consciously to best advantage.

17. Fiske and Kinder, as cited in note 12, p. 177.

18. Ibid., pp. 171, 177.

19. The evidence on the impact of education on cognition complexity is controversial. Paul Hagner and John Pierce "Conceptualization and Consistency in Political Beliefs: 1956-1976," *Midwest Political Science Association Paper*, 1981, p. 10. Hagner and Pierce concluded from the study of survey research data of presidential elections from 1956 to 1976 that the data from 1964 onward show that people with higher education think in more sophisticated ways. But other researchers dispute these findings and our data support the latter view. See, for instance, Stephen Earl Bennett, Robert W. Oldendick, Alfred J. Tuchfarber, and George F. Bishop, "Education and Mass Belief Systems: An Extension and Some New Questions," *Political Behavior*, 1, 1979, pp. 53–72; Charles M. Judd and Michael M. Milburn, "The Structure of Attitude Systems in the General Public," *American Sociological Review*, 45, 1980, pp. 627-643.

20. Fiske and Kinder, as cited in note 11, p. 182.

21. Karl A. Lamb, *As Orange Goes: Twelve California Families and the Future of American Politics*, New York, Norton, 1974, p. 70.

22. Teresa E. Levitin and Warren E. Miller, "Ideological Interpretations of Presidential Elections," *American Political Science Review*, 73, 1979, p. 752. Levitin and Miller have estimated, on the basis of 1972 survey data, that 45–55% of the population do not have a clear view what it means to be a conservative or liberal, even when they use these tags in self-identification. Moreover, most people do not know what the liberal versus conservative position is on most issues, unless it is clearly labelled.

23. Putnam, *The Beliefs of Politicians*, as cited in note 14, p. 34. For schema patterns emerging from an analysis of general television viewing, see, W. Russell Neuman, "Television and American Culture," *Public Opinion Quarterly*, 46, 1982, pp. 471–487.

# 10

# Conclusions, Implications, Applications

A book is like a long journey. After one has travelled the road, absorbed the sights and sounds, and formed initial impressions, one should pause at journey's end to contemplate the whole. What are the final conclusions? What is their significance? How can the new discoveries ease future journeys? And, finally, are there lessons that can be put immediately into practice? One may answer such questions cautiously, sticking strictly to what seems certain from the evidence. Or one may, within reason, gamble a bit and interpret the evidence boldly, trusting that it will ultimately prove to be robust enough to sustain the broader conclusions. Heartened by a spate of recent studies that corroborate many findings presented in this book, I am following the latter approach. Hence, in this concluding chapter, the broader term "people" will take the place of more cautious references to only "our panelists."

## HOW PEOPLE TAME THE INFORMATION TIDE

The first major conclusion drawn from this study of information processing is that people tame the information tide quite well. They have workable, if intellectually vulnerable, ways of paring down the flood of news to manageable proportions. When they finish reading their newspapers, 2 out of every 3 stories have been excluded. Perusal of the remaining stories is simplified by taking advantage of the inverted pyramid style of news reporting. In this style, the most important information appears in the initial paragraph, allowing the reader to skip the remainder with relative impunity. Nearly half of the stories that people notice are handled by way of such partial reading. Out of the total story offering in an average newspaper, only 18% of the stories are read in full.

A similar screening process goes on for televised and radio news. On an average, out of 15 to 18 stories in a television newscast, no more than 1 is retained sufficiently well so that it can be recalled in any fashion shortly afterwards. The total loss of information, however, is not as great as these numbers suggest. Many of the stories are ignored because the audience realizes that they are a repetition of previously reported information. Television and radio newscasts throughout a given day are especially repetitious. If one considers only genuinely new information, the proportion of actual "news" recalled is somewhat higher.

Although the initial news selection process is haphazard, in addition to being stringent, people manage to keep on top of the most important stories. When one focuses only on stories that are significant by the canons of elite journalism, the balance between skipping and paying attention is reversed. People who are exposed to high-quality news sources recollect to some degree 2 out of every 3 prominent stories that are likely to affect the course of politics substantially. The credit for this greater attentiveness to important stories is shared by newspeople. They use a series of prominence cues (e.g., story placement, headline size, story length, pictorial treatment, and frequent repetitions) to attract attention to news that political leaders and media gatekeepers deem significant.

In addition to paring down the flow of information by ignoring large numbers of stories, people use a processing mechanism that further reduces the amount of information needing to be stored. This mechanism is the schema process. It allows individuals to extract only those limited amounts of information from news stories that they consider important for incorporation into their thinking. The schema process also facilitates integration of new information into existing knowledge. Since news sources usually present the news in isolated snippets, without sufficient background, schemas allow the receivers to incorporate the news into a meaningful context. During relatedness searches, the information extracted from a news story may be integrated into a single schema, or it may be segmented and the segments incorporated into several schemas. Alternatively, the same segments may become a part of several schemas. In this way, a single story may be used to substantially broaden an individual's store of knowledge. If it becomes apparent that the new information is not needed because it is redundant or because it does not conform to previous knowledge that seems sound, the schema process allows the unwanted information to slip from readily available memory.

While the schema process does well in reducing the danger of information overload, it does not lead to the retention of a large amount of factual data. Understanding, rather than rote learning, is the goal. This explains why most people are unable to provide full particulars for news that they have processed. Despite the nature of the schema process, people nonetheless learn a limited amount of detail because many news stories recur frequently with essentially the same information items. For instance, most people can provide some details for stories about street crime, unemployment, pollution, and corruption among officeholders. Even when people cannot recall specifics from a particular story, they know, on the basis of comparisons with familiar information stored in memory that there has been "nothing new." Whenever information needs to be recalled, schemas can provide ready-made nonspecific answers. Schemas can even provide previously-stored story details for stories for which these details have been skipped.

Over time, an individual's fund of generalizations and specific knowledge grows, despite substantial amounts of forgetting. This is not surprising. Several daily lessons about current events, carried on year after year, with frequent repetition of the same lesson, are bound to leave their mark, even when learning is purely passive. Since most of these lessons are used to flesh out preformed beliefs, a good deal of systematic error is likely to occur whenever these beliefs are wrong. That is the price people must pay for the relief from information-processing burdens brought about by the use of prototypes.

From the standpoint of average Americans, haphazard news processing is quite satisfactory. Interest in news is comparatively low. Therefore, it does not justify great expenditure in time and effort when there are other things to do that have a higher priority for the individual. But despite lukewarm interest in the news, average Americans want to keep informed because they have been socialized to feel that this is a civic responsibility. Many of them also want daily reassurance that they are not missing news items that might be significant for their lives. This combination of normative and personal pressures impels people to give at least cursory attention to news on a regular basis.

Most Americans have also learned to look on news as a form of entertainment, so they try to satisfy two goals simultaneously, whenever possible. They scan the news for pieces of information that are important, diverting, and possibly both. The decision to select news for attention, or to reject it, therefore, is strongly influenced by an appraisal of the significance and the appeal of a particular piece of news. This makes it incumbent upon the media to cover essential stories in ways that capture and hold the public's interest.

## IMPLICATIONS FOR AMERICAN DEMOCRACY

The broader political implications of the kind of news-processing behavior that we have depicted need to be considered from two perspectives. The first of these is the capacity of average Americans to acquire enough political information so that they can fulfill the obligations of democratic citizenship. The second perspective requires a look at the implications for democratic living that flow from the substance of currently held schemas, as developed and sustained through daily mass media news reports.

### The Capacity for Political Learning

The American mass media supply a vast amount of current political information to average Americans. This is mixed in with an even larger amount of non-political information. In general, no single person, spending all waking hours in news consumption, could begin to pay attention to all of it, let alone absorb it successfully.

Our panelists demonstrated that people from all walks of life, endowed with varying capabilities, can manage to extract substantial amounts of political knowledge from this flood of information. All panelists had mastered the art of paying selective attention to news and engaging in the various forms of relatedness searches. All had acquired schemas into which they were able to fit incoming political information. All were able to work with an adequate array of schema dimensions, and all frequently used multiple themes in their various schemas. All had adopted culturally sanctioned values as the schematic framework into which schemas covering more specific matters were then embedded.

The differences among the panelists in the use of their processing skills were surprisingly minor. Largely, they were matters of degree of use of various skills, such as segmenting and checking, and differences in coping with highly complex information drawn from settings remote to the individual's life. Some of these differences were linked to life-style, because life-style generates needs for certain types of processing. Insofar as life-style overlaps demographic categories, such as age, sex, and ethnicity, life-style differences take on the appearance of demographic differences. There also are some processing differences linked to intellect, education, and motivation. Again, these result in differences in degree of performance, rather than substance.

On balance, the verdict is clear. Average Americans are capable of extracting enough meaningful political information from the flood of news to which they are exposed to perform the moderate number of citizenship functions that American society expects of them. They keep informed to a limited extent about the majority of significant publicized events. They also learn enough about major political candidates to cast a thoughtful vote and make some judgments about post-election performance. Our findings show that "no opinion" replies often turned out to be instances where individuals did have opinions but were afraid to express them until coaxed to do so. Their initial reluctance was due to fear of sounding stupid or concern about the merits of particular opinions that were not grounded in adequate information.

Ideally, one may wish that expectations for good citizenship were higher and demands for political learning more exacting. One may wonder whether changes in news production and news processing might enhance the quality of citizenship. However, answers to such questions are speculative and disputed. Critics of current patterns may question whether people have acquired sufficient political information to fulfill citizenship needs when they lack specific knowledge and when they base election choices largely on assessments of the candidates' personal qualities. Shouldn't well-informed people depend more on issue information for voting decisions? Doesn't effective citizenship require that one remembers the name of one's Representative or knows the length of a senatorial term? Isn't it essential for Americans in the 1980s to be able to locate Afghanistan on a map? The answer is *no*. One does not need to include issue information in candidate assessment to make a sound choice. One does not have to know the name of one's Representative or the length of a senatorial term in order to understand the role that Congress plays in the political process. One does not have to locate Afghanistan on a map to be aware that the Soviet Union is intervening militarily in adjacent countries.

People select their bases for political judgments in their own ways, despite lip service to the judgmental criteria advocated by political elites. Nor are people's judgmental criteria framed to meet the need of survey researchers to develop easily codable questions. Nonetheless, these choice criteria work well, judged from the perspective of personal efficiency. Take the example of selecting political leaders largely on the basis of personality. This makes eminently good sense

> given the capacities and inclinations of the average voter. Information about personal qualities is the only information which the average layman, remote from the political scene, can appraise intelligently. . . People may properly feel that a president who is "a good man, capable and experienced" can tackle any kind of problem. At the time of the election it may be uncertain in which areas a candidate's severest test will come. Therefore it may be best to concentrate on general leadership qualities and characteristics of integrity and trustworthiness, rather than dwelling on competence in a variety of areas."[1]

The intellectual ability of the average citizen has also been called into question because social scientists have not been able to find the kind of belief systems for which they were looking. We have seen that people do have belief systems, although they are not the grand edifices about which researchers have been speculating. Broad value principles provide the closest thing to an overarching belief structure. Beyond these, people do make causal and other connections among their schemas. The fact that processing involves relatedness searches also shows that there is continual awareness of similarities and connections.

The multiplicity of basic values in the schema structure leads to substantial flexibility and diversity in organizing information. This makes patterns of belief far less predictable than the patterns expected as the result of previous belief system research. In many respects, it also makes them far more realistic. One should not squeeze or stretch multifaceted problems into a single Procrustean bed. Ambivalence is sound when there are no clear-cut choices. Rather than worrying about the public's rationality, one may well wonder about "the unwillingness of many political leaders and commentators to accept the public's 'post-ideological' maturity, and their insistence that the public should either endorse the left's traditional affirmation of the state or the right's rejection of it."[2]

## The Impact of Schematic Thinking

Since schemas, once created, form the mold into which new information is integrated, previous schemas become extremely important. This highlights the significance of early socialization. The overarching cultural values appear to be internalized early in life. These, of course, are the values that account for the substantial consensus in American politics and for tolerance of a wide variety of views. It is this consensus, coupled with tolerance for a limited range of deviations, that makes a heterogeneous nation, like America, governable.

Early socialization also lays the groundwork for needed diversity. We know that children adopt party identifications early in life, as well as leanings towards liberalism and conservatism. These early identifications, carried throughout life, provide political symbols that have a significant, though limited, influence on subsequent political orientations.

When people fail to learn or create appropriate schemas for certain types of news, that news cannot be absorbed. Socialization of average Americans apparently leaves a number of gaps in the schema structure. These gaps then make it difficult to focus public attention on some important problems. News about most foreign countries and news about science are examples. Even when such news is presented in simple ways, much of the audience fails to make the effort to absorb it because appropriate schemas did not form part of past socialization.

One may ask why people learn many new schemas early in life but lose that capacity or inclination as adults. An analogy to language learning may provide the answer. Small children learn new languages with relative ease and without extensive practice in logical thinking. Most adults, despite their greater capacities for logic, find it difficult, and occasionally impossible, to learn new languages and use them for thinking as well as speech. To push the analogy a bit further, just as nearly all people with normal intelligence are able to learn a new language in childhood, so nearly all people with normal intelligence are able to learn schematic thinking during their early years of life. Higher intelligence may permit more sophisticated use of these abilities, but the basic capacities for language learning and for schematic thinking are shared by all. Like language learning, schema development and the creation of new schemas continue throughout life. But, as in language learning, the pace becomes much slower, except in the wake of extraordinary events.

The media play a significant part in early as well as later phases of socialization. Because of their pervasiveness, and the ready access of all Americans to the same news sources, this socializing role is an important factor in creating a basis for nationwide commonality in thinking. As Lane observed in his Eastport panel, people who take their cues from the media:

> reinforce one another's criticisms, they echo each other's solutions, and they share one another's sense of insecurity or of hope. In this they come to evolve common concepts of industrial and governmental responsibility, of what is appropriate for the individual to do, whether wives should work, whether taxes are driving industry from Eastern State, whether the Republicans should or should not be blamed. And these, arising from more basic views on the proper relationship between social classes, the proper role of government, the proper way to explain a social event of this damaging character, go into the communications network and filter into the political stream. . . .[3]

Regardless of whether people filter their news largely through the eyes of liberals or conservatives, the media to which the average American is exposed have a status-quo bias. They legitimize the American system by the deference they pay to its structure, its values, and its elected and appointed officials, in general, if not in specific ways.

The fact that the same basic values as well as some specific schemas about the political process are adopted by most Americans during childhood and adolescence means that public political thinking tends to lack flexibility. Depending on one's feelings about the substance of consensus among Americans, the stability inherent in schematic thinking is either a boon or a bane. However, incremental changes do occur fairly readily in the wake of changing circumstances. Only large, abrupt changes in thinking about political issues are rare, except when major upheavals occur or when serious new problems become obvious. When these unusual conditions are widely publicized and involve declarations by well-known opinion leaders, they are apt to shake the confidence of large numbers of people in the continued validity of their existing schemas. Vietnam, Watergate, and the Civil Rights' movement are recent examples of events that evidently produced major schema changes in a relatively brief period of time. The growing awareness of pollution problems, which was heightened by the activities of very visible political action groups, is another.

## The Substance of Schemas

In the preceding chapters, I outlined the chief political attitudes expressed by our panelists when they were reporting their reactions to current news. These attitudes evidently are shared by Americans in general. For example, Everett Carll Ladd and Seymour Martin Lipset, who examined scores of nationwide public opinion polls, described the political thinking of average Americans in the 1970s in terms which would be quite appropriate for describing our interview findings:

> Attempts to put a political label on the seventies can also be confusing because the words we use to characterize politics—liberal and conservative—do not sharply differentiate the values of most Americans . . . We are no longer as certain that as a nation we can solve our problems and come out on top. . .
>
> America's diminished self-certainty finds expression through a low level of professed confidence in the leaders of most institutions—governmental, business, labor, et al.—and sharp criticisms voiced about the way these institutions operate. But at the same time, the great majority of Americans remain strongly positive about the fundamentals of their nation. They bemoan the spotty performance of their leaders and institutions—yet they do not want to scrap, or even alter significantly, any core institutions. . .
>
> There is no shortage of examples of the profound ambivalence which now characterizes public opinion and values in the United States . . . Nearly every measure of public opinion shows this same general phenomenon—of Americans continuing to look to the state for answers and actions. At the same time, however,

the public is deeply troubled about governmental performance. It *does* believe the government is too intrusive, too profligate, too inefficient.[4]

The key word that characterizes such attitudes is "ambivalence." Today's Americans have mixed feelings about their government. This ambivalence goes beyond heterogeneity of beliefs among different groups. The ambivalence lies within the thinking of average individuals. Such ambivalence at the individual level allows political communicators to tap selectively into contradictory schemas held by individuals to evoke desired support or opposition. Individual ambivalence thus provides political communicators with a tremendous opportunity to lead the public in desired directions. By the same token, it may also become a booby trap that can lead to disaster when opposition leaders tap into schemas that suit their purposes.[5]

Many specific schemas have major political implications because they are so widely shared. An example is the generally negative view of government and politicians, coupled with a tolerance for their failings and a strong belief that, on balance, the American system is sound. Such a mixture of beliefs may be a prescription for excessive public acquiescence to governmental failures. It greatly reduces the shock value of media stories so that investigative journalism, which has focused on graphic illustrations of governmental misdeeds, raises little more than eyebrows. It usually fails to spawn "let's turn the rascals out" political campaigns. In fact, even the news value of many exposés has been comparatively small. Crooked politician stories lack the glamor of "man bites dog."

This does not mean that negative feelings never lead to action when the circumstances are right. The strong belief that government is wasteful apparently was a major component in accepting tax limitation propositions. So were the widely shared beliefs that government is inefficient and that taxes are unnecessarily high.[6] Other policy-relevant schemas that have been reflected in public opinion and public policies are the notion that big business is corrupt, the idea that government is the savior of last resort, and, above all, the belief that American democracy is the best form of government for the country and that ordinary people as well as politicians ought to behave in accordance with its tenets.

The fact that some types of schemas or schema themes are absent or under-developed affects democratic living just as strongly as the existence and full development of others. The nearly total lack of scenarios in people's schemas about the manner in which public institutions operate is an example. The sparsity of the themes included in schemas about a variety of important public policies is another. If people lack relevant schemas and schema dimensions in matters that ought to be of public concern, they are not likely to absorb information that might give them better insights into these matters. However, while one may regret that schemas lack richness, one must keep in mind that their chief purpose is efficiency in information storage and retrieval. Granted that purpose, the leanness of schemas is an advantage.

## CONTRIBUTIONS TO SOCIAL SCIENCE

The contributions of this book to social science knowledge fall under two major rubrics. The first of these concerns exploration of various aspects of the political learning process and their implications for current social science knowledge and procedures. The second rubric relates to the development and use of schema theory for political science research.

## The Political Learning Process

The findings presented in this study confirm that political communication is very much a transactional process. Mass media messages are not imprinted on the minds of media audiences in the precise manner in which they are offered. Rather, audience members condense the offerings in their own ways, select aspects of interest, and integrate them into their own thinking. Similar perceptions among audience members and the resemblance of these perceptions to the images provided by the media spring from two sources: (1) similarity in socialization and (2) lack of relevant schema themes to mold incoming news. Consequently, schemas reflect media offerings closely in some areas and hardly at all in others. There is, however, no hypodermic effect, as some communication scholars still argue, whereby a media message is internalized exactly as presented.[7]

Our findings also add support to those critics of cognitive balance theories who have pointed out that people have a preference for information which is in accord with their established beliefs, but that this preference is not absolute. In fact, many people like to hear what transpires on the other side of the opinion fence, either out of curiosity, or because of their belief in the value of openness in a democratic society. With few exceptions, we found no automatic rejection of discordant information.[8]

Our findings shed some new light on the nature of rationality in political thinking. Anthony Downs and his followers have long argued that citizens use a rational calculus for their political thinking and behavior. They absorb and use information only if the anticipated benefits to be derived from learning are commensurate with the costs entailed in acquiring information. Since the costs are usually estimated—rightly or wrongly—to be substantially higher than the likely benefits, most citizens keep political learning and political participation at a minimum.[9]

Similarly, our findings indicate that people calculate the cost of processing the news in terms of time and effort. They prefer a process that saves time and simplifies the complexities of political learning. Therefore, they use the thinking categories that are easiest for them to handle. This is hardly the rationale that social scientists, eager for serious deliberation of complex issues, would like citizens to use. But it represents rational thinking nonetheless. As M. Brewster Smith has pointed out, rationality can be judged by the steps in the decision process as well as by its products. Rational decisions are ones "that select appropriate means to attain specified goals at acceptable costs. . . ."[10]

The study brings to light a number of features that characterize people's memory for news. We found that memory for specific events decays rapidly. Flashbulb memories are the exception; they indicate that the capacity for long-term memory for news events exists. After people have forgotten specific story events, the attitudes distilled from these events are likely to be retained as part of a schema. Hence, individuals may remember that they had specific reasons for considering a politician capable or incapable, without being able to recall the reasons. Over the period of the study year, we did not find any evidence that basic schemas had been forgotten. But it seems likely that they, too, may ultimately be difficult to retrieve from memory if they are not activated occasionally.

The study provided evidence that rehearsal of information retards decay. For instance, election information learned at various times during the campaign was beyond recall until it was rehearsed during the presidential debates. Hence the journalistic habit of repeating the same information periodically refreshes memory and prevents information loss. Rehearsals may be crucial just before political activities, such as voting, take place. For example, candidate debates immediately prior to elections, even when they add no new information, become an important intellectual exercise because they refresh previously learned information when most needed for decision making.

Our findings contribute to the debate about significance of economic self-interest in political decisions made by average Americans. The findings support the contention that people take an altruistic approach to many social problems, rather than judging them purely from self-centered, pocketbook perspectives. However, they also show that there are limitations to the sociotropic argument. Schemas contain personal along with public welfare concerns. The personal angles tend to become dominant when individuals feel seriously, rather than mildly threatened. Since it is often difficult to connect public policies and events with personal concerns, serious threats to personal security often go unrecognized.[11]

Throughout this book, I have pointed to the fact that demographic categories, such as sex, ethnicity, age, and economic status are spurious variables when it comes to the analysis of thinking processes. In many ways, their use as if they were relevant variables is dangerous. It tends to perpetuate the stereotype that members of these groups think alike and that, somehow, this thinking is the inevitable outcome of unchangeable demographic factors. There are ample data, in addition to those presented in this study, to show that members of demographic groups differ in those opinions, attitudes, and thinking patterns that, presumably, are a mark of their group membership. To cite just two examples, many women oppose the feminist movement in whole or in part, and many Jews do not identify with the State of Israel. Yet research conventions, and the difficulty, at times, of obtaining large enough samples to demonstrate intragroup differences, have led to glossing over such differences. The consequences, in terms of continued public stereotyping, are profound and undesirable. This study may help in remedying this problem.

This study lends additional support to the troublesome finding that the information rich tend to get richer while the poor stay poor. Since information is a major asset in gaining political power, this means that social groups who lack information are likely to remain at the bottom of the power heap. This fact has implications for social policy. A society that is genuinely dedicated to equal opportunity for all, must provide the means whereby all citizens learn to hone their thinking facilities to the limit of their capacities.

As we have pointed out, segmenting and checking are great helps in processing information in the most productive ways and making it available for easy recall. Both of these skills can be taught and obviously are taught. But many people, especially those with a limited amount of formal education, apparently do not learn these skills well enough to apply them to best advantage. Better teaching along these lines is needed at all levels of public education. Unfortunately, lack of facility in processing information has an adverse spiral effect. If less information is processed, fewer schemas are available for future processing. Consequently, people who have limited funds of knowledge are further handicapped. They find it more difficult to retrieve information because they have fewer schemas from which the needed information can be extracted.

Finally, our findings again emphasize the need to reexamine survey research procedures so that better survey instruments can be designed. At the very least, they call attention to the errors introduced into survey results by the shortcomings of current methodologies. Specifically, survey researchers need to be more mindful of the fact that closed questions provide cues leading to specific schemas and hence predetermine the nature of answers. Consequently the validity of answers is impaired. Open-ended questions should be used more extensively. However, this approach also presents problems in addition to its currently high costs. Without the guidance that cues in closed questions provide for relatedness searches, people often are unable to tap into the schemas needed to answer particular questions. The researcher may then draw an unwarranted "don't know" even when the respondent has the necessary schemas to produce an answer. The solution here is more careful, imaginative probing.

Survey researchers also need to be more aware of the process by which slight changes in wording can tap into different schemas and can thereby drastically alter responses. Elizabeth Loftus, in a book dealing with the problems encountered in tapping the recollections of eyewitnesses during legal proceedings, provides many graphic examples. One of them concerns an experiment in which people saw a film about a car accident and were subsequently questioned about it. One group was asked "How fast were the cars going when they *smashed into each other*?" A second group was asked "How fast were the cars going when they *hit each other*?"[12] All subjects were then asked to estimate the speed of the colliding cars. The group whose car crash schemas were tapped by the word "smash" estimated much higher rates of speed than those whose schemas were tapped by the word "hit." A follow-up question, one week later, graphically revealed the difference that a single word can make in tapping different schemas. All subjects were asked whether they had seen any broken glass in the film. There had been none, but schemas of car crashes usually evoke notions of breakage. So it was not surprising that a sizeable number of the subjects reported seeing broken glass despite its absence. More surprisingly, the phrase "smashing into each other" was more potent in evoking visions of major damage than the phrase "hit each other." Accordingly, 32% of the "smash" group, compared to 14% of the "hit" group erroneously reported seeing broken glass.

## The Use of Schema Theory for Political Research

Our study demonstrates that schema concepts are valuable in studying political thinking. It presents evidence that schemas used for political thinking have the characteristics that cognitive psychologists have described for schemas dealing with simpler types of knowledge. Schemas about politics appear to be hierarchically organized with broad values encasing specifics and with specific incidents buttressing more general conclusions. Some cognitive psychologists have viewed schemas only in cognitive terms; others have argued that schemas contain memories of feelings and evaluations about the concepts in question. Our findings accord with the latter view.[13]

Specifically, the study demonstrates that average Americans have large numbers of schemas in their political thinking. But individual schemas have relatively few themes and are arranged along fairly simple dimensions. When new information is encountered, people usually are able to integrate selected portions into existing schemas through various types of relatedness searches. Pending research on schematic thinking in other knowledge domains, we do not know whether the processing strategies and schema patterns encountered in the political realm are universal.

In an article published in 1980, Susan Fiske and Patricia Linville ask the question: "What Does the Schema Concept Buy Us?"[14] This is an important question. Phrased in a way more relevant for political studies, we may ask: "What help does schema theory offer for the study of political phenomena that goes beyond the insights that flow from other theories?" Above all, schema theory provides a much richer, more realistic, model of the totality of the thinking process than hitherto used in political science. As Sears and Citrin point out, one can visualize schematized attitudes as "(1) reasonably well informed, (2) affectively consistent and interdependent, (3) based in some broader, more abstract conceptualization, and (4) stable over time." Within individual schemas, there is pressure toward affective and cognitive consistency. Schematic thinking makes individuals "more resistant to influence, and more likely to deduce attitudes on new issues from pre-existing attitudes. . . ."[15] The hypotheses generated by this formulation are richer than, and often different from, hypotheses based on other cognitive theories. They provide better answers to the many puzzles posed by seemingly inconsistent political thinking and behavior.

One example can be drawn from the research that has probed the thinking behind the spate of tax limitation proposals that swept the country in the early 1980s. Converse's "levels of ideological sophistication" concepts would predict that political experts would have more consistent belief structures than people with less political sophistication.[16] Schema theory, on the other hand, would predict that experts, having more schemas related to complex economic problems than average people, would have more dissonance within their schema array. A study of the beliefs underlying the attitudes of Massachusetts citizens towards a tax limitation proposal confirms this counter-intuitive prediction based on schema theory.[17]

# THE ROLE OF POLITICAL COMMUNICATORS

## Setting the Political Agenda

Aldous Huxley once said that:

> Words *do* have a magical effect—but not in the way that the magicians supposed, and not on the objects they were trying to influence. Words are magical in the way they affect the minds of those who use them. "A mere matter of words," we say contemptuously, forgetting that words have power to mold men's thinking, to canalize their feeling, to direct their willing and acting. Conduct and character are largely determined by the nature of the words we currently use to discuss ourselves and the world around us.[18]

What Huxley did not say, but what is implicit in his statement, is that words provide cues that evoke schemas in the audience. When political communicators, be they newspeople or politicians, choose particular words and verbal configurations, they bias the reaction and response. For example, public opinion poll results show that people favor support for "public assistance programs to the elderly and the disabled" as well as "public assistance programs for low-income families with dependent children." But when they are asked about "welfare" programs, their willingness to support aid for the poor drops sharply.[19] Obviously, a rose by any other name does not appear to smell as sweet.

Media also make major contributions to schema formation and development by providing the public with partially preprocessed information in various domains of knowledge and by signalling the relative importance of stories. This information is particularly pervasive in those areas of knowledge where people have few chances to acquire information through personal sources. Ease of access to non-media sources varies, of course. People, whose access is limited and whose schemas are not well-developed, are, therefore, more susceptible to media influence whenever they are exposed to media stories.

If the media fail to cover essential news, it has little chance of entering the minds of average individuals or even of political elites, because Americans rely very heavily on the mass media as their eyes and ears on the world. The crucial role that media play in creating the context which affects people's judgments has also been mentioned. News stories are not absorbed in isolation. In addition to more directly experienced environmental factors, the mood set by the context of major news stories and the schemas that they bring to the fore become major reference points for judging all stories that surface at a particular point in time.

We have stressed throughout this study that there are distinct limitations to the media's power to influence schemas. But these limitations should not be overemphasized. For many areas of public life, average Americans are totally dependent on media information. There simply are no other sources to acquire information. The information provided by the media may be suspect and conflicting, but, in the end, the individual must form schemas from whatever is presented. There is little opportunity for gaining different insights or verifying the accuracy of available information and interpretations.

Besides, many average Americans lack self-confidence in their ability to make political judgments and often defer to the judgments of newspeople. Public reactions to the Ford–Carter debates during the 1976 presidential campaign are instructive. Immediately after the second debate, in which President Ford had declared that Eastern Europe was free from Soviet domination, more respondents in a national survey named Ford, rather than Carter as the better debater. A day later, after media stories had criticized Ford, Carter's score rose by 51 percentage points making him the favorite. People had adopted the evaluation of the media, rather than holding to their own.[20] As Penny Liebman put it: "I thought that Ford had won, but the papers say it was Carter. So it must be Carter."

Some intriguing questions about the role of different types of news media are raised by the fact that there are variations in the ease with which meaningful information about abstract concepts can be extracted from printed news, as compared to televised news. Printed descriptions and analyses, once audiences overcome the hurdle of mastering reading, are much easier to process. Printed stories state meanings explicitly and provide preprocessed information from which to choose data that fit into available schemas. The verbal portions of telecasts are much sparser in their data. Moreover, while pictures are more plentiful and while one picture may be worth a thousand words, a problem arises. Faced with the equivalent of a thousand words or more, most people are unable to absorb the flood of information quickly enough, particularly when the pictures lack explicit cues to point out what is important. Given this difficulty, it is not surprising that 48% of the stories remembered by our panelists were attributed to newspaper sources, compared to 27% attributed to television and 25% to other sources. The interesting question raised by this situation concerns future political learning. What will happen to the quality of learning about public affairs if newspaper use continues to decline and electronic media capture an increasing share of the audience's attention?

## The Impossible Task of the Mass Media

Throughout this book, the media have come in for a goodly share of criticism for inadequacies in news presentation. That record, too, must be put into perspective. The task that democratic theory prescribes for American general-purpose mass media is extremely difficult at best, and, in most instances, impossible. To gain the attention of mass audiences, the media must tell political stories simply and interestingly. But most political stories are neither simple nor appealing to general audiences. Most cannot be condensed to fit the brief attention span of the public. The attempt to be both simple and interesting leads to oversimplifications and an emphasis on sensational human interest features of events. This, in turn, engenders adverse criticism of the media.

A number of institutional problems further complicate the media's task. Complex stories cannot be adequately told unless there is sufficient time available. But electronic newscasts, for a variety of institutional reasons, are generally so brief that they allow for little more than presentation of headlines and a few brief story lines to accompany the pictures. Even newspaper space is too constrained to satisfy the requirements of adequate explanations, without undue sacrifice of variety in coverage. Space and time pressures are magnified by the need to repeat background material in every story because media audiences are in constant flux. Since many people read the news irregularly, they require quick recapitulations about what transpired before they paid attention. Such summaries take up substantial amounts of scarce media space and time. High quality presentation is further hampered by the abominable dictatorship of deadlines. Given current news production conventions in the United States, news must be produced quickly, leaving little opportunity for research and reflection. Speed and "the scoop," unfortunely, are prized more than depth and insight.

Finally, media people must work in a transactional environment without knowing very much about the audience with whom they are interacting. Hence, it is nearly impossible to know what types of information various members of the media audience need and want to flesh out in their schemas and how that information should be presented so that it fits readily into the schema structure of audience members. To meet audience needs more completely, newspeople will have to engage increasingly in scientific audience analysis, as advertisers, political campaign consultants, and other marketing professionals are now doing. The use of focus groups may prove especially helpful. Such groups represent a small number of individuals with diverse schema systems. Group discussion can test how these systems react to new information. It may also disclose the nature of relevant schemas.

Political information processing could be facilitated if newspeople learned to cast information into formats that closely matched those used by audience members for storing information. In an era when most political information was made available through mass media directed to huge audiences, personalized news casting was impossible. This era may be reaching its end. The age of electronic narrow-casting and interactive media communication has arrived, and with it the possibility to personalize political information transmission sufficiently to match a much wider variety of processing needs.

Whether "better" communication, in the sense of tailoring messages more carefully to the predilections of audiences, would be "worse" communication because it would be more persuasive, is an open question. As stated at the outset, the findings presented in this study confirm that average Americans can successfully scrutinize the merits of people and policies from a variety of perspectives. They can recognize their own limits and those of others in information-processing capabilities. They do not make judgments based on a single ideology or the recommendations of a single source. Average people know how to accept and reject information, and they are, therefore, not likely to be manipulated into large-scale acceptance of schemas that conflict with the basic tenets of American culture. For all these reasons, I cast my vote in favor of more effective political communication.

## Notes

1. Doris A. Graber, "Press Coverage and Voter Reaction in the 1968 Presidential Election," *Political Science Quarterly*, 89, 1974, pp. 96–97.

2. Everett Carll Ladd, "Politics in the 80s: An Electorate at Odds with Itself," *Public Opinion*, 5, 1983, p. 3.

3. Robert E. Lane, *Political Ideology: Why the American Common Man Believes What He Does*, New York, Free Press, 1962, p. 443.

4. Everett Carll Ladd, and Seymour Martin Lipset, "Anatomy of a Decade," *Public Opinion*, 1980, pp. 2–4.

5. Doris A. Graber, *Verbal Behavior and Politics*, Urbana, Ill., University of Illinois Press, 1976, pp. 289–321.

6. David O. Sears and Jack Citrin, *Tax Revolt: Something for Nothing in California*, Cambridge, Mass., Harvard University Press, 1982, p. 92.

7. The continuing public debate about the impact of television crime shows on juvenile and adult crime rates provides many examples of arguments based on the hypodermic model.

8. Also see, Lewis Donohew and Philip Palmgreen, "A Reappraisal of Dissonance and the Selective Exposure Hypothesis," *Journalism Quarterly*, 48, 1971, pp. 412–420.

9. Anthony Downs, *An Economic Theory of Democracy*, New York: Harper, 1957, pp. 38–45, 241–244, 271–272.

10. M. Brewster Smith, "Personality in Politics: A Conceptual Map, with Application to the Problem of Political Rationality," in O. Garceau (ed.), *Political Research and Political Theory*, Cambridge, Mass., Harvard University Press, 1968, p. 94.

11. The debate between proponents and opponents of the sociotropic approach is outlined in Gerald H. Kramer, "The Ecological Fallacy Revisited: Aggregate-versus Individual-Level Findings on Economics and Elections, and Sociotropic Voting," *American Political Science Review*, 77, 1983, 92–111; also see, M. Stephen Weatherford, "Economic Voting and the "Symbolic Politics" Argument: A Reinterpretation and Synthesis," *American Political Science Review*, 77, 1983, pp. 158–174.

12. Elizabeth F. Loftus, *Eyewitness Testimony*, Cambridge, Mass., Harvard University Press, 1979, pp. 77–78.

13. The link between cognition and affect is discussed in Robert B. Zajonc, "Feeling and Thinking: Preferences Need No Inferences," *American Psychologist*, 35, 1980, pp. 151–175.

14. Susan T. Fiske and Patricia Linville, "What Does the Schema Concept Buy Us?," *Personality and Social Psychology Bulletin*, 6, 1980, pp. 543–557.

15. Sears and Citrin, as cited in note 6, p. 78.

16. Philip E. Converse, "Public Opinion and Voting Behavior," in Nathan Polsby

and Fred Greenstein (eds.), *Handbook of Political Science*, vol. 4, Reading, Mass., Addison-Wesley, 1975, pp. 100–107.

17. Richard R. Lau, Robert F. Coulam, and David O. Sears, "Proposition 2½ in Massachusetts: Self-Interest, Anti-Government Attitudes, and Political Schemas," *Midwest Political Science Association Paper*, 1983, pp. 17–22.

18. Aldous Huxley, "Words and Their Meanings" in Max Black (ed.), *The Importance of Language*, Englewood Cliffs, N.J., Prentice-Hall, 1962, pp. 1–2.

19. Sears and Citrin, as cited in note 6, pp. 184–185.

20. Frederick T. Steeper, "Public Response to Gerald Ford's Statements on Eastern Europe in the Second Debate," in George F. Bishop, Robert G. Meadow, and Marilyn Jackson-Beeck (eds.), *The Presidential Debates: Media, Electoral, and Policy Perspectives*, New York, Praeger, 1978, pp. 84–87.

# Bibliography

Ajzen, Icek, and Martin Fishbein. *Understanding Attitudes and Predicting Social Behavior.* Englewood Cliffs, N.J.: Prentice-Hall, 1980.

Allison, Graham T. "Conceptual Models and the Cuban Missile Crisis." *American Political Science Review*, *63*, 1969, 689–718.

Allport, Gordon W., and Leo J. Postman. "The Basic Psychology of Rumor." *Transactions of the New York Academy of Sciences*, 8 (Series 2), 1945, 61–81.

Anderson, John R. (ed.). *Cognitive Skills and Their Acquisition.* Hiilsdale, N.J.: Lawrence Erlbaum, 1981.

Asch, Soloman E. "The Process of Free Recall." In Constance Scheerer (ed.), *Cognition: Theory, Research, Promise.* New York: Harper & Row, 1964.

Atkin, Charles K. "A Conceptual Model of Information Seeking, Avoiding, and Processing." In Peter Clarke (ed.), *New Models for Mass Communication Research.* Beverly Hills: Sage, 1973.

———. "Instrumental Utilities and Information Seeking." In Peter Clarke (ed.), *New Models of Mass Communication Research.* Beverly Hills: Sage, 1973.

———. "Communication and Political Socialization." In Dan D. Nimmo and Keith R. Sanders (eds.), *Handbook of Political Communication.* Beverly Hills: Sage, 1981.

Axelrod, Robert. "Schema Theory: An Information Processing Model of Perception and Cognition." *American Political Science Review*, *67*, 1973, 1248–1266.

———. *Structure of Decision: The Cognitive Maps of Political Elites.* Princeton: Princeton University Press, 1976.

Bachman, Jerald G., and Patrick O'Malley. "When Four Months Equal a Year: Inconsistencies in Student Reports of Drug Use." *Public Opinion Quarterly*, *45*, 1981, 536–548.

Baron, Jonathan. "Intelligence and General Strategies." In Constance Scheerer (ed.), *Cognition: Theory, Research, Promise.* New York: Harper & Row, 1964.

Bauer, Raymond A. "The Obstinate Audience." *American Psychologist*, *19*, 1964, 319–328.

Beck, Paul Allen. "The Structure of Policy Thinking: State versus National Issues." *American Political Science Association Paper*, 1982.

Beck, Paul Allen, and M. Kent Jennings. "Pathways to Participation." *American Political Science Review*, *76*, 1982, 103–110.

Becker, Lee B. "Two Tests of Media Gratifications: Watergate and the 1974 Election." *Journalism Quarterly*, 53, Spring 1976, 26–31.

————. "Measurement of Gratifications." *Communication Research*, *6*, 1979, 54–73.

Becker, Lee B., Maxwell E. McCombs, and Jack M. McLeod. "The Development of Political Cognitions." In Steven H. Chaffee (ed.), *Political Communication: Issues and Strategies for Research*. Beverly Hills: Sage, 1975.

Becker, Lee B., Idowu Sobowale, and William E. Casey. "Newspaper and Television Dependencies: Their Effects on Evaluations of Public Officials." *Journal of Broadcasting*, *23*, 1979, 465–475.

Bem, Daryl J. *Beliefs, Attitudes, and Human Affairs*. Belmont, Calif: Brooks-Cole, 1970.

————. "Self-Perception Theory." In Leonard Berkowitz (ed.), *Cognitive Theories in Social Psychology*. New York: Academic Press, 1978.

Bennett, James. *Oral History and Delinquency: The Rhetoric of Criminology*. Chicago: University of Chicago Press, 1981.

Bennett, Stephen Earl, Robert W. Oldendick, Alfred J. Tuchfarber, and George F. Bishop. "Education and Mass Belief Systems: An Extension and Some New Questions." *Political Behavior*, *1*, 1979, 53–72.

Bennett, W. Lance. "Perception and Cognition: An Information-Processing Framework for Politics." In Samuel L. Long (ed.), *The Handbook of Political Behavior* (vol. 1). New York: Plenum Press, 1981.

————. *The Political Mind and the Political Environment*. Lexington, Mass.: Lexington Books, 1975.

Berelson, Bernard, Paul Lazarsfeld, and William McPhee. *Voting: A Study of Opinion Formation in a Presidential Campaign*. Chicago: University of Chicago Press, 1954.

Bishop, George, Robert W. Oldendick, and Alfred J. Tuchfarber. "Effects of Presenting One versus Two Sides of an Issue in Survey Questions." *Public Opinion Quarterly*, *46*, 1982, 69–85.

Bishop, George, Robert W. Oldendick, and Alfred J. Tuchfarber. "Political Information Processing: Question Order and Context Effects." *Political Behavior*, *4*, 1982, 177–200.

Blumler, Jay G. "The Role of Theory in Uses and Gratifications Studies." *Communication Research*, *6*, 1979, 9–36.

Blumler, Jay G., and Katz, Elihu (eds.). *The Uses of Mass Communications: Current Perspectives on Gratifications Research*. Beverly Hills: Sage, 1974.

Bobrow, Daniel G., and Allan Collins (eds.). *Representation and Understanding: Studies in Cognitive Science*. New York: Academic Press, 1975.

Borgida, Eugene, Anne Locksley, and Nancy Brekke. "Social Stereotypes and Social Judgment." In Nancy Cantor and John F. Kihlstrom (eds.). *Personality, Cognition, and Social Interaction*. Hillsdale, N.J.: Lawrence Erlbaum: 1981.

Brody, Richard A., and Paul M. Sniderman. "From Life Space to Polling Place: The Relevance of Personal Concerns for Voting Behavior." *British Journal of Political Science*, *7*, 1977, 337–360.

Brown, Steven R. "Intensive Analysis in Political Research." *Political Methodology*, *1*, 1974, 1–25.

————. *Political Subjectivity: Applications of Q Methodology in Political Science*. New Haven: Yale University Press, 1980.

Brown, Thomas S., and Patricia M. Wallace. *Physiological Psychology*. New York: Academic Press, 1980.

Bryant, Barbara Everitt. "Marketing Newspapers with Lifestyle Research." *American Demographics*, *3*, 1981, 21–25.

Campbell, Angus, Philip E. Converse, Warren E. Miller, and Donald E. Stokes. *The American Voter*. New York: Wiley, 1960.

Campbell, Angus, Gerald Gurin, and Warren Miller. *The Voter Decides*. Evanston, Ill.: Row, Peterson, 1954.

Campbell, Bruce A. "On the Utility of Trait Theory in Political Science." *Micropolitics*, *1*, 1981, 177–190.

Cantor, Nancy. "A Cognitive-Social Approach to Personality." In Nancy Cantor and John F. Kihlstrom (eds.), *Personality, Cognition, and Social Interaction*. Hillsdale, N.J.: Lawrence Erlbaum, 1981.

Cantor, Nancy, and John F. Kihlstrom (eds.). *Personality, Cognition, and Social Interaction*. Hillsdale, N.J.: Lawrence Erlbaum, 1981.

Cantor, Nancy, and Walter Mischel. "Prototypes in Person Perception." In Leonard Berkowitz (ed.), *Advances in Experimental Social Psychology* (vol. 12). New York: Academic Press, 1979.

Carmines, Edward G., and James A. Stimson. "Racial Issues and the Structure of Mass Belief Systems." *Journal of Politics*, *44*, 1982, 2–20.

———. "The Two Faces of Issue Voting." *American Political Science Review*, *74*, 1980, 78–91.

Carroll, John S., and John W. Payne (eds.). *Cognition and Social Behavior*. Hillsdale, N.J.: Lawrence Erlbaum, 1976.

Carterette, Edward C., and Morton P. Friedman (eds.). *Handbook of Perception: Perceptual Processing* (vol. 9). New York: Academic Press, 1978.

Chaffee, Steven H. (with Marilyn Jackson-Beeck, Jean Durall, and Donna Wilson). "Mass Communication in Political Socialization." In Stanley Renshon (ed.), *Handbook of Political Socialization*. New York: Free Press, 1977.

Clarke, Peter, and Eric Fredin. "Newspapers, Television and Political Reasoning." *Public Opinion Quarterly*, 42, 1978, 143–160.

Cohen, Claudia E. "Goals and Schemata in Person Perception: Making Sense From the Stream of Behavior." In Nancy Cantor and John F. Kihlstrom (eds.), *Personality, Cognition, and Social Interaction*. Hillsdale, N.J.: Lawrence Erlbaum, 1981.

Collins, Allan M., and Elizabeth F. Loftus. "A Spreading-Activation Theory of Semantic Processing." *Psychological Review*, *82*, 1975, 407–428.

Collins, W. Andrew. "Social Scripts and Developmental Patterns in Comprehension of Televised Narratives." *Communication Research*, *9*, 1982, 380–398.

Conover, Pamela Johnston. "Political Cues and the Perception of Candidates." *American Politics Quarterly*, *9*, 1981, 427–448.

Conover, Pamela Johnston, and Stanley Feldman. "Belief System Organization in the American Electorate: An Alternate Approach." In John C. Pierce and John L. Sullivan (eds.), *The Electorate Reconsidered*. Beverly Hills: Sage, 1980.

———. "The Origins and Meaning of Liberal/Conservative Self-Identification." *American Journal of Political Science*, *25*, 1981, 617–645.

———. "Schema Theory and the Use of Q-Methodology in the Study of Mass Belief Systems." *American Political Science Association Paper*, 1982.

———. "Group Identification, Values, and the Organization of Political Beliefs." *Midwest Political Science Association Paper*, 1983.

Converse, Philip E. "Attitudes and Non-Attitudes: The Continuation of a Dialogue." In Edward Tufte (ed.), *The Quantitative Analysis of Social Problems*. Reading, Mass.: Addison-Wesley, 1970.

———. "The Nature of Belief Systems in Mass Publics." In David Apter (ed.), *Ideology and Discontent.* New York: Free Press, 1964.

———. "Public Opinion and Voting Behavior." In Nathan Polsby and Fred Greenstein (eds.), *Handbook of Political Science,* (vol. 4). Reading, Mass.: Addison-Wesley, 1975.

———. "Rejoinder to Judd and Milburn." *American Sociological Review, 45,* 1980, 644–646.

Cronkhite, Gary, and Jo R. Liska. "The Judgment of Communicant Acceptability." In Michael E. Roloff and Gerald R. Miller (ed.), *Persuasion: New Directions in Theory and Research.* Beverly Hills: Sage, 1980.

Cundy, Donald T. "Affect, Cue-Giving and Political Attitude Formation: Survey Evidence in Support of a Social Conditioning Interpretation." *Journal of Politics, 41,* 1979, 55–74.

Cutler, Neal E., and James A. Danowski. "Process Gratification in Aging Cohorts." *Journalism Quarterly, 57,* 1980, 269–276.

Dance, Frank E. X., and Carl E. Larson. *The Functions of Human Communication.* New York: Holt, Rinehart & Winston, 1976.

Davis, Dennis K., and Stanley J. Baran. *Mass Communication and Everyday Life: A Perspective on Theory and Effects.* Belmont, Calif.: Wadsworth, 1981.

Dawson, Paul A. "The Formation and Structure of Political Belief Systems." *Political Behavior, 1,* 1979, 99–122.

Dennis, Jack (ed.). *Socialization to Politics: A Reader.* New York: Wiley, 1973.

Donohew, Lewis, and Philip Palmgreen. "A Reappraisal of Dissonance and the Selective Exposure Hypothesis." *Journalism Quarterly, 48,* 1971, 412–420.

Downs, Anthony. *An Economic Theory of Democracy.* New York: Harper, 1957.

Eiser, J. Richard. *Cognitive Social Psychology: A Guidebook to Theory and Research.* London: McGraw-Hill, 1980.

Erbring, Lutz, Edie N. Goldenberg, and Arthur H. Miller. "Front-Page News and Real-World Cues: A New Look at Agenda-Setting by the Media." *American Journal of Political Science, 24,* 1980, 16–49.

Erikson, Robert S., Norman R. Luttbeg, and Kent L. Tedin. *American Public Opinion: Its Origins, Content, and Impact* (2nd ed.). New York: Wiley, 1980.

Feldman, Stanley. "Economic Self-Interest and Political Behavior." *American Journal of Political Science, 26,* 1982, 446–466.

Field, John O., and Ronald Anderson. "Ideology in the Public's Conceptualization of the 1964 Election." *Public Opinion Quarterly, 33,* 1969, 380–398.

Fishbein, Martin, and Icek Ajzen. *Belief, Attitude, Intention and Behavior: An Introduction to Theory and Research.* Reading, Mass.: Addison-Wesley, 1975.

Fisher, B. Aubrey. *Perspectives on Human Communication.* New York: Macmillan, 1978.

Fiske, Susan T., David A. Kenny, and Shelley E. Taylor. "Structural Models of the Mediation of Salience Effects on Attribution." *Journal of Experimental Social Psychology, 18,* 1982, 105–127.

Fiske, Susan T., and Donald R. Kinder. "Involvement, Expertise, and Schema Use: Evidence from Political Cognition." In Nancy Cantor and John F. Kihlstrom (eds.), *Personality, Cognition, and Social Interaction.* Hillsdale, N.J.: Lawrence Erlbaum, 1981.

Fiske, Susan T., and Patricia Linville. "What Does the Schema Concept Buy Us?" *Personality and Social Psychology Bulletin, 6,* 1980, 543–557.

Foti, Roseanne J., Scott L. Fraser, and Robert G. Lord. "Effects of Leadership Labels and Prototypes on Perceptions of Political Leaders." *Journal of Applied Psychology*, 67, 1982, 326–333.

Free, Loyd A., and Hadley Cantril. *The Political Beliefs of Americans: A Study of Public Opinion*. New York: Simon & Schuster, 1968.

Freedman, Philip E., and Anne Freedman. "Political Learning," In Samuel L. Long (ed.), *The Handbook of Political Behavior* (vol. 1). New York: Plenum Press, 1981.

Freeman, Samuel. "The Elitist-Populist Debate on Mass Belief Systems." *Midwest Political Science Association Paper*, 1981.

Gant, Michael M., and Dwight Davis. "Negative Voter Support in Presidential Elections." *Midwest Political Science Association Paper*, 1982.

Gardner, Riley W. "The Development of Cognitive Structures," In Constance Scheerer (ed.), *Cognition: Theory, Research, Promise*. New York: Harper & Row, 1964.

Glucksberg, Sam. "General Discussion of Issues: Relationships Between Cognitive Psychology and the Psychology of Personality." In Nancy Cantor and John F. Kihlstrom (eds.), *Personality, Cognition, and Social Interaction*. Hillsdale, N.J.: Lawrence Erlbaum, 1981.

Gopoian, J. David. "Issue Preference and Candidate Choice in Presidential Primaries." *American Journal of Political Science*, 26, 1982, 523–546.

Graber, Doris A. "Press Coverage and Voter Reaction in the 1968 Presidential Election." *Political Science Quarterly*, 89, 1974, 68–100.

———. *Verbal Behavior and Politics*. Urbana: University of Illinois Press, 1976.

———. "Agenda-Setting: Are There Women's Perspectives?" In Laurily Keir Epstein (ed.), *Women and the News*. New York: Hastings House, 1978.

———. "Problems in Measuring Audience Effects of the 1976 Debates." In George F. Bishop, Robert G. Meadow, and Marilyn Jackson-Beeck (eds.), *The Presidential Debates: Media, Electoral, and Policy Perspectives*. New York: Praeger, 1978.

———. *Crime News and the Public*. New York: Praeger, 1980.

———. "Hoopla and Horse-Race in 1980 Campaign Coverage: A Closer Look." In Winfred Schulz and Klaus Schoenbach (eds.), *Mass Media and Elections in Democratic Societies*, in press.

Graber, Doris A., and Young Yun Kim. "Why John Q Voter Did Not Learn Much from the 1976 Presidential Debates." In Brent D. Ruben (ed.), *Communication Yearbook 2*. New Brunswick, N.J.: Transaction Books, 1978.

Greenstein, Fred. "Personality and Politics." In Fred I. Greenstein and Nelson W. Polsby (eds.), *Handbook of Political Science: Micropolitical Theory* (vol. 2). Reading, Mass.: Addison-Wesley, 1978.

Grunig, James E. "The Message-Attitude-Behavior Relationship." *Communication Research*, 9, 1982, 163–200.

Hagner, Paul R., and John C. Pierce. "Conceptualization and Consistency in Political Beliefs: 1956-1976." *Midwest Public Opinion Association Paper*, 1981.

Hagner, Paul R., John C. Pierce, and Kay G. Wolsborn. "Ideological Conceptualization and the Opinion Bases of Partisan Choice." *Midwest Political Science Association Paper*, 1983.

Hastie, Reid. "Schematic Principles in Human Memory." In E. Tory Higgins, C. Peter Herman, and Mark P. Zanna (eds.), *Social Cognition: The Ontario Symposium* (Vol. 1). Hillsdale, N.J.: Lawrence Erlbaum, 1981.

Herzon, Frederick D. "Ideology, Constraint, and Public Opinion: The Case of Lawyers." *American Journal of Political Science*, 24, 1980, 233–258.

Higgins, E. Tory, and Gillian King. "Accessibility of Social Constructs: Information

Processing Consequences of Individual and Contextual Variability." In Nancy Cantor and John F. Kihlstrom (eds.), *Personality, Cognition, and Social Interaction*. Hillsdale, N.J.: Lawrence Erlbaum, 1981.

Hill, David B. "Attitude Generalization and the Measurement of Trust in American Leadership." *Political Behavior*, 3, 1981, 257–270.

Himmelweit, Hilde T., Patrick Humphreys, Marianne Jaeger, 'and Michael Katz. "Structure of Political Attitudes: Randomness or Ideology." In *How Voters Decide: A Longitudinal Study of Political Attitudes and Voting Extending Over 15 Years*. London: Academic Press, 1981.

Hinckley, Barbara. "The American Voter in Congressional Elections." *American Political Science Review*, 74, 1980, 641–650.

Hochschild, Jennifer L. *What's Fair? American Beliefs about Distributive Justice*. Cambridge: Harvard University Press, 1981.

Hopple, Gerald W. *Political Psychology and Biopolitics: Assessing and Predicting Elite Behavior in Foreign Policy Crises*. Boulder: Westview, 1980.

Horowitz, Mardi Jon. *Image Formation and Cognition* (2nd ed.). New York: Appleton-Century-Crofts, 1978.

Hunt, Morton. *The Universe Within*. New York: Simon and Schuster, 1982.

Insko, Chester A. *Theories of Attitude Change*. New York: Appleton-Century-Crofts, 1967.

Iyengar, Shanto. "Television News and Issue Salience: A Re-examination of the Agenda-Setting Hypothesis." *American Politics Quarterly*, 7, 1979, 395–416.

Iyengar, Shanto, Mark D. Peters, and Donald R. Kinder. "Experimental Demonstrations of the 'Not-So-Minimal' Consequences of Television News Programs." *American Political Science Review*, 76, 1982, 848–858.

Jackman, Mary R., and Mary Scheuer Senter. "Images of Social Groups: Categorical or Qualified?" *Public Opinion Quarterly*, 44, 1980, 341–360.

Jacoby, Jacob, and Wayne D. Hoyer, "Viewer Miscomprehension of Televised Communication: Selected Findings." *Journal of Marketing*, 46, 1982, 12–26.

Janis, Irving, L., and Leon Mann. *Decision Making: A Psychological Analysis of Conflict, Choice, and Commitment*. New York: Free Press, 1977.

Jennings, M. Kent. "Another Look at the Life Cycle and Political Participation." *American Journal of Political Science*, 23, 1979, 755–771.

Judd, Charles M., and Michael M. Milburn. "The Structure of Attitude Systems in the General Public." *American Sociological Review*, 45, 1980, 627–643.

Katz, Elihu, Jay G. Blumler, and Michael Gurevitch. "Uses and Gratifications Research." *Public Opinion Quarterly*, 37, 1973, 509–523.

Kelley, Harold H. *Causal Schemata and the Attribution Process*. Morristown, N.J.: General Learning Press, 1972.

Kerlinger, Fred N. "Social Attitudes and their Critical Referents: A Structural Theory." *Psychological Review*, 74, 1967, 110–122.

Kessel, John. *Presidential Campaign Politics: Coalition Strategies and Citizen Response*. Homewood, Ill.: Dorsey Press, 1980.

Key, V. O. Jr. (with the assistance of Milton C. Cummings, Jr.). *The Responsible Electorate*. Cambridge, Mass.: Harvard University Press, 1965.

Kihlstrom, John F. "On Personality and Memory." In Nancy Cantor and John F. Kihlstrom (eds.), *Personality, Cognition, and Social Interaction*. Hillsdale, N.J.: Lawrence Erlbaum, 1981.

Kinder, Donald R. "Presidents, Prosperity and Public Opinion." *Public Opinion Quarterly*, *45*, 1981, 1–21.

———. "Sociotropic Politics: The American Case." *British Journal of Political Science*, *11*, 1981, 129–162.

———. "Enough Already about Ideology: The Many Bases of American Public Opinion." *American Political Science Association Paper*, 1982.

Kinder, Donald R., Shanto Iyengar, Jon A. Krosnick, and Mark D. Peters. "More than Meets the Eye: The Impact of Television News on Evaluations of Presidential Performance." *Midwest Political Science Association Paper*, 1983.

Kinder, Donald R., and D. Roderick Kiewiet. "Economic Grievances and Political Behavior: The Role of Personal Discontents and Collective Judgments in Congressional Voting." *American Journal of Political Science*, *23*, 1979, 495–527.

Kinder, Donald R., Mark D. Peters, Robert P. Abelson, and Susan T. Fiske. "Presidential Prototypes." *Political Behavior*, *2*, 1980, 315–337.

Kitchin, William. "Hemispheric Lateralization and Political Communication." *American Political Science Association Paper*, 1982.

Klapp, Orrin E. *Opening and Closing: Strategies of Information Adaptation in Society*. Cambridge: Cambridge University Press, 1978.

Klingemann, Hans D. "The Background of Ideological Conceptualizations." In Samuel H. Barnes et al. (eds.), *Political Action: Mass Participation in Five Western Democracies*. Beverly Hills: Sage, 1979.

———. "Ideological Conceptualization and Political Action." In Samuel H. Barnes et al. (eds.), *Political Action: Mass Participation in Five Western Democracies*. Beverly Hills: Sage, 1979.

———. "Measuring Ideological Conceptualizations." In Samuel H. Barnes et al (eds.), *Political Action: Mass Participation in Five Western Democracies*. Beverly Hills: Sage, 1979.

Knapp, Mark L., Cynthia Stohl, and Kathleen K. Reardon. "'Memorable' Messages." *Journal of Communication*, *31*, 1981, 27–41.

Knoke, David. "Stratification and the Dimensions of American Political Orientations." *American Journal of Political Science*, *23*, 1979, 772–791.

Kramer, Gerald H. "The Ecological Fallacy Revisited: Aggregate-versus Individual-Level Findings on Economics and Elections and Sociotropic Voting." *American Political Science Review*, *77*, 1983, 92–111.

Kraus, Sidney, and Dennis Davis. *The Effects of Mass Communication on Political Behavior*. University Park, Pa.: Pennsylvania State University Press, 1976.

Krugman, Herbert E. "Brain Wave Measures of Media Involvement." *Journal of Advertising Research*, *11*, 1971, 3–9.

Lachman, Roy, Janet L. Lachman, and Earl C. Butterfield. *Cognitive Psychology and Information Processing: An Introduction*. Hillsdale, N.J.: Lawrence Erlbaum, 1979.

Ladd, Everett Carll. "Politics in the 1980s: An Electorate at Odds with Itself." *Public Opinion*, *5*, 1983, 2–5.

Ladd, Everett Carll, and Seymour Martin Lipset. "Anatomy of a Decade." *Public Opinion*, *3*, 1980, 2–9.

Lamb, Karl A. *As Orange Goes: Twelve California Families and the Future of American Politics*. New York: Norton, 1974.

Lane, Robert E. *Political Ideology: Why the American Common Man Believes What He Does*. New York: Free Press, 1962.

Lane, Robert E. "Patterns of Political Belief." In Jeane Knutson (ed.), *Handbook of Political Psychology*. San Francisco: Jossey-Bass, 1974.

Langer, E. "Rethinking the Role of Thought in Social Interaction." In John H. Harvey, William J. Ickes, and Robert F. Kidd (eds.), *New Directions in Attribution Research* (vol. 2). Hillsdale, N.J.: Lawrence Erlbaum, 1978.

Langton, Kenneth P., and Octavian Petrescu. "Cognitive and Situational Antecedents to Worker Participation." *American Political Science Association Paper*, 1982.

Lasswell, Harold D. "The Structure and Function of Communication in Society." In Wilbur Schramm (ed.), *Mass Communication*. Urbana: University of Illinois Press, 1949.

Lau, Richard R. "The Origins of Health Locus of Control Beliefs." *Journal of Personality and Social Psychology*, *42*, 1982, 322–334.

Lau, Richard R., and Karen A. Hartman. "Common Sense Representations of Common Illnesses." *Health Psychology*, *2*, 1983, 167–185.

Lau, Richard R., Robert F. Coulam, and David O. Sears. "Proposition 2½ in Massachusetts: Self-Interest, Anti-Government Attitudes, and Political Schemas." *Midwest Political Science Association Paper*, 1983.

Lau, Richard R., David O. Sears, and Richard Centers. "The 'Positivity Bias' in Evaluation of Public Figures: Evidence Against Instrument Artifacts." *Public Opinion Quarterly*, *43*, 1979, 347–358.

Lazarsfeld, Paul, Bernard Berelsonm and Hazel Gaudet. *The People's Choice*. New York: Columbia University Press, 1944.

Levitin, Teresa E., and Warren E. Miller. "Ideological Interpretations of Presidential Elections." *American Political Science Review*, *73*, 1979, 751–771.

Levy, Mark R. "The Audience Experience with Television News." *Journalism Reports* (No. 55), 1978.

Lindblom, Charles E. "Another State of Mind." *American Political Science Review*, *76*, 1982, 9–21.

Lindsay, Peter H., and Donald A. Norman. *Human Information Processing*. New York: Academic Press, 1977.

Lingle, John H., and Thomas M. Ostrom. "Principles of Memory and Cognition in Attitude Formation." In Richard E. Petty, Thomas M. Ostrom, and Timothy C. Block (eds.), *Cognitive Responses in Persuasion*. Hillsdale, N.J.: Lawrence Erlbaum, 1981.

Lippmann, Walter. *Public Opinion*. New York: Harcourt Brace, 1922.

Lodge, Milton, and John C. Wahlke. "Politicos, Apoiliticals, and the Processing of Political Information." *International Political Science Review*, *3*, 1982, 131–150.

Loftus, Elizabeth F. *Eyewitness Testimony*. Cambridge, Mass.: Harvard University Press, 1979.

Lowery, David, and Lee Sigelman. "Understanding the Tax Revolt: Eight Explanations." *American Political Science Review*, *75*, 1981, 963–974.

Lynd, Robert S., and Helen Merrell Lynd. *Middletown*. New York: Harcourt Brace, 1929.

———. *Middletown in Transition: A Study in Cultural Conflicts*. New York: Harcourt Brace, 1937.

MacKuen, Michael B. "Broadcast and Contextual Cues for Partisan Voting." *Midwest Political Science Association Paper*, 1983.

MacKuen, Michael B., and Steven Lane Coombs. *More than News: Media Power in Public Affairs*. Beverly Hills: Sage, 1981.

Mandler, Jean Matter, and George Mandler. *Thinking: From Association to Gestalt*. New York: Wiley, 1964.

Manheim, Jarol B. *The Politics Within: A Primer in Political Attitudes and Behavior* (2nd ed.). New York: Longman, 1982.

Mann, Thomas E., and Raymond E. Wolfinger, "Candidates and Parties in Congressional Elections." *American Political Science Review*, 74, 1980, 617–632.

Markus, Gregory B. "The Political Environment and the Dynamics of Public Attitudes: A Panel Study." *American Journal of Political Science*, 23, 1979, 338–358.

Markus, Hazel. "Self-Schemata and Processing Information about the Self." *Journal of Personality and Social Psychology*, 35, 1977, 63–78.

Markus, Hazel, and K. Sentis. "The Self in Social Information Processing." In J. Suls (ed.), *Social Psychological Perspectives on the Self*. Hillsdale, N.J.: Erlbaum, 1980.

Markus, Hazel, and Jeanne Smith. "The Influence of Self-Schema on the Perception of Others." In Nancy Cantor and John F. Kihlstrom (eds.), *Personality, Cognition, and Social Interaction*. Hillsdale, N.J.: Lawrence Erlbaum, 1981.

May, Ernest R. *"Lessons" of the Past*. New York: Oxford University Press, 1973.

McArthur, Leslie Zebrowitz. "What Grabs You: The Role of Attention in Impression Formation and Causal Attributions." In E. Tory Higgins, C. Peter Herman, Mark P. Zanna (eds.), *Social Cognition: The Ontario Symposium*. Hillsdale, N.J.: Lawrence Erlbaum, 1981.

McCombs, Maxwell E. "The Agenda-Setting Approach." In Dan D. Nimmo and Keith R. Sanders (eds.), *Handbook of Political Communication*. Beverly Hills: Sage, 1981.

McFarland, Sam G. "Effects of Question Order on Survey Responses." *Public Opinion Quarterly*, 45, 1981, 208–215.

McLeod, Jack M., and Lee B. Becker. "Testing the Validity of Gratification Measures through Political Effects Analysis." In Jay G. Blumler and Elihu Katz (eds.), *The Uses of Mass Communications: Current Perspectives on Gratifications Research*. Beverly Hills: Sage, 1974.

McLeod, Jack M., and Lee B. Becker. "The Uses and Gratifications Approach." In Dan D. Nimmo and Keith R. Sanders (eds.), *Handbook of Political Communication*. Beverly Hills: Sage, 1981.

Miller, Arthur, Patricia Gurin, Gerald Gurin, and Oksana Malanchuk. "Group Consciousness and Political Participation." *American Journal of Political Science*, 25, 1981, 494–508.

Miller, Arthur A., and Michael MacKuen. "Informing the Electorate: A National Study." In Sidney Kraus (ed.), *The Great Debates: Carter vs. Ford, 1976*. Bloomington: Indiana University Press, 1979.

Miller, Arthur H., and Warren E. Miller. "Ideology in the 1972 Election: Myth or Reality." *American Political Science Review*, 70, 1976, 832–849.

Miller, Arthur H., Martin P. Wattenberg, and Oksana Malanchuk. "Cognitive Representations of Candidate Assessments." *American Political Science Association Paper*, 1982.

Miller, Gerald R. "On Being Persuaded." In Michael E. Roloff and Gerald R. Miller (ed.), *Persuasion: New Directions in Theory and Research*. Beverly Hills: Sage, 1980.

Miller, Warren E., and Teresa E. Levitin. *Leadership and Change*. Cambridge, Mass.: Winthrop, 1976.

Miller, Warren E., Arthur H. Miller, and Edward J. Schneider. *American National Election Studies Data Sourcebook, 1952-1978*. Cambridge, Mass.: Harvard University Press, 1980.

Mischel, Walter. "Personality and Cognition: Something Borrowed, Something New?" In Nancy Cantor and John F. Kihlstrom (eds.), *Personality, Cognition, and Social Interaction*. Hillsdale, N.J.: Lawrence Erlbaum, 1981.

Modigliani, Andre, and William A. Gamson. "Thinking About Politics." *Political Behavior*, *1*, 1979, 5–30.

Mueller, John E. "Public Expectations of War during the Cold War." *American Journal of Political Science*, *23*, 1979, 301–329.

Neisser, Ulric. *Cognition and Reality*. San Francisco: Freeman, 1976.

Neuman, W. Russell. "Differentiation and Integration: Two Dimensions of Political Thinking." *American Journal of Sociology*, *86*, 1981, 1236–1268.

Neuman, W. Russell. "Television and American Culture: The Mass Medium and the Pluralist Audience," *Public Opinion Quarterly*, *46*, 1982, 471–487.

Nie, Norman H., and James N. Rabjohn. "Revisiting Mass Belief Systems Revisited: Or, Doing Research Is like Watching a Tennis Match." *American Journal of Political Science*, *23*, 1979, 139–175.

Nie, Norman H., Sidney Verba, and John R. Petrocik. *The Changing American Voter*. Cambridge, Mass.: Harvard University Press, 1976.

Nisbett, Richard E., and Lee Ross. *Human Inference: Strategies and Shortcomings of Social Judgment*. Englewood Cliffs, N.J.: Prentice-Hall, 1980.

Nisbett, Richard E., and Timothy DeCamp Wilson. "Telling More than We Can Know: Verbal Reports on Mental Processes." *Psychological Review*, *84*, 1977, 231–259.

Noelle-Neuman, Elizabeth. *Die Schweigespirale*. Munich: R. Piper, 1980.

Norman, Donald R., and David G. Bobrow. "On the Role of Active Memory Processes in Perception and Cognition." In Charles Cofer (ed.), *The Structure of Human Memory*. San Francisco: Freeman, 1976.

O'Keefe, Garrett J., and L. Erwin Atwood. "Communication and Election Campaigns," In Dan D. Nimmo and Keith R. Sanders (eds.), *Handbook of Political Communication*. Beverly Hills: Sage, 1981.

Ostrom, Elinor (ed.). *Strategies of Political Inquiry*. Beverly Hills: Sage, 1982.

Ostrom, Thomas M., John B. Pryor, and David D. Simpson. "The Organization of Social Information." In E. Tory Higgins, C. Peter Herman, and Mark P. Zanna (eds.), *Social Cognition: The Ontario Symposium* (vol. 1). Hillsdale, N.J.: Lawrence Erlbaum, 1981.

Palmgreen, Philip, Lawrence A. Wenner, and J. D. Rayburn. "Relations between Gratifications Sought and Obtained." *Communication Research*, *7*, 1980, 161–192.

Patterson, Thomas E. *The Mass Media Election: How Americans Choose Their President*. New York: Praeger, 1980.

Patterson, Thomas E., and Robert D. McClure. *The Unseeing Eye: The Myth of Television Power in National Elections*. New York: Putnam, 1976.

Perloff, Richard M., and Timothy C. Brock. "And Thinking Makes It So: Cognitive Responses in Persuasion." In Michael E. Roloff and Gerald R. Miller (eds.), *Persuasion: New Directions in Theory and Research*. Beverly Hills: Sage, 1980.

Peterson, Steven A. "Neurophysiology and Rationality in Political Thinking." *American Political Science Association Paper*, 1982.

Petty, Richard E., and John T. Cacioppo. "Effects of Message Repetition and Position on Cognitive Response." *Journal of Personality and Social Psychology*, *37*, 1979, 97–109.

———. "Issue Involvement Can Increase or Decrease Persuasion by Enhancing Message-

Relevant Cognitive Responses." *Journal of Personality and Social Psychology, 37,* 1979, 15–26.

———. *Attitudes and Persuasion: Classic and Contemporary Approaches.* Dubuque, Iowa: Wm. C. Brown, 1981.

Petty, Richard E., Stephen G. Harkins, and Kipling D. Williams. "The Effects of Diffusion of Cognitive Effort on Attitudes: An Information Processing View." *Journal of Personality and Social Psychology, 38,* 1980, 81–92.

Petty, Richard E., Thomas M. Ostrom, and Timothy C. Brock (eds.). *Cognitive Responses in Persuasion: A Text in Attitude Change.* Hillsdale, N.J.: Lawrence Erlbaum, 1981.

Pierce, John C. "Party Identification and the Changing Role of Ideology in American Politics." *Midwest Journal of Political Science, 14,* 1970, 25–42.

———. "The Relationship between Linkage Salience and Linkage Organization in Mass Belief Systems." *Public Opinion Quarterly, 39,* 1975, 102–110.

Pierce, John C., and Paul R. Hagner. "Conceptualization and Party Identification: 1956–1976." *American Journal of Political Science, 26,* 1982, 377–387.

Pomper, Gerald M. (with Susan Lederman). *Elections in America* (2nd ed.). New York: Longman, 1980.

Putnam, Robert D. *The Beliefs of Politicians: Ideology, Conflict, and Democracy in Britain and Italy.* New Haven: Yale University Press, 1973.

———. *The Comparative Study of Political Elites.* Englewood Cliffs, N.J.: Prentice-Hall, 1976.

Rabinowitz, George, James W. Prothro, and William Jacoby. "Salience as a Factor in the Impact of Issues on Candidate Evaluation." *Journal of Politics, 44,* 1982, 41–63.

Rapoport, Ronald B. "The Sex Gap in Political Persuading: Where the Structuring Principle Works." *American Journal of Political Science, 25,* 1981, 32–46.

———. "Sex Differences in Attitude Expression: A Generational Explanation." *Public Opinion Quarterly, 46,* 1982, 86–96.

Reese, Stephen D., and M. Mark Miller. "Political Attitude Holding and Structure." *Communication Research, 8,* 1981, 167–188.

Renshon, Stanley Allen (ed.). *Handbook of Political Socialization.* New York: Free Press, 1977.

Robinson, John, and John Holm. "Ideological Voting Is Alive and Well." *Public Opinion, 3,* 1980, 52–58.

Rock, Irving, and John Ceraso. "Toward a Cognitive Theory of Associative Learning." In Constance Scheerer (ed.), *Cognition: Theory, Research, Promise.* New York: Harper & Row, 1964.

Rogers, Timothy B. "A Model of the Self as an Aspect of the Human Information Processing System." In Nancy Cantor and John F. Kihlstrom (eds.), *Personality, Cognition, and Social Interaction.* Hillsdale, N.J.: Lawrence Erlbaum, 1981.

Rokeach, Milton. *The Open and Closed Mind: Investigations into the Nature of Belief Systems and Personality Systems.* New York: Basic Books, 1960.

———. *Understanding Human Values, Individual and Societal.* New York: Free Press, 1979.

Roloff, Michael E. "Self-Awareness and the Persuasion Process: Do We Really Know What We Are Doing?" In Michael E. Roloff and Gerald R. Miller (eds.), *Persuasion: New Directions in Theory and Research.* Beverly Hills: Sage, 1980.

Rosenberg, Shawn W. "The Study of Political Reasoning: An Alternative to the Belief Systems Approach." *American Political Science Association Paper,* 1982.

Rumelhart, David E., and Donald A. Norman. "Analogic Processes in Learning." In John R. Anderson (ed.), *Cognitive Skills and Their Acquisition*. Hillsdale, N.J.: Lawrence Erlbaum, 1980.

Rumelhart, David E., and Andrew Ortony. "The Representation of Knowledge in Memory," In R. C. Anderson, R. J. Spiro, and W. E. Montague (eds.), *Schooling and the Acquisition of Knowledge*. Hillsdale, N.J.: Erlbaum, 1977.

Russell, D. "The Causal Dimension Scale: A Measure of How Individuals Perceive Causes." *Journal of Personality and Social Psychology*, *42*, 1982, 1137–1145.

Salomon, Gavriel. *Interaction of Media, Cognition, and Learning*. San Francisco: Jossey-Bass, 1979.

Schank, Roger C., and Robert P. Abelson. *Scripts, Plans, Goals, and Understanding: An Inquiry Into Human Knowledge Structures*. Hillsdale, N.J.: Lawrence Erlbaum, 1977.

Scheerer, Constance (ed.). *Cognition: Theory, Research, Promise*. New York: Harper & Row, 1964.

Schlozman, Kay Lehman, and Sidney Verba. *Injury to Insult: Unemployment, Class, and Political Response*. Cambridge: Harvard University Press, 1979.

Schneider, David J., Albert H. Hastorf, and Phoebe C. Ellsworth. *Person Perception*. Reading, Mass: Addison-Wesley, 1979.

Schuman, Howard, Stanley Presser, and Jacob Ludwig. "Context Effects on Survey Responses to Questions about Abortion." *Public Opinion Quarterly*, *45*, 1981, 216–223.

Searing, Donald D. "A Study of Values in the British House of Commons." In Milton Rokeach (ed.), *Understanding Human Values, Individual and Societal*. New York: Free Press, 1979.

———. "Rules of the Game in Britain: Can the Politicians Be Trusted?" *American Political Science Review*, *76*, 1982, 239–257.

Sears, David O., and Jack Citrin. *Tax Revolt: Something for Nothing in California*. Cambridge, Mass.: Harvard University Press, 1982.

Sears, David O., Carl B. Hensler, and Leslie K. Speers. "Whites' Opposition to 'Busing': Self-Interest or Symbolic Politics?" *American Political Science Review*, *73*, 1979, 369–384.

Sears, David O., and Richard R. Lau. "Inducing Apparently Self-Interest Political Preferences." *American Political Science Review*, *77*, 1983.

Sears, David O., Richard R. Lau, Tom R. Tyler, and Harris M. Allen, Jr. "Self-Interest vs. Symbolic Politics in Policy Attitudes and Presidential Voting." *American Political Science Review*, *74*, 1980, 670–684.

Sennett, Richard, and Jonathan Cobb. *The Hidden Injury of Class*. New York: Random House, 1972.

Shaffer, Stephen D. "Balance Theory and Political Cognitions." *American Politics Quarterly*, 9, 1981, 291–320.

Shimanoff, Susan B. *Communication Rules: Theory and Research*. Beverly Hills: Sage, 1980.

Sigal, Leon V. *Reporters and Officials: The Organization and Politics of Newsmaking*. Lexington, Mass.: D.C. Heath, 1973.

Sigel, Roberta H., and Marilyn Brookes Hoskins. "Perspectives on Adult Political Socialization—Areas of Research." In Stanley Allen Renshon (ed.), *Handbook of Political Socialization*. New York: Free Press, 1977.

Sigelman, Lee. "Question-Order Effects on Presidential Popularity." *Public Opinion Quarterly*, *45*, 1981, 199–207.

———. "The Presidency: What Crisis of Confidence?" In Doris A. Graber (ed.), *The President and the Public*. Philadelphia: Institute for the Study of Human Issues, 1982.

Sigelman, Lee, and Pamela Johnston Conover. "Knowledge and Opinions about the Iranian Crisis: A Reconsideration of Three Models." *Public Opinion Quarterly*. *45*, 1981, 477–491.

Simon, Herbert. *Models of Man*. New York: Wiley, 1957.

Smith, M. Brewster. "Personality in Politics: A Conceptual Map, with Application to the Problem of Political Rationality." In O. Garceau (ed.), *Political Research and Political Theory*. Cambridge, Mass.: Harvard University Press, 1968.

Smith, M. Brewster, Jerome S. Bruner, and Robert W. White. *Opinions and Personality*. New York: Wiley, 1956.

Smith, Eric R. A. N. "The Levels of Conceptualization: False Measures of Ideological Sophistication." *American Political Science Review*, *74*, 1980, 685–696.

Smith, Eliot R., and Frederick D. Miller. "Limits on Perception of Cognitive Processes: A Reply to Nisbett and Wilson." *Psychological Review*, *85*, 1978, 355–362.

Smith, Tom W. "America's Most Important Problem—A Trend Analysis, 1946–1976." *Public Opinion Quarterly*, *44*, 1980, 164–180.

Smith, Tom W. "Can We Have Confidence in Confidence? Revisited." In Denis F. Johnston (ed.), *The Measurement of Subjective Phenomena*. Washington, D.C.: U.S. Government Printing Office, 1981.

Sniderman, Paul M., Richard A. Brody, Jonathan Siegel, and Percy H. Tannenbaum. "Evaluative Bias and Issue Proximity." *Political Behavior*, *4*, 1982, 115–131.

Sprague, John. "Is There a Micro Theory Consistent with Contextual Analysis?" In Elinor Ostrom (ed.), *Strategies of Political Inquiry*. Beverly Hills: Sage, 1982.

Stamm, Keith R., and M. Daniel Jacoubovitch. "How Much Do They Read in the Daily Newspaper: A Measurement Study." *Journalism Quarterly*, *57*, 1980, 234–242.

Steeper, Frederick T. "Public Response to Gerald Ford's Statements on Eastern Europe in the Second Debate." In George F. Bishop, Robert G. Meadow, and Marilyn Jackson-Beeck (eds.), *The Presidential Debates: Media, Electoral, and Policy Perspectives*. New York: Praeger, 1978.

Stephenson, William. *The Play Theory of Mass Communication*. Chicago: University of Chicago Press, 1967.

Sullivan, John L., James E. Pierson, and George E. Marcus. "Ideological Constraint in the Mass Public: A Methodological Critique and Some New Findings." *American Journal of Political Science*, *23*, 1978, 233–249.

Sullivan, John L., James E. Pierson, George E. Marcus, and Stanley Feldman. "The More Things Change, the More They Stay the Same: The Stability of Mass Belief Systems." *American Journal of Political Science*, *23*, 1979, 176–186.

Swanson, David L. "The Uses and Misuses of Uses and Gratifications." *Human Communication Research*, *3*, 1977, 214–221.

———. "Political Communication Research and the Uses and Gratifications Model: A Critique." *Communication Research*, *6*, 1979, 37–53.

———. "A Constructivist Approach." In Dan D. Nimmo and Keith R. Sanders (eds.), *Handbook of Political Communication*. Beverly Hills: Sage, 1981.

Tannenbaum, Percy H. "The Indexing Process in Communication." *Public Opinion Quarterly*, *19*, 1955, 292–302.

Tanenhaus, Joseph, and Mary Ann Foley. "Separating Objects of Specific and Diffuse Support: Experiments on Presidents and the Presidency." *Micropolitics*, *1*, 1981, 345–367.

Taylor, Shelley E. "The Interface of Cognitive and Social Psychology." In John H. Harvey (ed.), *Cognition, Social Behavior, and the Environment*. Hillsdale, N.J.: Lawrence Erlbaum, 1981.

Taylor, Shelley E., and Jennifer Crocker. "Schematic Bases of Social Information Processing." In E. Tory Higgins, C. Peter Herman, and Mark P. Zanna (eds.), *Social Cognition: The Ontario Symposium* (vol. 1). Hillsdale, N.J.: Lawrence Erlbaum, 1981.

Taylor, Shelley E., and Susan T. Fiske. "Salience, Attention and Attribution: Top of the Head Phenomena." In Leonard Berkowitz (ed.), *Advances in Experimental Social Psychology* (vol. 11). New York: Academic Press, 1978.

———. "Getting Inside the Head: Methodologies for Processing Analysis." In J. H. Harvey et al. (eds.), *New Directions in Attribution Research* (vol. 3), Hillsdale, N.J.: Lawrence Erlbaum, 1980.

Taylor, Shelley E., Susan T. Fiske, Nancy L. Etcoff, and Audrey J. Ruderman. "Categorical and Contextual Bases of Person Memory and Stereotyping." *Journal of Personality and Social Psychology*, *36*, 1978, 778–793.

Tedeschi, J. B., J. B. Schlenker, and T. Bonoma, "Cognitive Dissonance: Private Ratiocination or Public Spectacle." *American Psychologist*, *26*, 1971, 685–695.

Tetlock, Philip E., Faye Crosby, and Travis Crosby. "Political Psychobiography." *Micropolitics*, *1*, 1981, 191–214.

Tichenor, Philip J., George A. Donohue, and Clarice A. Olien. "Mass Media Flow and Differential Growth in Knowledge." *Public Opinion Quarterly*, *34*, Summer 1970, 159–170.

Underwood, Geoffrey (ed.). *Strategies of Information Processing*. London: Academic Press, 1978.

Volgy, Thomas J., and John E. Schwarz. "On Television Viewing and Citizens' Political Attitudes, Activity and Knowledge." *Western Political Quarterly*, *33*, 1980, 153–166.

Ward, Dana. "Genetic Epistemology and the Structure of Belief Systems: An Introduction to Piaget for Political Scientists." *American Political Science Association Paper*, 1982.

Warr, Peter B., and Christopher Knapper. *The Perception of People and Events*. London: Wiley, 1968.

Weatherford, M. Stephen. "Economic Voting and the 'Symbolic Politics' Argument: A Reinterpretation and Synthesis." *American Political Science Review*, *77*, 1983, 158–174.

Weaver, David H. "Political Issues and Voter Need for Orientation." In Donald Shaw and Maxwell E. McCombs (eds.), *The Emergence of American Political Issues: The Agenda-Setting Function of the Press*. St. Paul, Minn.: West, 1977.

Weaver, David H., Doris A. Graber, Maxwell E. McCombs, and Chaim H. Eyal. *Media Agenda-Setting in a Presidential Election; Issues, Images, and Interest*. New York: Praeger, 1981.

Weisberg, Herbert F. "A Multidimensional Conceptualization of Party Identification." *Political Behavior*, *2*, 1980, 33–60.

Wells, William D. (ed.). *Life Style and Psychographics*. Chicago: American Marketing Association, 1974.

White, Elliott. "Sociobiology, Neurobiology and Political Socialization." *Micropolitics*, *1*, 1981, 113–144.

Williams, Robin M. "Change and Stability in Values and Value Systems: A Sociological Perspective." In Milton Rokeach (ed.), *Understanding Human Values: Individual and Societal*. New York: Free Press, 1979.

Wilson, C. Edward. "The Effect of Medium on Loss of Information." *Journalism Quarterly*, *51*, 1974, 111–115.

Witkin, Herman A. "Origins of Cognitive Style." In Constance Scheerer (ed.), *Cognition: Theory, Research, Promise*. New York: Harper & Row, 1964.

Wray, J. Harry. "Comment on Interpretation of Early Research into Belief Systems." *Journal of Politics*, *41*, 1979, 1173–1181.

Wyer, Robert S., Jr., and Donald E. Carlston. *Social Cognition, Inference, and Attribution*. Hillsdale, N.J.: Lawrence Erlbaum, 1979.

Wyer, Robert S. Jr., and Thomas K. Srull. "The Processing of Social Stimulus Information: A Conceptual Integration." In Reid Hastie et al. (eds.), *Person Memory: The Cognitive Basis of Social Perception*. Hillsdale, N.J.: Lawrence Erlbaum, 1980.

Zajonc, Robert B. "Cognitive Theories in Social Psychology." In Gardner Lindzey and Elliot Aronson (eds.), *The Handbook of Social Psychology* (2nd ed., vol. 1). Reading, Mass.: Addison-Wesley, 1968.

———. "Feeling and Thinking: Preferences Need No Inferences." *American Psychologist*, *35*, 1980, 151–175.

Zielske, Hubert A. "The Remembering and Forgetting of Advertising." *Journal of Marketing*, *23*, 1959, 239–243.

Zucker, Harold G. "The Variable Nature of News Media Influence." In Brent D. Ruben (ed.), *Communication Yearbook 2*. New Brunswick, N.J.: Transaction Books, 1978.

Zukin, Cliff. "Mass Communication and Public Opinion." In Dan D. Nimmo and Keith R. Sanders (eds.), *Handbook of Political Communication*. Beverly Hills: Sage, 1981.

# Index